MARIO FERRARI

on WINE and FOOD

with Joan Dew

Dedication

This book is dedicated to my mother, Maria, and my father, Carlo, who together taught me love and respect for food and wine, and gratitude for the celebration of life that it represents.

Mario Ferrari
Nashville Tennessee
September 1985

<Mario with Joan Dew

EDITORIAL STAFF

Editorial Manager	Mary Jane Blount
Cookbook Editors	Georgia Brazil
	Mary Cummings
	Jane Hinshaw
	LaNita Stout
Design, Typography	Shirley Edmondson

First Printing: 5,000 Editions

©Mario Ferrari MCMLXXXV
  1915 West End Avenue, Nashville, Tennessee 37203
Library of Congress Cataloging-in-Publication Data
Ferrari, Mario, 1932-
    Mario Ferrari on wine and food.
    Includes index.
    1. Wine and wine making. 2. Gastronomy. I. Dew,
Joan. II. Title. III. Title: On wine and food.
TP548.F414 1985   641.2'2   85-21936
ISBN 0-87197-203-4

CONTENTS

On Mario Ferrari 6
What is Wine? 9
The Pairing of Food and Wine 19
Wines Around the World 31
    United States 32
    France 52
    Italy 63
    Germany 79
    Spain and Portugal 82
Cooking with Wine 85
Menus from Wine Connoisseurs 86
Special Recipes for Wine Lovers 107
Wine Glossary 142
Index 145

MARIO FERRARI

When I was a boy growing up in Italy, I learned at an early age how my family felt about food and wine.

These were the years of World War II, and we didn't have much. Nobody did. I didn't own a pair of shoes until I was 12, and then I had to join Mussolini's Boy Scouts to get them.

Food was scarce. We ate polenta (Italian cornmeal), vegetables from our small garden, and chickens my grandmother raised in the backyard. But there was always a barrel of homemade wine fermenting in the basement. The care and love my mother and grandmother put into making their simple meals couldn't have been more important to them if they'd been preparing a Papal feast.

I was the oldest of three sons, and always big for my age, so I was given manly chores from boyhood. When my Papa, Carlo, made his wine it was my job to stomp the grapes. Why else would God have blessed him with a son whose feet were bigger than shoeboxes? For hours on end I had to jump around in the big crushing vat, squishing grapes under my feet until my skin turned purple all the way up to my ankles.

Like all Italian men, Papa took great pride in his homemade wine, and from him I learned respect for the vino.

My mother, Maria, took just as much pride in her cooking. It was Italian tradition for the oldest son to help out in the kitchen and she had her hands full with me. I was big and clumsy and always knocking something over. She would smack me one minute, then the next she'd be laughing, "Figlio mio, figlio mio" (my son, my son), putting her arms around me so I wouldn't cry.

Every day when she cooked polenta I stood over the pot on the wood-burning stove and stirred continually so it wouldn't lump. If I stopped to let my arm rest, I got another smack. Meanwhile, my grandmother would be calling me to the backyard to kill a chicken for dinner. I also had to feed the chickens every morning and afternoon, so to me they were like pets. I hated killing them so much that to this day I don't eat anything with feathers.

When we sat down to lunch or dinner at the big table in the kitchen it was a special time, no matter how simple the food. My mother and grandmother always treated their family to the best they could make, even when they couldn't get the basics like sugar and salt. And there was always Papa's good homemade wine. He would send me down into the basement with a carafe to be filled from the wine barrel, making me whistle all the way there and back

My "Sweetheart," Robin.

President Gerald R. Ford

so he would know I wasn't sneaking a sip of the vino. The children were always given a few drops of wine in their water — it was our soda pop — but he didn't want me tapping the barrel until I was old enough. When the meal was over, and the table had been cleaned off, the wine carafe was always put back in case anyone wanted a glass later.

When I was about 13, the Germans left my home town, Trieste, and soon the Americans, French and English moved in. The Germans were so stiff and regimented that we kids had been afraid to go near them. But the Americans were so friendly we were all over them in no time. They shared their "C" rations, teased us, and tried to teach us English. I learned to say, "Gimme gum" and "Gimme cigarettes for my Papa." It was being around these good-natured American G.I.'s that made me want to come to the United States.

Trieste, which is located on the Adriatic Sea, resembles San Francisco, and it is a city of sailors. Had it not been for the War, I would have gone to the Academy to become a merchant seaman like so many other men in my family had done. Instead, I left home at 16 to go to Genoa where I knew I could get work on a ship bound for America.

I was soon signed on in the galley of a merchant ship headed for the "promised land." When we docked in New York harbor, I put on two pairs of pants, three shirts, and jumped ship. Arrivederci Italy; Hello America!

I had 20 dollars in my pocket, no friends, no relatives here, and I spoke almost no English. ("Gimme gum" doesn't get you very far in New York City!) I got jobs by lying about my experience. I would go to the back door of an Italian restaurant, talk them into hiring me as a busboy, then get fired 2 days later because it was obvious I didn't know what I was doing. Then I'd go to another restaurant and get another job, learning a little more each time until I had worked my way up to waiter.

I registered for the Draft

Governor Lamar Alexander (left) and Sheriff Fate Thomas

Anthony Quinn

right away because I knew I could get my citizenship papers by serving in the Military. When my call came I joined the Marines and served in the Korean action for 3 years, first as a mess Corporal, then in Intelligence because they needed interpreters and I spoke several languages (though I'm not sure you could count English as one of them!). When I was discharged from Camp Pendleton I stayed on in California and began working in restaurants in the Los Angeles area.

Eventually I went on to Dallas to work as a bartender before coming to Nashville to manage the Old Executive Club on West End Avenue.

When I got the opportunity to open my first restaurant, Mario's, a few years later, I was determined to give the food and wine the same respect my parents had given theirs at home.

In the past 20 years I've learned a lot about the restaurant business (but that's another book), and a lot about people and their eating and drinking habits.

In Nashville, I've seen the same awakening to new ideas in cuisine and wine that has taken place across the entire country during this period.

When I first came to America I was shocked to learn that wine was either considered a drink for the elite, or something winos hid in a brown sack to sip in an alleyway. Now Americans are coming to accept wine for what it is — a healthy, natural drink that goes better with food than any other liquid.

I wanted to write this book for the same reason I wanted to open a restaurant 20 years ago. I saw a need. In studying wine books during the 3 years I've been writing a weekly wine column for the Nashville Banner, I never found one volume that contained all the information I wanted, especially one that focused on the marriage of wine and food.

The study of wine is so complex that I have often said to myself, "Forget it! You know what you like and what you don't like, and that's *all* you need to know to enjoy wine."

But the romance of wine always draws me back to learn more. It's like being in love with a beautiful woman. Wine is a living thing, and therefore, like a woman, constantly changing. You know her, yet you don't. She is familiar, yet she is full of surprises. The more you learn about her, the more you want to know.

I hope this book will make you fall in love with the study of wine (and especially wines with food) as I have, and that it will not only serve as a reliable reference source but as an inspiration to encourage you in further study.

Mario Ferrari

WHAT IS WINE?

"If food is the body of good living, wine is its soul." —Clifton Fadiman

Throughout the ages, wine has been romanticized as much *more* than an enjoyable drink.

This is partly due to the fact that it has enjoyed such a colorful history, recorded as far back as drawings on the walls of caves and long before the written word. Poets and philosophers have exalted it; artists have been inspired by it; and authors have written countless volumes explaining it.

But the plain truth is much less romantic. Put simply, *wine is fermented grape juice.*

All that is needed to turn grape juice into wine is the natural process of fermentation. The formula for fermentation is: Sugar + Yeast = Alcohol + Carbon Dioxide (CO_2).

Both sugar and yeast are present naturally in the ripe grape. (The yeast is in the grape skin.) The fermentation process ends when all the sugar has been converted into alcohol, killing off the yeast. When the grape skin is broken, the yeast goes to work on the sugar in the pulp. When the alcohol level reaches about 15 percent, the yeast dies, and the result is wine.

The decanting of a jeroboam of Chateau Lafite, 1970, with Judge Wiseman

Over the centuries, man has found ways to tamper with this natural fermentation process in order to make wines of varying styles and flavors. It's now a process that is sophisticated, precise and high tech. But men were enjoying wine, made solely by natural fermentation centuries before modern machinery and technical know-how came along.

The accompanying chart by the Sebastiani Vineyards in Sonoma, California, describes the basic process of wine making much better than I could.

HOW WINE IS MADE

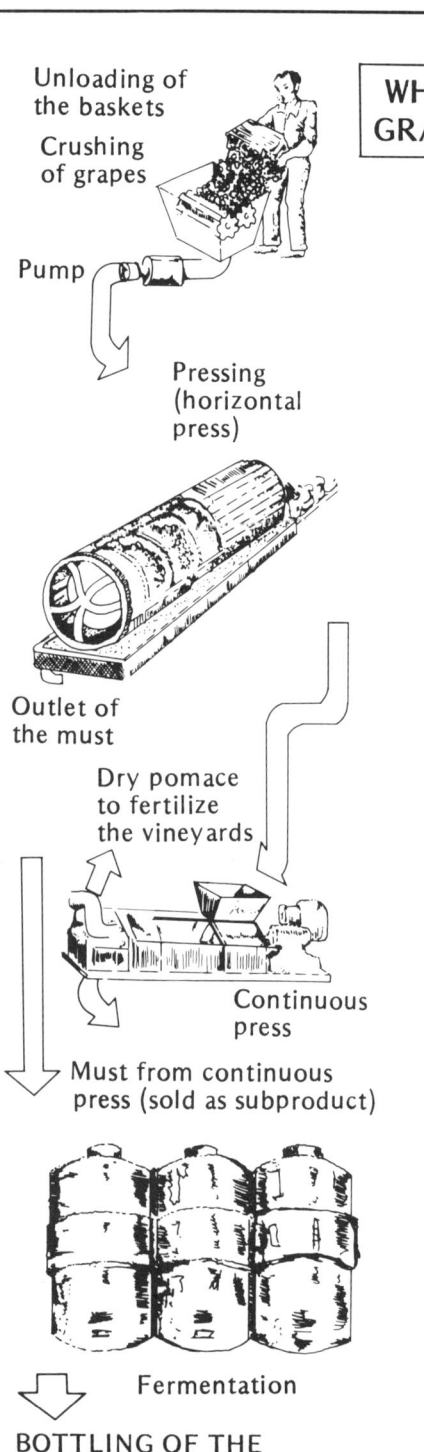

WHITE GRAPES

Unloading of the baskets
Crushing of grapes
Pump
Pressing (horizontal press)
Outlet of the must
Dry pomace to fertilize the vineyards
Continuous press
Must from continuous press (sold as subproduct)
Fermentation

BOTTLING OF THE FINISHED WINE IN THE MONTH FOLLOWING FERMENTATION!

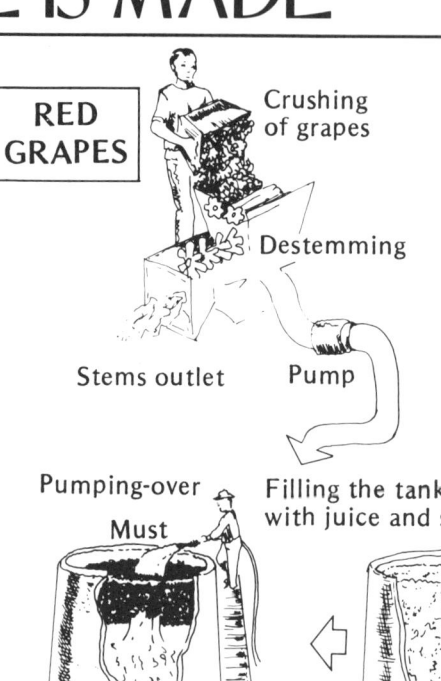

RED GRAPES

Crushing of grapes
Destemming
Stems outlet
Pump
Pumping-over
Must
Filling the tank with juice and skins
Fermentation tank

In 24 hours skins will rise to the top of the tank. During fermentation this "cap" of skins is sprayed with the fermenting wine to extract color.

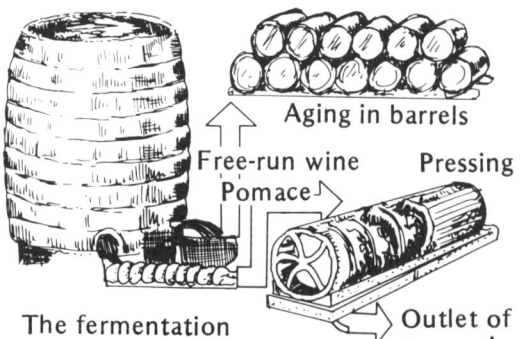

Aging in barrels
Free-run wine
Pomace
Pressing
Outlet of press wine

The fermentation finishes in 7 to 15 days. The wine is drained from the tank (free-run wine) to age in barrels.

The pomace is pressed (press wine). This press wine is then conveyed separately to another group of barrels.

TYPES and STYLES of WINES

The 3 major types of wines are Table Wine, Sparkling Wine and Fortified Wine. Within these groups are more specific categories.

Table Wine

Table wines are any wines that do not fall under the heading of Sparkling or Fortified. They include red wine, made basically from red grapes; white wine, made from green grapes; and Rose. Rose may be made either from a blend of white wine with red, or in the classical method. This natural process makes the Rose from red grapes when the skins are left in contact with the white juice (all grape juice is white if there is no skin contact) just long enough to give it a pinkish color.

Varietal table wines are wines made predominantly from a single grape variety, such as Cabernet Sauvignon, Pinot Noir or Chenin Blanc.

Generic table wines are made from blending wines of several different grapes (usually not top grade), such as American "Burgundy" or "Chablis." These are called "jug wines," although a number of California wineries are now making varietal wines in "jug" (1.5 litre) size bottles.

In all the above Table Wine categories, the taste of the wine can range from bone dry to sugar sweet.

Sparkling Wine

All Champagne is sparkling wine, but not all sparkling wine is Champagne.

Real Champagne comes only from the wine region of France bearing its name and is made by a very laborious and expensive process. (See page 62). The better Sparkling Wines from other countries also use the *Methode Champenoise* process. However, others that usually sell for about $3 a bottle are made by less expensive processes, such as allowing fermentation to take place in large containers rather than individual bottles, or by simply adding carbon dioxide to the wine (the way that soda pop is made).

Fine Sparkling Wines are made in many places other than the Champagne district of France. *Vins Mousseux* are French sparkling wines made outside the Champagne district. *Spumante*, meaning sparkle, is made in Italy. Germans call their sparkling wine *Sekt.* The Spanish produce many fine sparklers (usually good bargains, too!). Two of the best known in this country are Codorniu and Freixenet.

New York State and California are the 2 main producers of sparkling wine in this country. In the past few years, several Champagne makers of France have begun making fine sparkling wines in California (Domaine Chandon and Piper-Sonoma, to name 2) and numerous California winemakers have their own brands of sparklers. These include Korbel, Mirassou, Schramsberg, Chateau St. Jean, Sebastiani, Heitz, Beaulieu, Geyser Park, Wente Brothers and Hanns Kornell.

Fortified Wine

These wines have had Brandy added. Any wine could be fortified with the addition of alcohol beyond the point where natural fermentation will take it (usually about 14 percent). But the ones for which fortification has become a vital part of the production process are Port, Sherry, Madeira and Marsala.

Varietal Wine

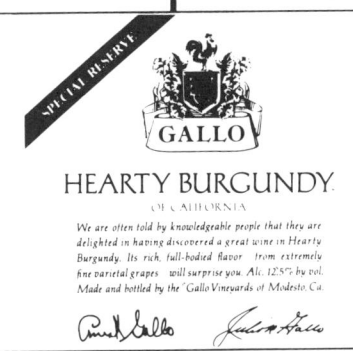

Generic Wine

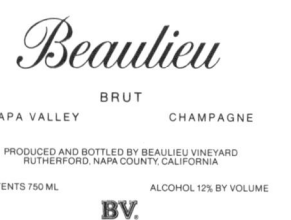

WINE GRAPES

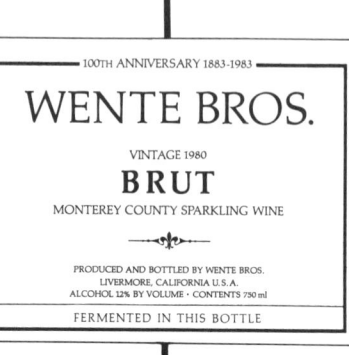

The flavor of wine depends on the type of grape used, the fermentation process, and how long the wine is aged.

There are more than 5,000 grape varieties in the world, but only about 50 are used in wine making.

The major wine producing grapes throughout the world are:
- Arinto
- Barbert
- Cabernet (Franc and Sauvignon)
- Catawba
- Chardonnay (Pinot Chardonnay)
- Chenin Blanc
- Condord
- Delaware
- Furmint
- Gamay
- Gewurztraminer
- Grenache
- Malbec
- Merlot
- Muller-Thurgau
- Muscat
- Nebbiolo
- Nerello
- Palomino
- Pedro Ximenex
- Petit Verdot
- Pinot Blanc
- Pinot Noir
- Riesling
- Rulander
- Sangioveso
- Sauvignon Blanc
- Savagnin
- Semillon
- Sercial
- Soave
- Sylvaner
- Syrah
- Tintas
- Traminer
- Ugni Blanc
- Verdelho
- Zinfandel

Most wines are a blend of several grape varieties, with one predominating. Some wines are blended for taste, some for economy.

Even the most dedicated wine connoisseur would have a tough time recognizing the characteristics of all the wine producing grapes, but it is important to know something about the most popular varieties.

- *Chardonnay* — The white Burgundy grape (Montrachet, Chablis, Meursault, Pouilly-Fuisse). One of the grapes of Champagne and the best white grape of California. Gives firm, full, strong wine with scent and character that ages well.
- *Cabernet Sauvignon* — A small, tough-skinned grape that is spicy, herby and tannic. The first grape of the Medoc and the one which gives distinction to the red wines of Bordeaux. Always blended with Merlot there, and sometimes Malbec. Also makes the best California red. All Cabernet wines gain by aging in the bottle as well as in wood.
- *Muscat* — Easily recognizable by its pungent hothouse taste and smell. Can be black or white. Mostly used to make perfumed sweet wines.
- *Semillon* — Like the Riesling, it "rots nobly" on the vine, producing luscious creamy wine like golden Sauternes.

- *Sauvignon Blanc* — Number one white grape of Bordeaux, producing a distinctive aromatic, herbal and sometimes smoky scented wine. Combined with Semillon and Muscadelle to make dry Graves and sweet Sauternes. Also used in parts of California. Sometimes known as Fume Blanc.
- *Chenin Blanc* — The leading white grape of the middle Loire Valley producing intense wine, whether dry or sweet. Also used to make sparkling wine. In California, sometimes incorrectly called White Pinot.
- *Pinot Noir* — Burgundy's noble red (Chambertin, Romanee, Corton, Beaune) is said to be the best red-wine grape in the world when grown in the right climate and soil conditions. At best, the scent, flavor, texture and body of wine from this grape is unsurpassed. Also used in making Champagne and some white wines.
- *Grenache* — A sweet grape used to make Tavel, one of the best French Roses, and in a blend to make Chateauneuf-du-Pape.
- *Riesling* — The classical German grape, also grown in California, Austria and Alsace, and Australia. It is a modest bearer and ripens late, but can make the ultimate honeyed, delicate, flower-scented nectar.

BOTTLE SIZES

Wines are bottled in different sized containers for different reasons — sometimes as a marketing tool, but usually (especially in France) because the larger the bottle the better the wine will age. In fine wines you don't get a bargain by buying a larger bottle. In other words, a magnum (two regular-sized bottles) will cost more than double that in a single bottle.

See chart on this page for bottle sizes and their designations.

VINTAGES

The vintage is the annual harvest of grapes that takes place in September or October in the Northern Hemisphere, and February and March in the Southern Hemisphere. It is also the wine produced from that harvest.

In the sense that vintage means the annual harvest, every year is a vintage year. However, in the world of wine, it has come to mean wines from particularly "good" years, years when Mother Nature was kind to the vineyards with the proper amount of rain and sun.

The quality of a wine depends on many things — the grapes used, the age of the vines, the soil, the climate, the fermentation and aging process, *and*, in the case of countries such as France, where the climate can vary a great deal from one year to the next, the *vintage*.

Every wine making country has its "vintage" years, but in some parts of the world, such as California, the variation in weather conditions is slight from year to year and "vintage" years are not nearly so important as in places where a sudden hailstorm could ruin the crop for that year.

If you were to try to memorize vintage years of fine wines, the place to start would be Bordeaux where vintage makes a great deal of difference, due to the unpredictable weather. The best of the older Bordeaux vintages are 1900, 1929, 1945 and 1961. The best of the most recent vintages are 1978, 1979, 1981, 1982 and 1983.

BOTTLE SIZES AND THEIR DESIGNATIONS

Name	Bottles	Litres or Centilitres	U.S. Ounces
Split	¼	18.7 cl.	6.76
Fillette of half	½	37.5 cl.	12.68
Single	1	75.0 cl.	25.36
Magnum	2	1.5 l.	50.71
Double Magnum	4	3.0 l.	101.42
Jeroboam	6	4.5 l.	152.16
(sparkling wine)	4	3.0 l.	101.42
Rehoboam	8	6.0 l.	202.85
(sparkling wine)	6	4.5 l.	152.16
Imperial	8	6.0 l.	202.85
Methuselah	8	6.0 l.	202.85
Salmanazar	12	9.0 l.	304.32
Nebuchadnezzar	14–20	12.0–16.0 l.	355.04–507.20

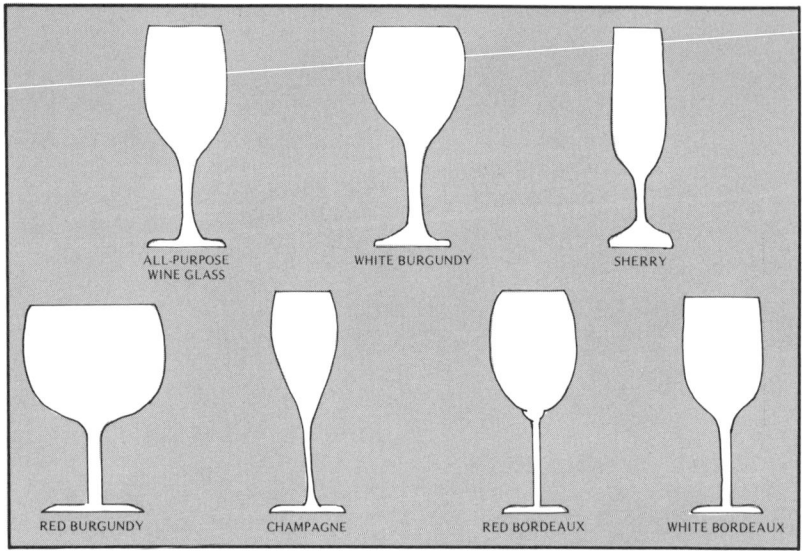

SERVING WINE

Several things are important to remember when serving wine. The first, of course, is whether or not it is the appropriate wine to serve with the meal. For that reason a large portion of this book is devoted to the pairing of wines and food.

Temperature

Equally important in the serving of wine is the temperature of the wine. Most red wines should be served at room temperature, between 60 and 65 degrees. One exception is Beaujolais, which many people prefer slightly chilled. White wines and sparkling wines should always be chilled to around 50 degrees. Roses should be cool, say 55 degrees.

Never put wine in the freezer to chill quickly. This ruins the taste of a fine wine. Also, it is not a good idea to chill a wine, let it come to room temperature, then rechill it again later. Here again the fine taste is lost.

The best way to chill wine is in an ice bucket, filled with half water and half ice. You can refrigerate wine, but if left too long, it becomes too cold and you will "chill" the flavor out of the wine.

Glasses

Wines are not drunk from stemmed glasses just for appearance's sake. A stemmed glass is very important for the full appreciation of wine. It is essential to hold the glass by the stem instead of the bowl, because the heat from your hands will change the wine's temperature as you drink it.

It is also extremely important to use sparkling clean glasses. Any residue or oil on the glass will affect the taste of the wine. Do not use colored glasses. The visual pleasure of the color of the wine is lost.

There is also a reason for serving different wines in different shaped glasses. Wider bowled glasses are best for enjoying the aroma or "nose" of fine red wines. Narrower openings are best for Sherry and white wines.

It has, unfortunately, become popular in the United States to serve sparkling wine in the "birdbath" shaped wide bowl glass. You'd be better off drinking Champagne from a fruit jar. Sparkling wine will go flat and get warm in a "birdbath" glass almost as fast as it would in your cupped hands.

Had it not been for Marie Antoinette's ego, that shape glass would have never been introduced as a vessel for Champagne. As a fashion trend-setter, she ordered the new design made in the shape of her breast, and it immediately became *the* Champagne glass at Louis XVI's court. It should have gone out with powdered wigs, but it came to the New World instead. Only now are people here realizing that the only proper glass for drinking sparkling wine is the tall, tulip shape. It holds the bubbles much longer and allows the visual pleasure of watching the bubbles rise to the surface.

STORING WINE

The ideal place to store wine, of course, is a wine cellar. Since most people don't have one, there are certain rules that must be observed if you intend to keep the wine for more than a few weeks before drinking it.

1. Stand the wine bottle upright for a day or so, for the sediment, if there is any, to settle to the bottom of the bottle. Then store on its side — label up. It is important to keep the cork moist; a dry cork will allow air to enter the bottle, spoiling the wine.

2. Do not store wines near air-conditioning or heating vents. Wine should be stored in a dark, cool room, and left as undisturbed as possible.

3. Do not refrigerate wine until serving time. Long refrigeration deadens the taste of the wine.

STARTING A WINE CELLAR

Some people think you have to be rich to have a wine cellar. Not true. You just have to like wine enough to want to collect it, but not so much that you can't resist drinking whatever you've got on hand.

Starting your own cellar can be a great hobby — one that will bring you pleasure for years to come — and it doesn't have to be expensive.

First, where do you put it? A place that's dark and cool, where there's not a lot of traffic. Wine likes to sleep in the dark, and the temperature should be as constant as possible — somewhere between 50 and 70 degrees. The ideal temperature is 55 degrees, but it is more important that the temperature not vary much from season to season. And where do you find a traffic-free area? The basement, an unused closet, under a staircase, or make a hole in the kitchen floor and go under the house. Be creative.

If you can't find a place with all interior walls, then insulate the best you can. Styrofoam on the walls will help. The area you choose must not be too dry (50 percent humidity is best, and Nashville has plenty of that); it must be well ventilated (keep a fan going if necessary); away from the kind of vibrations caused by motorized appliances; and without sunlight.

To stack the wine, use anything from custom-made shelving to cardboard wine boxes collected from a liquor store. Ceramic drain pipes stacked up against the wall in an unused bedroom make a great wine cellar. Stack the wines that need the most aging on the bottom, up to current drinking ones at eye level. Store white wines on lower shelves (it's cooler); reds and Roses higher and Brandies and liqueurs on the very top. (The higher alcoholic content stands up better to heat.) Store reds horizontally, but do not let the neck slant down. The sediment must collect on the bottom side of the bottle, not the cork.

What do you collect? You don't have to collect expensive wines to have a good cellar. Buy wines that will last and improve with age. Do not collect wines that are meant to be drunk young, such as Beaujolais *Nouveau*. But most wines, including many whites, will hold well for several years. When in doubt, buy from a retailer who has someone on the staff knowledgeable enough to advise you. When possible, it's a good idea to buy one case of each wine you intend to store in your cellar. This allows you the pleasure of sampling the wine through its aging process. Buy quality wines for cellaring, but don't only buy gold medal winners and First Growths. Some of your best bottles can come from under-rated vintages or overlooked producers.

The First Beaujolais Nouveau in Nashville

HOW TO HOLD A WINE TASTING

In Italy we have a saying: *gusti sono gusti*. A taste is a taste. It means people have different tastes — about food, about love, about art, about fashion. And certainly about wine!

No one else can tell you which wine is good, or which wine is bad. *Your* taste buds have to make that decision, no matter what the "experts" say; no matter what you've read or heard about a certain wine. And the only way to decide is to taste many different wines.

One of the best ways of doing this is to have a wine tasting party.

Ask as many guests as you like, but I prefer to keep it small — no more than 10 people. And don't offer more than 6 wines to be tasted. Any more than that confuses and tires the palate. Since you don't want to pour more than one to two ounces of wine per person for tasting, one bottle of each wine will be more than enough for 10 guests.

There are basically 2 kinds of wine tastings: *vertical* and *horizontal*.

Horizontal tastings are wines from different chateaux or different districts but all of the same vintage; *vertical tastings* compare different vintages of the same wine.

But, remember the purpose of a wine tasting is simply to expose your palate to more and different wines in order to determine which you prefer. So, at many wine tastings I serve both whites and reds, not only from different vintages and winemakers, but from different countries as well.

At an "official" wine tasting, food is not served, but bread and cheese is sometimes offered as a palate cleanser between tastes. That's not the way I do it, because wine *is* food and from its earliest beginning it was meant to be drunk with food. Therefore I think it should be tasted with food. So, I always serve something to eat. This way I can experiment pairing the wines with a food when I am tasting them. The exception would be a *vertical tasting,* for you are trying to determine the difference between wines from the same winery but different vintages.

For your tasting:

1. Use clear wine glasses so you can fully appreciate the wine's color.

2. Hold the glass by the stem so the warmth of your hand won't change the wine's temperature.

3. Check the color by holding it up to the light. Is it cloudy, dull, bright, crystalline? Red wines may range in color from light red, to mahogany to amber, depending on maturity, vintage and district. (Bordeaux, for example, are purple or deep violet color when young; glowing red-brown when mature.)

4. Sniff the wine. Professional tasters say they learn more from the wine's perfumes than any test. At the first sniff, look for any disagreeable odors — mustiness, sulphur, cork. Then check the aroma as a whole.

5. Now swish the wine in a circle in the glass about 3 times to release the bouquet and to examine the "legs" of the wine as they trickle down the side of the glass. The legs are the key to the body of the wine.

6. Now smell the wine again. This time the previously closed-in odors will come forth.

7. Take a sip of the wine by sucking the wine into your mouth. If you simply take a drink of the wine, the tongue will give you the taste, but if you suck it in, then swirl it around inside your mouth (pretend you're rinsing your mouth), more bouquet will be set free.

After swallowing the wine, note the aftertaste. It should be lingering and pleasant. Then take a sip of water between wines to rinse the taste buds.

You should supply your guests with rating cards so they can make notes about each wine. Then compare them. This is where individual taste comes in. There is no wrong or right. If you like a wine that no one else in the room likes, it simply means you have different taste than theirs.

Some of the terms most commonly used to describe the tastes of wines are acidity (tartness); fruity or grapey; mature; mellow; nutty (as in Sherry); rough (not well balanced or too astringent); tart (agreeable acidity); powerful, robust, earthy, clean and fresh tasting. See Wine Glossary on page 142.

16

HEALTH and WINE

When Louis Pasteur, the "father of pasteurization," described a drink as "the most *healthful* and most *hygienic* of all beverages" he was not talking about milk. He was talking about wine! The famous French scientist did as much work on the problem of spoilage in wines as he did on pasteurizing milk, and he concluded that wine is as good *for* you as it is good.

I've always known it was healthy to drink wine in moderation. After all, we Italians are a hearty, robust people, and we start drinking vino with water as children. But I never knew exactly why it was so good for you until I read Marjorie Michaels' book, *Drink Wine and Stay Healthy* (Dial Press).

Among its other beneficial properties, her book states that wine aids digestion, acts as a gentle tranquilizer, helps prevent heart attacks, helps us live longer, is a natural disinfectant, reduces nervous and muscular tension, and heightens sexual sensitivity. *Viva il vino!*

In Europe, wine has been accepted for centuries as a tonic for everything from insomia and premature wrinkles to diabetes and heart disease, but it took modern science to tell us how it works.

The reason wine is so good at helping us digest our food, for example, is because it is the only natural beverage that resembles human gastric juices. When consumed in reasonable amounts wine increases salivation and stimulates both gastric activity and appetite. There are some of us, like me, who don't need our appetites stimulated. But wine is great for dieters, too. It is low in calorie count (a 3-ounce glass of dry red or white wine contains less calories than 1 cup skim milk). However, wine calories, unlike those of other simple carbohydrate foods, are not converted by the body into fat. Nor is the alcohol broken down into unnecessary fatty acids or sugars.

Wine is also a high energy nutrient. Table wines, especially Port, Bordeaux and Burgundy are rich in iron. And both sweet red and dessert wines have a lot of B vitamins, as well as essential minerals, such as phosphorus, sulphur, calcium, magnesium and potassium.

Wine helps us live longer because the alcohol content dilates blood vessels, permitting freer circulation and temporarily reducing blood pressure. Two 3-ounce glasses of any wine can lower blood pressure for up to 4 hours.

United States Senator Albert Gore, Jr. (left) and Tennessee Speaker of the House of Representatives Ned Ray McWherter

Dr. John P. Kane of the Cardiovascular Research Institute of the University of California at San Francisco conducted a study that showed moderate wine drinkers had fewer heart attacks than teetotalers because of the effect of alcohol on high density lipoproteins (HDL), a "good" form of cholesterol believed to protect against atherosclerosis.

Wine is one of the best natural disinfectants available. After fermentation, the natural plant pigments in grapes become strong fighters against bacteria and viruses. At the Bonn Institute in West Germany, a wine and water mixture actually worked better against specific bacteria than strong doses of penicillin.

There's an old saying that alcohol and *amore* don't mix. Supposedly alcohol increases the desire, but diminishes the performance. That's undoubtedly true of hard liquor, but a reasonable amount of vino has the opposite effect! In another study documented in Michaels' book, the subjects surveyed agreed that a glass or 2 of wine before lovemaking enhanced their performance and made them feel more amorous. The scientific explanation was that the sedative and inhibition releasing effects of wine also heighten sexual sensitivity. It also awakens the sense of smell. Researchers, like Masters and Johnson, have found there is a strong physiological connection between the olfactory nerves and sexuality.

Personally, I don't care how it works, I'm just glad it does!

In these times when so many people are worried about the alcohol consumption in our country, it's important to note the difference between drinking wine and other alcoholic beverages.

According to Dr. Paul Scholten, medical professor at the University of California, San Francisco, "It is time to stop ignoring the differences among alcoholic beverages, which have long been known to the medical profession. When wine is served in its traditional manner, alongside food at the dinner table, evidence identifies it as the least intoxicating and, therefore, the most temperate of all alcoholic beverages. The drinker of wine with food raises his blood-alcohol level less than a third as much as if he drank the same amount of alcohol in whiskey, vodka, or gin the way these drinks are usually consumed, on an empty stomach at the cocktail hour."

It's *what* you drink that makes the difference and wine in moderation is one of the healthiest drinks in the world.

Papillon Mignon, recipe on page 117

THE PAIRING OF WINE AND FOOD

You've heard about the marriage of food and wine? Shrimp and Fowl married Sauvignon Blanc and Chardonnay, and Beef is living happily ever after with Cabernet Sauvignon.

For many people this is where it stops, but for those who would like to follow the story beyond the honeymoon I've compiled the following list of food and wine pairings to use as a *guideline.* I say "guideline" because *no one,* not even the greatest wine connoisseur in the world, can tell you what wine is the *perfect* companion for a certain food. Only your own palate can do that.

The rule that you drink white wine with fish and fowl, red wine with meat must be something the Americans came up with because that's not the way we do it in Europe.

There we say "white wine to drink; red wine to eat."

In France and Italy especially, white wine is served more as a refreshment — an aperitif or cocktail before the meal — and red wine is served with the food.

I remember when I was a boy in Italy, there was always a bottle of white wine in the refrigerator and the adults would take a glass when they were thirsty, like water.

I very seldom drink white wine with food, except perhaps with a salad for lunch. Otherwise, I like red wine with almost any food, including pasta.

Recently, I was dining with friends and we were eating a course of homemade pasta covered in a white cream sauce topped with freshly ground pepper and lots of freshly grated Italian Parmesan. They wanted white wine with their pasta because that's what they always drank with a cream sauce entree. I persuaded them to try a red — a magnificent Aloxe-Corton Burgundy. They loved it, and agreed the red complemented the dish better because the strong flavor of Parmesan overpowers a lighter white wine.

I think the reason many Americans don't try more red wines is because, at one time or another, they've tasted a cheap domestic jug wine that was sour, or they drank a red wine "before its time," and concluded all reds are harsh and tannic. Any red wine that is drunk too young will have a high tannin content and it won't taste at all like the same wine when it matures. But there is no more sublime taste in the world than a fine, mature red wine. Let your palate come in contact with a splendid Bordeaux, a great Burgundy, a robusto Brunello or Amarone before you decide you don't like red wine!

If you doubt whether a vintage is mature enough to drink, ask your wine merchant before purchasing it. Generally speaking, a red Bordeaux needs to age in the bottle longer than red Burgundies. In Burgundy, a wine is still considered young at 2½ years. In Bordeaux, a 4 year old is still young, and some estate bottled wines don't mature until they have aged 20 years.

Beaujolais can be drunk very young — within a year after appearing on the market — to fully appreciate its fruitiness, liveliness and true character.

California Pinot Noir should not be drunk before 3 years; Zinfandel 2 or more, but Gamay Beaujolais can be drunk the year it is released. Cabernet Sauvignon, on the other hand, needs time to mature. A 3 year old Cabernet is still too young to drink.

When a red wine is fairly young, the taste will be greatly improved by opening it and letting it breathe for 30 to 45 minutes before you serve it.

I admit, it's harder to find a good, inexpensive red wine than it is white. But there are a number of very nice red wines available in the $5 to $8 range.

The following list gives you the names of several wines that are compatible with each dish, but *your* taste will have to determine whether they are destined to become a casual date, a love affair or a lifelong marriage.

Craig Claiborne

FOOD		WINE
APPETIZERS AND FIRST COURSES		
ANTIPASTO		Dry white, such as Pinot Grigio; Orvieto; Greco di Tufo. Light red, such as Chianti; Dolcetto; Valpolicella; Bardolino.
ARTICHOKE	stuffed	Sauvignon Blanc; Pouilly-Fume; dry Rose.
	vinaigrette	Young red, such as Beaujolais.
	Hollandaise	Full-bodied dry; or medium-dry white, such as Macon Blanc or Rheinpfalz.
ASPARAGUS		Fume Blanc; St.-Veran; dry Sylvaner; Chardonnay; Tavel Rose.
AVOCADO	stuffed with seafood	Dry or medium-dry white, such as Pinot Blanc; Fume Blanc; dry Johannisberg Riesling; Grey Riesling. Dry Rose, such as Tavel.
	guacamole	Sangria (Spanish wine punch. See recipe on page 132.)
	vinaigrette	Light red, or fino Sherry. (The vinegar tends to kill the wine taste, but try these.)
CAVIAR		Iced Vodka; Champagne or other sparkling wine.
COLD MEATS	ham, roast beef, duck	Light red, such as Beaujolais. Blush, such as Pinot Noir Blanc or White Zinfandel.
COQUILLES ST. JACQUES		Pouilly-Fume; Fume Blanc.
CRUDITES		Fruity dry white, such as Macon Blanc; Italian Chardonnay. Light red, such as Cotes du Rhone. Dry Rose, such as Cabernet d'Anjou.
ESCARGOT		Red or white Burgundy.
FOIE GRAS		Sauternes; Alsace Gewurztraminer or Champagne Rose.
PATE	liver	Vouvray; Alsace Gewurztraminer; Sancerre; Chablis; Macon Blanc; White Graves.
PATE OR TERRINES	country or Terrines	Medium-bodied red, such as a Cru Beaujolais (Brouilly, Fleurie, Morgon); lighter red Bordeaux, such as Cotes du Rhone.

FOOD		WINE

APPETIZERS AND FIRST COURSES (continued)

PROSCIUTTO AND MELON		Johannisberg Riesling; Gewurztraminer; sweet enough to contrast with the salty meat; or, go the other way with dry, fruity white, such as Macon; Pinot Blanc; Pinot Grigio.
SAVORY CANAPES	salted nuts and cheeses	Fino Sherry; Manzanilla; Champagne; dry Vermouth.
SHRIMP	cocktail	Champagne; a California sparkler. (Cocktail sauce tends to kill the wine taste, but try these.)
	scampi	Chardonnay; Sauvignon Blanc; French Chablis.

MAIN DISHES

CHILI CON CARNE		Young reds, such as Beaujolais; Sangre de Toro; Chianti; light Zinfandel.
PAELLA		Spanish red, dry white or Rose, such as Panades; Rioja; Vinho Verde.
PASTA		The choice of wine depends on the sauce.
	with Cream Sauces	Dry white, such as Pinot Grigio; Gavi; Orvieto; Frascati.
	with Vegetables	Same as above; Light red, such as Cabernet del Friuli; Beaujolais; Bordolino; Valpolicella.
	with Meat and Tomato Sauce	Heartier red, such as Chianti; Barbera.
	with Fish Sauce	Dry white, such as Verdicchio; Soave; Pinot Grigio.
	with Herb Sauce	Zinfandel; Grignolino.
PIZZA		Medium-bodied, dry Italian red, such as Chianti.
QUICHE		Dry white with body, such as Alsace; Graves; Sauvignon Blanc; Young, red depending on ingredients.
SOUFFLES	fish	Dry white Burgundy; Bordeaux; Chardonnay.
	cheese	Red Burgundy; Bordeaux; Cabernet Sauvignon.
STUFFED PEPPERS		Vigorous red, such as Chianti; Zinfandel.

FOOD		WINE
SOUPS		
BISQUES		Dry white with good body, such as Verdicchio; Pinot Gris; Graves; French Chablis.
BOUILLABAISSE OR CIOPPINO		Light red, such as young Burgundy; Bordeaux Superieur; Italian Merlot. Dry full-bodied white, such as French Chablis; Corton-Charlemagne; Meursault.
GAZPACHO		Dry Manzanilla or Montilla; not-too-sweet Sangria.
ONION		Beaujolais; Cotes du Rhone.
SOUPS, OTHER	tomato base	Light reds.
	cream base	Dry whites.

MEATS		
BEEF	boiled	Reds, such as Cru Bourgeois Bordeaux; Cotes du Rhone-Villages.
	corned beef hash	Zinfandel; Chianti; Cotes du Rhone Red.
	hamburger	Beaujolais-Villages; Merlot; Napa Gamay.
	roast	Full-bodied reds, such as mature Cabernet Sauvignon; Brunello di Montalcino; Bordeaux; Zinfandel; Chianti Classico Riserva.
	spareribs, barbecued	Beaujolais; Zinfandel; Dolcetto.
	steak	Same as for Roast.
	steak, Teriyaki	Zinfandel.
	stew	Pomerol; St. Emilion.
	stroganoff	Barolo; Valpolicella; Amarone; Late-Harvest Zinfandel.
	Sukiyaki	Young, fruity reds, such as Beaujolais Crus Fleurie or Brouilly.
BRAINS		Beaujolais, or other light red. Dry Riesling.
CASSOULET	and meaty casseroles	Barbera; Petite Sirah; Cabernet Sauvignon; Merlot.

FOOD		WINE
MEATS (continued)		
CHICKEN	roast or grilled	Medium-bodied reds, such as Cabernet Sauvignon; Merlot; Cotes du Rhone; Gattinara. Full-bodied dry whites, such as French Chablis. Montrachet; big California Chardonnays. Actually, chicken, which is one of the most versatile of meats because it can be prepared so many ways, is also one of the easiest to pair with wine as it will go with most any you choose — from fine old reds, to young, dry whites.
	barbecued	Beaujolais; Zinfandel; Petite Sirah.
	sauteed in cream sauce	White Graves; White Burgundy; California Chardonnay.
	provencale	Cotes du Rhone; Morgon.
	Coq au Vin	French red Burgundy.
	salad	Riesling; dry Chenin Blanc; California Gewurztraminer; Vouvray.
DUCK OR GOOSE		Red Burgundy; California Pinot Noir; Riesling Spatlese; Alsace Gewurztraminer; Rheinpfalz Spatlese. Also, Pinot Noir; Gamay Beaujolais; Zinfandel.
FRANKFURTERS		Riesling; Beaujolais; Beer.
GAME	venison	Big, robust reds, such as Brunello di Montalcino; Amarone; Chambertin; Zinfandel; Barolo.
	hare	Young Italian red, such as Bardolino; Valpolicella.
GAME BIRDS		Lighter red Burgundy, such as Pommard; Oregon Pinot Noir; a light Chianti.
GOULASH		Strong red, such as Sangre de Toro; Zinfandel; Bulgarian Cabernet.
HAM		Pinot Noir Blanc; Vin Gris; Tavel Rose; Beaujolais; German Rhein Spatlese; Johannisberg Riesling.
KIDNEYS		Pomerol; St. Emilion; Rhone; Barbaresco; California or Australian Cabernet.
LAMB	roast	Mature Bordeaux; Cabernet Sauvignon; Spanish Rioja Reserva.
	stew	Younger reds than for roast.

FOOD		WINE

MEATS (continued)

LIVER		Fruity reds, such as Beaujolais; light Bordeaux. Lighter Burgundy, such as Volnay; Beaune.
PORK	chops	Dry white, medium-bodied Italian, such as Corvo Bianco; Soave; Tocai. French Pouilly-Fuisse; Pouilly-Fume. Light reds, such as Merlot; Beaujolais.
	roast with fruit or herb stuffing	Riesling Kabinett; Spatlese.
	roast, less spicey	Light reds, such as Fleurie; Morgon; Chenas.
TURKEY	roast, with dressing	Sutter Home Zinfandels; Reds, such as Inglenook; Ridge; San Luis; Clos du Bois; Firestone Merlot. Roses, such as Chateau Ste. Michelle Rose of Cabernet; Firestone Rose of Cabernet; Simi Rose of Cabernet. Blushes, such as Sebastiani Eye of the Swan; Sutter Home White Zinfandel. Whites, such as Chateau Ste. Michelle Chenin Blanc; Chappellet Chenin Blanc.
	without dressing	Light, dry white, such as Est! Est! Est!; Frascati (both Italian); Macon-Village (French); French Colombard or Gewurztraminer.
VEAL	chops, stew, scallops with mushrooms or Marsala	Medium-bodied Bordeaux; Cabernet Sauvignon; Chianti Classico.
	with cream sauce	White Burgundy; Chardonnay.
	Milanese	Gattinara.

FISH AND SHELLFISH

ABALONE		Dry, full-bodied Rose, such as Tavel; Blush, such as white Zinfandel. Dry or medium-white, such as Sauvignon Blanc; Chardonnay; Verdicchio.
BASS	freshwater	Light dry white, such as Soave; Pinot Bianco; Fume Blanc.
	sea bass	Full-bodied white Burgundy, such as Meursault; Puligny-Montrachet; California Chardonnay.

FOOD		WINE

FISH AND SHELLFISH (continued)

FOOD		WINE
COD		Fine dry or medium white, such as Chablis; white Graves; German Kabinetts.
CRAB	cold	Fume Blanc; Pouilly-Fume.
	steamed, or in sauce	California Chardonnay.
	soft-shelled	Dry to medium-bodied white, such as Sancerre; Macon; St.-Veran.
HADDOCK		Dry white, such as Meursault; California Chardonnay.
HERRING		Acidic white, such as Muscadet; young Alsace Riesling.
LOBSTER		California Chardonnay; Chablis Grand Cru; white Burgundy; Italian Frascati.
LOBSTER OR CRAB SALAD		White nonvintage Champagne; Alsace Riesling; Chablis Premier Cru.
	richly sauced	Vintage Champagne; Fine white Burgundy; white Graves; California Chardonnay.
MACKEREL		Sauvignon Blanc from Bergerac or Touraine; white Rioja.
MONKFISH		Full-bodied California Chardonnay.
MUSSELS		Muscadet; Pinot Grigio; California Chablis.
OYSTERS	raw or fried	French Chablis; Muscadet; California Fume Blanc; Champagne; white sparkling wine.
	smoked	Amontillado Sherry; Tokay d'Alsace.
RED SNAPPER		St.-Veran; Pouilly-Fuisse; white Burgundy.
SALMON	cold, poached	Sauvignon Blanc.
	baked or grilled	California Chardonnay; Montrachet; Meursault. Medium reds, such as Beaune; Volnay; Merlot.
	smoked	Fino Sherry; Alsace Gewurztraminer; Chablis Grand Cru; Champagne.
SARDINES	grilled	Crisp, dry white, such as Vino Verde or Muscadet.
	smoked	Dry Sherry.
SCALLOPS		Sauvignon Blanc; Pouilly-Fume; Sancerre; French Chablis; Italian Gavi; California Chardonnay.

FOOD		WINE
FISH AND SHELLFISH (continued)		
SHRIMP	fried	Muscadet; Pinot Blanc; dry Chenin Blanc.
	scampi	Chardonnay; Sauvignon Blanc; French Chablis.
	Newburg	Muscadet.
SOLE		Alsace Riesling; Riesling Kabinett; Pinot Bianco; light Chardonnay.
SUSHI, SASHIMI		Light, dry or off-dry whites; Sake.
SWORDFISH	grilled	Sauvignon Blanc; light red Burgundy.
TROUT	grilled	Delicate white, such as Mosel Riesling; dry Chenin Blanc; Macon.
	stuffed or with sauce	Fuller dry white, such as Montrachet; French Chablis.
	smoked	Riesling Kabinett; Pinot Blanc; Sancerre.
TUNA	salad	Light, fruity white, such as Macon; dry Chenin Blanc; dry Rose.
	fresh, grilled	Medium-bodied red, such as Merlot; Pomerol.
TURBOT		Rich, full-bodied white, such as California Chardonnay; white French Burgundy; Meursault.

FOOD	WINE
SPECIAL FOODS	
CHINESE	Spicy whites, such as Gewurztraminer; Tocai; Tokay d'Alsace. Roses, such as Grenache Rose; Rose d'Anjou.
CURRY	Orvieto Abboccato; Riesling Spatlese. With lamb or beef curry, try chilled Beaujolais or young, fruity Zinfandel.
MEXICAN	Sangria; Rioja Blanco; Mexican Beer; California Sparkling Wine.

CHEESE		WINE
ASIAGO		Barbera d'Alba; Rubesco; Nebbiolo d'Alba.
	aged	Bigger red, such as Barbaresco.
BEL PAESE		Gattinara; Valtellina reds; mature Bordeaux; Cabernet Sauvignon.
BLUE,	creamy	Fruity whites, such as Riesling. Fruity reds, such as Beaujolais.
	piquant	Sturdy reds from Bordeaux or the Rhone, such as Vino Nobile; Rioja Reserva; Barbaresco; Cabernet Sauvignon.
	pungent	Sauternes; Barsac; Muscat; Beaumes-de-Venise; Late Harvest Zinfandel; Amarone; Ruby Port.
BRIE		Dry Sherry; Chianti; Sauvignon Blanc; California Petite Sirah; Rioja.
CAMEMBERT		Hermitage; Red Burgundies; Sancerre; Vouvray; Pouilly-Fume; Semillon; Zinfandel; Chardonnay.
CARAWAY (including Kumin Ost)		Bordeaux reds; White Burgundies.
CHEDDAR		Port; Barolo; Rhone; California Pinot Noir; Johannisberg Riesling; Cabernet Sauvignon.
CHESHIRE		Fleurie; Bourgogne Rouge; Cotes du Rhone.
CREAM CHEESE		Full-bodied whites; medium-bodied reds; Champagne.
EDAM		Medium-dry Sherry; Red Bordeaux or Burgundies; Port; Tavel Rose; Cocktail Sherry.
EPOISSES		Nuits-St.-Georges; Chambolle-Musigny; Pommard; Corton-Bressandes.
FONTINA VAL D'AOSTA		Nebbiolo d'Alba; Gattinara; Valtellina reds.
GOAT		Sancerre; Fume Blanc; St.-Veran; also Rhone reds and Cru Beaujolais.
GOUDA		Fruity whites, such as Riesling.
	aged	Sturdy reds, see Cheddar.
GRUYERE, EMMENTHALER		Medium-bodied dry whites, especially from the Rhone, such as Crozes-Hermitage; Blanc Condrieu; most reds.

CHEESE		WINE
LIEDERKRANZ		Burgundy; St. Emilion; Chianti.
LIMBURGER		Chelois; California Cabernet Sauvignon; Barbera.
JACK	Monterey	Fruity reds, such as Napa Gamay; Gamay Beaujolais. Fruity whites, such as Chenin Blanc; Colombard; Riesling.
	dry	Firm Cabernet Sauvignon; Merlot; claret-style Zinfandel.
MUENSTER		Grenache Rose; Red & White Bordeaux; California Burgundy.
	Alsace	Alsace Gewurztraminer; robust reds.
PARMIGIANO-REGGIANO		Full-bodied Italian reds, such as Barbaresco; Barbera; Vino Nobile; Brunello di Montalcino; Ruffino Riserva Ducale Chianti.
PECORINO		Same as for Parmigiano-Reggiano.
PORT SALUT, SAINT NECTAIRE, PYRENEES MOUNTAIN CHEESE		Fruity whites, such as Vouvray; Riesling. Medium reds, such as Cotes du Rhone; Corbieres; Cahors; light Bordeaux.
PORT DU SALUT		Red or White Burgundy, such as Vouvray; Anjou Rose; Johannisberg Riesling.
PROVOLONE		Baco Noir Burgundy; Chelois.
REBLOCHON		Red Burgundy; California Pinot Noir; Hermitage; Chateauneuf-du-Pape.
RICOTTA SALATA (young Percorine)		Dry white, such as Orvieto Secco; Vernaccia di San Gimignano; Sancerre; Fume-Blanc.
ROQUEFORT		Sauternes; Barsac; Late-Harvest Zinfandel.
SEMISOFT CHEESE		Same as Port du Salut.
STILTON		Vintage or Ruby Port.
SWISS		Red Burgundies, such as Rhone; Zinfandel; Medoc; Orvieto.

CHEESE — WINE

CHEESE	WINE
TELEMES	Light, fruity California whites or reds.
TILSIT	Chablis; Bordeaux; California and Alsatian Riesling; Gruner Veltliner; Tokay d'Alsace; dry Riesling; medium-bodied to fairly sturdy reds.
TOMMES (semifirm mountain cheeses)	Medium-bodied Rhone reds, such as Zinfandel; Barbera.
VACHERIN MONT D'OR	Mature Pomerol; red Burgundy from the Cote de Beaune.
WENSLEYDALE	Dry, fruity whites or light reds.

DESSERTS — WINE

DESSERTS	WINE
APPLE PIE	Sweet German, Austrian or Hungarian white.
APPLES	Vintage port.
BAKED ALASKA	Sweet Champagne; Asti Spumante.
CAKES	German Auslese; Beerenauslese; Sweet Muscats; Asti Spumante; Extra Dry Champagne; Bual or Malmsey Madeira; Oloroso or Cream Sherry.
CHEESECAKE	Sweet white from Vouvray or Coteaux du Layon, Quarts de Chaume.
CHOCOLATE CAKE, MOUSSE, SOUFFLES	No wine.
CHRISTMAS PUDDING	Sweet Champagne; Asti Spumante.
CREAMS AND CUSTARDS	Sauternes; Monbazillac; Sweet Vouvray.
CREME BRULEE	Sauternes; German Beerenauslese; or the best Madeira; Tokay.
CREPES SUZETTE	Sweet Champagne; Asti Spumante.
FRUIT FLANS peach, raspberry	Sauternes; Monbazillac; Sweet Vouvray.
FRUITS fresh	Off-dry whites, such as Riesling; Gewurztraminer; Chenin Blanc; sweet Coteaux du Layon.

DESSERTS / WINE

DESSERTS		WINE
FRUITCAKE		Bual or Malmsey Madeira; Ruby or Tawny Port; dry Oloroso Sherry.
FRUIT SALADS		No wine.
FRUIT FLAMBEES (crepes suzettes, cherries jubilee, bananas Foster)		Brandy.
FRUIT TARTS		Sauternes; Barsac; Riesling Auslese.
ICE CREAM		Too sweet for most wines, except perhaps Marsala. Best with fruit liqueurs.
PLUM PUDDING		Ruby Port; Late-Harvest Zinfandel.
RASPBERRIES		Light, fruity reds, such as Beaujolais; Zinfandel. Light, such as sweet Rieslings or Muscats.
SORBETS		Best with fruit liqueurs, such as Cassis, Blackberry, Fraise des Bois.
SOUFFLES	dessert	Sauternes; Late-Harvest Rieslvings; Tokay Aszu.
STEWED FRUITS	apricots, pears	Muscat de Beaumes de Venise; Moscato di Pantelleria.
STRAWBERRIES AND CREAM		Sauternes; Vouvray.
STRAWBERRIES	and cream	Sauternes; Vouvray.
	fresh	Lightly chilled red, such as Beaujolais; Zinfandel.
	shortcake	Sweet Vouvray.
	wild	Red Bordeaux.
SUMMER PUDDING		Fairly young Sauternes of good vintage.
TRIFLE		Sherry.
ZABAGLIONE		Marsala.

WINES AROUND THE WORLD

George Fehrmann (left), Bailli of Nashville Chapter of Chaine des Rotisseurs, and Tom Milan

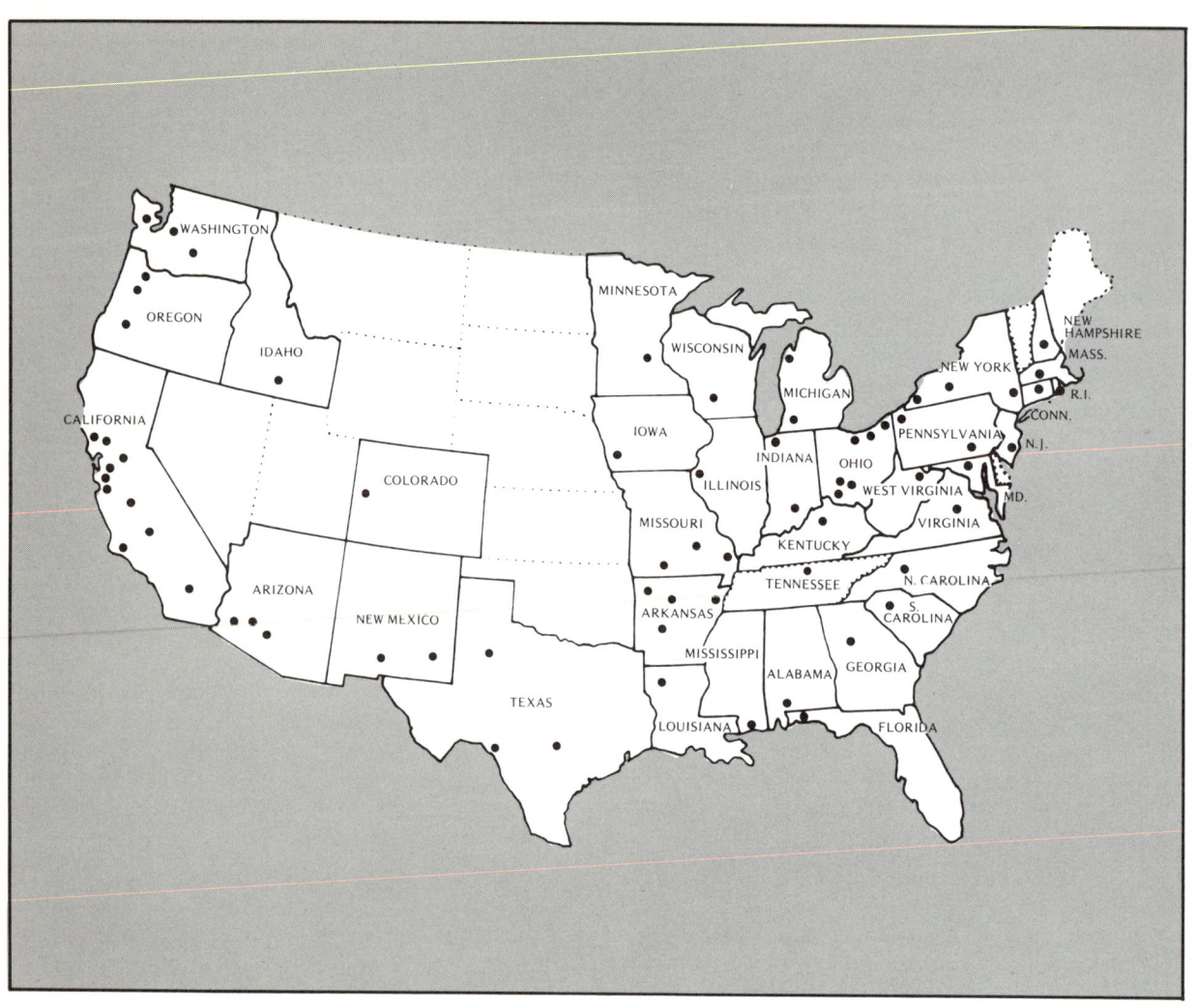

UNITED STATES

Compared to the great wine-producing nations of Europe, the United States is still a kid. Though vineyards were planted by the New World's first settlers as early as the 17th century, the United States' wine industry, as we know it, began taking shape with the Repeal of Prohibition in 1933.

From that point through the 1960's a great deal was accomplished. Modern technology and the perseverance of winemakers, who earnestly believed great wine could be made from American soil, brought us to where we are now.

After World War II, wineries concentrated on boosting the United States' level of wine consumption, which was one of the lowest in the world — less than a half gallon per person per year. So they made wines that would appeal to the most basic consumer taste: no varietals; no vintages; no aging requirements.

By the late 1960's, however, the industry was producing large quantities of very good wine. Growing consumer interest and admiration was fueling increased production, and by 1973, table wine accounted for more than half of California's wine production.

Now, of course, California is recognized as one of the world's fine wine regions. Meanwhile, states such as New York, Washington and Oregon are striving to establish their own reputations for producing fine wines. Today, many of America's fine wines fare well when compared in blind tastings to the best from Europe.

As for production, the United States currently ranks sixth worldwide, behind Italy, France and Spain, as well as the Soviet Union and Argentina.

As you can see by the map on the opposite page, almost every state in the United States produces wine of some kind, but only about 40 have one or more bonded wineries. California has the most, at close to 650, or more than 50 percent of all those in the nation. They produce 90 percent of the total wine made in the United States.

For the purpose of this book, we will concentrate on California wines, touching briefly on a few other states.

If you have never visited the California wine country, you have missed one of the most interesting, exciting and educational trips you could make in this country.

The first vines planted in California were brought north from Mexico in 1769 by the Franciscan Father Junipero Serra. As he moved slowly up the coast founding missions, he left a trail of grapevines behind. The vines were plentiful, but not very good. The first premium varietals were planted in the 1830's by Jean Louis Vignes, a Frenchman from Bordeaux.

The most colorful character in the early development of California wine making was a Hungarian named Agoston Haraszthy. He called himself a Count and lived like royalty on his Sonoma estate, Buena Vista. It was a showplace with a huge mansion, formal gardens, fountains and vast vineyards.

In 1861, the governor of California sent Haraszthy to Europe to bring back cuttings from the choicest vines. He returned with more than 100,000 of these from about 300 grape varieties and personally distributed them up and down the state. Most experts believe one of these varieties was the mysterious Zinfandel. Its unknown

How to Read an American Wine Label

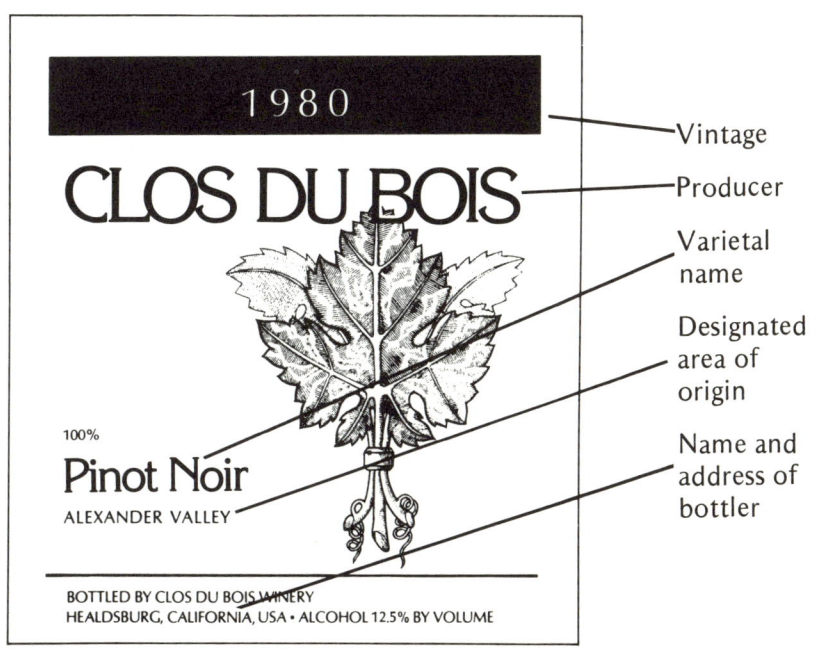

origins have made it unique to California, and it is the most widely planted grape in the state.

The fabulous Buena Vista estate was eventually abandoned, after an attack of phylloxera destroyed most of the vineyards and the 1906 earthquake demolished the storage tunnels. It was revived in 1943 by San Francisco newspaperman, Frank Bartholomew, and continues as one of Sonoma's leading wineries today.

And what happened to Haraszthy, "the father of California viticulture?" He disappeared in Nicaragua in 1869. He had gone there to look for new adventure and apparently found more than he bargained for in the form of hungry reptiles. Reportedly, he was eaten by alligators while crossing a river.

In 1870, the California wine industry was all but wiped out by the dreaded vine louse, phylloxera. Vineyard owners were just recovering from that disaster when they were hit by another — Prohibition. So it wasn't until the 1940's that California winemakers were able to lay the foundation for the industry that has brought them worldwide acclaim today.

California is divided into four major wine districts — the *North Coast,* including Napa Valley, Sonoma and Mendocino Counties; the *North Central Coast,* including Santa Clara and San Benito Counties, Monterey County, Salinas Valley, and the Santa Cruz Mountains; the *South Central Coast,* including San Luis Obispo and Santa Barbara; and the *Central Valley,* which runs more than half the length of the state.

Napa Valley and Sonoma County are the most well known districts, but the bulk of California wine comes from the San Joaquin Valley, within the Central Valley Section, where most jug wines are produced.

"Jug wine" is what we call "table wine" in Italy. These are everyday drinking wines, usually labeled with a generic name such as Chablis or Burgundy. They are neither real Chablis nor real Burgundy, of course, since those wines are made only in France. But most California jug wines, which are made from a blend of grapes, are very drinkable.

Ernest and Julio Gallo, the Italian-American brothers who have been credited with single-handedly turning American drinking habits from whiskey toward wine, make more jug wines than any other producer in the world. Their winery is not only the largest in the San Joaquin Valley, but in the United States, as well. Their annual sales are estimated at close to 50 million cases, more than all the Napa wineries combined.

Each region in California where wine is made has a different climate and within those regions microclimates can vary even in the same vineyard. The winemaker must know which variety of grapes will do best where, and it sometimes takes years of trial and error to learn this.

On my most recent visit to the California wine country I visited Napa, Sonoma, Santa Clara and Santa Barbara. They are all different, both in physical appearance and in atmosphere.

Roast Leg of Lamb with Wine Sauce, recipe on page 140

Mario Ferrari at Clos du Bois with owner Frank Woods, formerly from Nashville

Mario Ferrari with Robert Mondavi

NORTH COAST

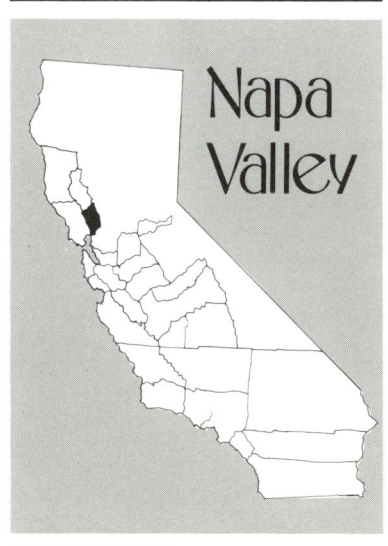

Napa Valley

The feeling in Napa Valley is that wine is not only their livelihood, but their life as well.

The valley itself is small — 30 miles long, less than 5 miles at its widest point, bordred on both sides by mountains, with majestic Mount St. Helena standing guard at the north. There are only 27,000 plantable acres, and 24,000 are planted in vines now, which makes the land very dear.

Of the principal grape varieties grown in Napa, the noble Cabernet Sauvignon and Chardonnay are by far the most popular. Other varieties planted in the region include Pinot Noir, Zinfandel, Chenin Blanc, White Riesling, Gamay, Sauvignon Blanc, Petite Sirah and Merlot.

Fine Napa Valley wines made from the Cabernet Sauvignon and Chardonnay grapes often rival the great clarets of Bordeaux and the whites of Burgundy. Cabernet Sauvignon has long been the star product of the valley, but with Americans still favoring white wine over red, winemakers are producing more and more Chardonnay.

When you approach Napa Valley from the north, through Calistoga, you hit a stretch on Highway 29 where wineries are built very close together. The buildings vary in style from restored Victorian mansions to modern concrete, and familiar names whiz by faster than you can write them down — *Stonegate, Sterling, Hanns Kornell, Stony Hill, Freemark Abbey, Charles Krug, Beringer, Sutter Home, Louis Martini, Heitz, Raymond, Grgich Hills, Beaulieu.* And those are only the ones you can see from the road before you get down to the busy stretch of road where *Mondavi* is located. There are more than 100 bonded wineries in Napa now, compared to fewer than 30 in 1971.

I was impressed to see the brotherhood of California winemakers firsthand. They couldn't be more supportive of one another, and yet they are most competitive. The publisher of the *St. Helena Star* once called it "the old barn-raising spirit." It reminds me of Italian families. We might fight among ourselves, but we stick together against everybody else.

The man who embodies this spirit is Robert Mondavi, "The King of Napa Valley." Mondavi, more than any other single winery owner, put California wines on the world map, helping them to gain credibility and respectability.

Bob is a crusader. His cause is *wine*. The passion and drive he puts into improving it, promoting it, and educating people about it, is as fervent as any crusade in history.

famous in their own right, like Warren Winiarski and Mike Grgich, founders of Stag's Leap and Grgich Hills Winery, respectively.

Mondavi encourages the talented young people who work for him to strike out and "do their own thing." He did this at age 54, when he started over from scratch and went on to build the largest premium winery in California.

He had left the family business, the Charles Krug Winery, after the death of his father. He and his brother, Peter, (who still owns Krug) could not agree on how to make and market wines.

Bob, who has the kind of drive and ambition that led him to go to work at 13 in order to put himself through Stanford University, was determined to prove his theories. So he borrowed $100,000, found two partners (whom he later bought out) and moonlighted as a consultant to other wineries to support his family until he got Mondavi off the ground.

Now in his early seventies, Bob is still doing it his way, always ahead of the pack, breaking new ground, setting the pace for other winemakers. Many of his innovative ideas for marketing and for making wine, are now standard practice in California.

Napa Boutique Wineries

While in Napa Valley, I also toured Silverado, Chappellet, Groth and St. Clement. These are small boutique wineries, represented and marketed by Wilson Daniels, Inc.

Jack Daniels, one of the partners in the firm, took us to the wineries, where the owners or winemakers held special tastings. I don't know when I've ever sampled so many fine wines in such a short period of time, each with its own unique character.

Visiting the huge mission-style Mondavi Winery was one of the highlights of my visit to the California wine country. It's like being on a college campus where all the students are filled with school spirit. They do more experimenting and innovative wine making at Mondavi than anywhere I've ever seen. You get the feeling they're all expecting the next breakthrough at any second.

We found Bob's son, Tim, who is Mondavi's winemaker, in one of the laboratories, surrounded by test tubes, vials and apprentices in white coats — like a doctor and his interns in a teaching lab.

Bob's eldest son, Michael, is president of Mondavi and his daughter, Marcia, is the Eastern Rep for the company. His wife, Margarit, plans all the wine-with-art events they hold in the winery. These include jazz concerts, theatrical performances, art exhibits and their Great Chefs series, where they import the finest chefs in the world to do week-long cooking seminars, emphasizing the marriage of wine and food.

The Mondavi operation is a real family affair, and everyone who works at the winery becomes a member of the "family." Many "graduate" to go on and become

At *Silverado*, which is owned by Walt Disney's widow, Lillian, and her daughter and son-in-law, Diane and Ron Miller, we drank their Gold Medal-winning Cabernet Sauvignon. Very fruity, silky and elegant — an outstanding wine.

In the office at Silverado, there is a large framed picture of Mickey Mouse with a brass plate under it that reads "OUR FOUNDER." I liked their sense of humor, but believe me, this is no Mickey Mouse wine! They specialize in Cabernet, Sauvignon Blanc and Chardonnay, and all are of exceptionally high quality.

The winery itself is a magnificent facility, high on a hill with a sweeping view of Napa Valley. But just to prove you don't have to have an impressive building to make fine wine, our next stop was the *Groth Winery*. This was no more than a concrete slab with wine making equipment sitting on it.

At Groth, which is a young, up-and-coming winery, they had been so busy making wine that they had not had time to finish the building! And thanks to the talents of their winemaker, Nils Venge, they were already producing award-winning Cabernet Sauvignon and Sauvignon Blanc. When their 1982 Cabernet hit the market, wine writers called it "great," "seductive," "pure velvet" and on and on. Their praise for Groth's 1983 Sauvignon Blanc was equally generous.

Chappellet is another award-winning winery, where we sampled some outstanding vino. Donn Chappellet, a man almost as big as the mountain his winery is built on, greeted us with Cabernets, Chardonnays and Chenin Blancs for tasting.

The winery, tucked away in the woods 1700 feet above the Napa Valley, is built in the shape of a pyramid with a towering roof of steel parted by long panels of glass. A spectacular sight! Some experts consider Donn's 1974 Cabernet Sauvignon the finest Cabernet ever made in California. There's none left now, but the last jeroboam (equal to 4 standard bottles) sold at a Napa Valley wine auction for $6000!

At *St. Clement*, I attended a very special wine tasting hosted by the owners, Dr. and Mrs. William Casey and their winemaker, Dennis Johns. There were 7 wine writers present, including Gerald Asher who writes the wine column for *Gourmet* magazine.

First, we were asked to sample and evaluate 6 St. Clement Chardonnays — 1978 through 1983. This was followed by 6 St. Clement Cabernet Sauvignons — 1975-76 through 1981. It was really interesting to watch this round table of pros analyzing the wines. It's like a science with them. With me, it boils down to "I like it" or "I don't like it." I liked all the St. Clements I tasted that day, even though some of the Cabernets were still too young to be at their best.

I especially like the style of their 1983 Chardonnay, which is clean and crisp and not overpowered by oak.

After the wine tasting, we were served a delicious luncheon on the patio of the beautiful old Victorian home that serves as the winery headquarters. The house, built in 1876, looks exactly like the picture on the St. Clement wine label. Dr. Casey (a famous San Francisco eye surgeon) and his wife, Alexandra, have restored the house to its original splendor. It is now one of the showplaces of Napa.

Actually, everywhere you go in Napa you see "showplace" wineries. Many are fabulous old mansions; many are ultra-modern structures, but they all have individual character — even Groth's concrete slab, which hopefully, by the time you read this will have a roof built over it.

Other Napa boutique wineries making excellent wines include Far Niente, Domaine Chandon and Schramsberg Vineyards (outstanding sparkling wines); Stag's Leap; Sterling Vineyards; and Cain Cellars. Larger Napa wineries that produce consistently good product include Clos du Val, Beaulieu, Charles Krug, Joseph Phelps, and Sutter Home.

Sonoma County

Back in the 1920's, Sonoma produced more wine than any other area in California. Since then, Napa has pushed ahead as the state's most famous region, although Sonoma has more acreage. But in the past decade, a whole new crop of wineries has sprung up in Sonoma, such as *Clos du Bois, Jordan, Chateau St. Jean* and *Kenwood.* These are now winning prestigious awards in the industry and high praise from consumers. Sonoma's future has never looked brighter.

The best-known districts within the region include Sonoma Valley, the site of the state's oldest plantings north of San Francisco. The valley's most famous wines are Zinfandel and Chardonnay, with Pinot Noir considered promising. Principal grape varieties are Cabernet Sauvignon, Zinfandel and Chardonnay. Others include Pinot Noir, Carignane, White Riesling, French Colombard and Petite Sirah.

Alexander Valley is well known for its Cabernet, Zinfandel and Chardonnay, as well as its Gewurztraminer and White Riesling. Dry Creek Valley, parallel to Alexander Valley, is best known for its Zinfandel, though fine

Donn Chappellet of Chappellet Winery

Sally Jordan at Jordan Winery

Cabernets and Chardonnays are produced there as well.

Knights Valley is a small area, first planted in the 1960's. It has shown promise with White Riesling. Russian River Valley, with a wide range of soils and microclimates, is especially versatile as a growing region.

The wineries of Sonoma are more diverse than those of Napa, and the growers emphasize this diversity.

My first stop in Sonoma was at the Jordan Winery where they make one of my all-time favorite Cabernet Sauvignons.

The history of this winery is my kind of story because it illustrates what determination can do.

From the time they were married in 1959, Tom and Sally Jordan dreamed of owning a fabulous chateau in Bordeaux where they could make First Growth wine.

Sally taught English at Colorado Woman's College, and Tom was an exploration geologist. Most people wouldn't have given them 100-to-1 odds on seeing their dream come true.

Then, in the early '70s, Tom struck it rich with the discovery of a major oil deposit in New Guinea. He knew exactly what he was going to do with the money. He and Sally immediately began chateau shopping in Bordeaux. It wasn't long before they found one they liked. Then they learned that the French government has a law against selling First Growth Chateaux to Americans (or any other nationality except French).

They were told they could buy a *lesser* chateau, but a first growth was off limits to foreigners. Jordan wanted Premier Grand Cru or nothing, so he told the French what they could do with their other growths and came home.

A few weeks later, he was having dinner at Ernie's in San Francisco. The wine steward brought him a bottle of old Beaulieu (BV), Georges de Latour from Napa Valley. One glass convinced Jordan that a truly great red wine *could* be made in California, so he got out his geologist tools and set about sampling land. He settled on Sonoma and planted 275 acres in 1972, bottling his first "estate" Cabernet in 1976. While waiting for the wine's release in 1980, Tom and Sally began building a chateau that would measure up to any in France.

The first glimpse of the Jordan Winery is awesome. You drive through electronically controlled gates onto the 270-acre estate winding up and around an oak-lined drive. Then, on a knoll above, majestically overlooking the Alexander Valley, you see a huge yellow stucco chateau with a terra cotta roof, French windows and red shutters. It looks as though a giant had plucked it from the countryside in Bordeaux and plopped it back down again across the Atlantic in Sonoma.

Off to the left, through the trees, you can see the Jordans' private chateau of the same yellow stucco and orange roof, and ahead, a gravel courtyard surrounded by a perfectly manicured lawn.

We were given our pick of three guest suites above the winery on the chateau's second floor. Choosing was not easy. All three looked like pictures from *Architectural Digest:* open redwood-beamed ceilings, walls of coordinated fabrics and wallpapers, huge fireplaces with antique mantels, Louis XV furniture, tile floors covered in Oriental rugs, bathrooms with marble sinks and gold gooseneck faucet handles and wet bars furnished with fruit baskets, cheese, Perrier, Scotch, and yes, even chilled Jordan Chardonnay. All the suites had French doors overlooking the winery itself. You could step onto the balcony, then walk down a catwalk to stand above millions of dollars worth of Jordan Cabernet, Merlot, and Chardonnay sleeping in row after row after row of oak barrels below you. Incredible sight!

The next morning, we toured the winery and talked with Rob Davis, Jordan's handsome young winemaker.

Rob is a University of California-Davis graduate who started his career at Jordan in 1976 when the winery was brand new. He works with Jordan's consultant, Andre Tchelistcheff. He told me that being with the 83-year-old Tchelistcheff is an education in itself. They spend time each year in Europe, studying methods in wineries there.

Rob is a perfectionist. He said he and Tom Jordan are not yet satisfied with their wines and may never be. "We continually experiment to make them better," he said. "That's one of the things I love about being a winemaker. There's so much to learn. It's very exciting."

I can't emphasize enough how impressed I was with the young winemakers I met in California. They all looked like college kids (I don't think even one was over 30) and many of them are young

women. Their knowledge and dedication was obvious, but it was their enthusiasm for their work that got to me. Just imagine the quality of wines these young people will be making with about 20 more years experience!

Clos du Bois

My second Sonoma stop was the Clos du Bois Winery in Healdsburg.

We arrived to find the owner, and former Nashvillian, Frank Woods, back in the fermentation room with his sleeves rolled up, working alongside his cellar master, Barry Johnson.

Barry was wearing a gas mask, and when I smelled sulphur, I knew what he had been doing. He was burning out barrels with a sulphur wick to cleanse them for storage. I used to do the same thing for my Papa when I was a kid in Italy.

Frank is my kind of boss. He doesn't sit behind a desk and give orders. He's a "hands on" winemaker, and he is also one of the smartest businessmen I know. It takes that combination to be a successful winemaker in today's competitive market.

One thing I learned in California: the wineries that fail do so because the owners don't know enough about business and marketing, not because they don't know how to make wine.

The Chateau built over the Jordan Winery

Frank's background *is* business and marketing. He was an executive with Procter & Gamble before starting his own marketing firm, and the idea of owning a winery lured him away from the corporate world.

Before that, he was a Nashville boy whose father ran the old Maxwell House Hotel and later owned Nobles Restaurant. It was at Nobles that Frank got his first real taste of management, while he was still going to Hillsboro High School.

The wine making bug didn't bite until after he'd moved to San Francisco to start his marketing firm. When it did, he took it slowly. First, he planted vineyards in Sonoma and, for the next ten years, sold the grapes to other wineries while the vines matured enough to produce the fruit he wanted for his own label.

In 1974, he decided his grapes were ready to be marketed under the Clos du Bois name, but he still didn't go into the wine business full time until his vino was ready to hit the market in 1977. Then, Frank hit the market with it. He traveled all over the country promoting Clos du Bois, and he still does, spending about 60 percent of his time on the road.

After touring the winery, Frank took us over to his Dry Creek farmhouse where we were to spend the night.

The house, which was built in 1890, sits in the middle of acres of vineyards, with majestic Mount St. Helena off in the distance. Even though this volcano has not erupted for two million years, the ash from its last blowup still affects the mineral content of the soil, making it perfect for vine growing.

Frank has restored the exterior of the white clapboard farmhouse to its original state and modernized the inside, making it one of the most attractive, comfortable homes I have ever visited.

The first thing I noticed upon entering the house was the wonderful aroma coming from the kitchen. Myra Hoefer, who, with her husband Wade, oversees and manages the Dry Creek Vineyard, was cooking pasta for lunch. One whiff and I knew I was in for a good time!

Inez Ferrari, Frank's public relations director, had thoughtfully brought along Pavarotti tapes, so we sat down to a lunch of delicious peasant pasta (see Myra's recipe on page 110), Italian opera and outstanding Clos du Bois wines. *Heaven!*

We sampled 9 wines that day — Chardonnays, Merlots, Marlstone, Pinot Noir, Cabernet Sauvignons and late harvest Johannisberg Riesling — and I promise you, each and every one of them was outstanding.

Frank told me wine making is one of the riskiest businesses imaginable. "You have to be willing to make more changes and more often than any business I know," he said, "but your margin for error is much less. I always remember what George Latour, the founder of Beaulieu Vineyards, once said, 'There are 3 principal ways to go broke: the fastest is to own a racehorse; the most enjoyable is to have an expensive mistress; but the surest way is to plant a vineyard!' "

Frank's risk-taking has paid off. In 1984, with his winery less than a decade old, he won more awards in California competitions than any other winery in the state.

Sebastiani

Another Sonoma winery that impresses me is Sebastiani's. In the early days of the California wine industry, all the wineries were family owned and operated. But now, so many big corporations have moved in and either bought out or bought controlling interest in California wineries that it's unusual to find one still owned and operated by the founding family. That's what makes the Sebastiani so interesting — one family, three generations, but amazing differences.

Sam Sebastiani took over the winery in 1980 when his father, August, died. (August's father, Samuele, founded the winery in 1904.) The winery had grown in sales from 550,000 cases in 1974 to *3 million* cases in 1979, making it the 10th largest winery in the country.

But August had not increased his staff and was still using the same outdated equipment, although his volume was *six* times greater, and things had gotten out of control. In addition, Sebastiani had no premium product.

Sam saw premium California wines as the wave of the future. His father had been content with making good jug wines at fair prices. That year Sam cut his grape buys by 3,000 tons because of poor quality. Doing without grapes meant making less wine, which meant less sales. Sam knew the risk he was taking because it takes years to upgrade a line of wines. You only have one vintage a year, and that means only one chance a year to change the product with better raw materials.

Sam invested $3.5 million on new French and American oak barrels; made an eight-fold increase in laboratory operations including an experimental "winery within a winery"; and began an eight-acre experimental vineyard with University of California at Davis, whick is the University's only experimental vineyard in Sonoma.

In just 5 short years, Sam Sebastiani upgraded the quality of his wines (while keeping the prices low) to where they now consistently win competition medals as well as critics' praise.

In addition to an impressive line of premium varietals, they are also making some of the best jug wine on the market. Their "Country" series — Cabernet Sauvignon, Fume Blanc and White Zinfandel — are exceptionally good values. They are now also bottling their famous Pinor Noir Blanc "Eye of the Swan," a superior blush wine, in 1.5 liter jug size.

The Sebastianis were among the first California winery owners to emphasize and promote pairing wines and foods. Sam's wife, Vicki, and his mother, Sylvia, are both noted gourmet cooks and have written several cookbooks. They were kind enough to contribute some great recipes for this book.

Mendocino Lake Counties

At St. Clement wine tasting with Mrs. William Carey and Jack Daniels of Wilson-Daniels Winery

This is the northernmost wine district of California. It is beautiful country with a wide variety of soils and terrain: steep mountain slopes, redwood forests, deep valley canyons and gently curved hillsides bisected by the Russian River.

There are only about 30 wineries in this rural area now, but many observers feel the district is a real comer due mainly to the fact that they've had such good luck with red wines.

Wineries, such as *Parducci, Fetzer, Weibel* and *Cresta Blanca,* are producing excellent Cabernets, Pinot Noirs and Zinfandels. There are about 11,000 acres of grapes with the principal varieties being Carignane, Zinfandel, French Colombard, Cabernet Sauvignon, Petite Sirah, Pinot Noir, White Riesling and Gewurztraminer.

I've met two of the Mendocino winemakers — John Parducci and Bob Fetzer — and I was impressed by both.

John Parducci is a farmer, a real man of the land, whose winery is known as the post-Prohibition pioneer of that area. He doesn't like the flavor that wood aging gives wines, believing, as I do, that oak often overwhelms the fruit. He makes wonderful Chardonnays that have never seen wood. Most of his reds are aged in redwood to soften them and even the ones that spend time in oak don't stay long enough to pick up wood flavors.

I met Bob Fetzer when he came to Nashville to hold a wine tasting. His family's operation reminds me of winemakers in the Old Country. Over there, the children are put to work in the vineyards, and the business is passed on from father to son.

Bob's father, Barney Fetzer, put his *eleven* kids to work in the vineyards before they were old enough to go to school. When he died in 1981, the winery was passed on to his daughters as well as his sons. (Only one of them, a daughter, Cathy, is not with the vineyard, but Bob says she might as well be, because she's their number one consumer!)

I arrived at the Fetzer wine tasting just in time to catch Bob finishing a beer. When I teased him, he laughed and said, "My father used to say it takes a lot of cold beer to make wine, and Fetzers still believe that."

The Fetzers may love beer, but it was evident at the tasting that they love their wine as well, from the ground up. As Bob explained, they think of themselves as farmers, whose first love is the land, then the vine and finally the wine. This is also the Old Country way.

From the consumer's viewpoint, one of the best things about the Fetzer operation is that they are dedicated to making *good* wine that will sell for under $10 a bottle.

NORTH CENTRAL COAST

With 36,000 acres of vineyards, Monterey is second in size only to Sonoma among coastal counties. White Riesling, Chardonnay and Chenin Blanc grapes dominate the acreage, with plantings of Cabernet Sauvignon, Zinfandel, and Pinot Noir evident as well.

Since an estimated 30,000 acres were planted from 1970 through 1974, many of the area's wines are still undergoing experimentation. Monterey's cool climate suits White Riesling quite well, and some Chardonnays have been produced here, too, though they are not as consistent.

Salinas Valley, the county's main area, produces some good whites in the north end, while the

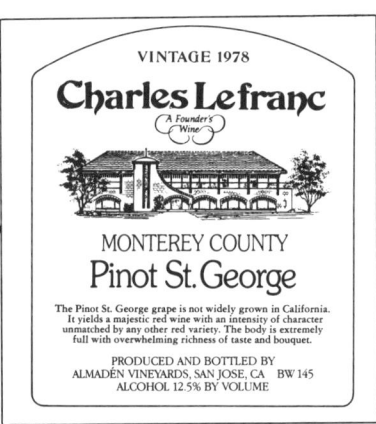
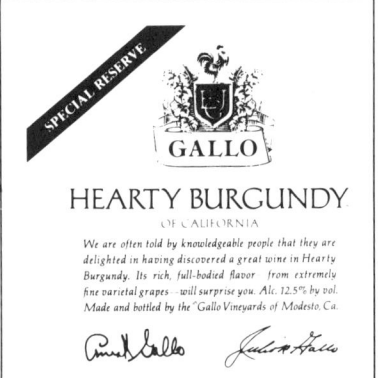

south appears to be quite versatile. In addition, some very good Cabernets and Chenin Blancs have come from nearby Carmel Valley. Monterey Vineyards is the best-known winery in this area.

San Benito County vineyards are almost all owned by Almaden, approximately 3,800 acres with over 2 *million* vines.

As one of the largest California producers, Almaden also owns vineyards in Monterey and Alameda counties, plus five wineries, with over 40 million gallons of wine in cooperage. They bottle their premium wines under the Charles LeFranc label.

Almaden and Paul Masson wineries share the same early history. Both date from 1852 when Etienne Thee, a Bordeaux farmer, planted his vineyards near Los Gatos in the Santa Clara Valley. His son-in-law, Charles LeFranc, inherited the vineyards and later, his son-in-law, Paul Masson, a native of Burgundy, went into wine making with him. In 1892, Masson bought out Charles LeFranc's son's share of the business and formed the Paul Masson Champagne Company, which eventually became Paul Masson Wines. But the original Santa Clara vineyards, named Almaden for a local quicksilver mine, stayed in the LeFranc family, then went dormant during Prohibition, and were finally bought by Louis Benoist, in 1941. The vineyards and winery grew by leaps and bounds under his direction and today they own a total of about 7,000 *acres* of vineyards.

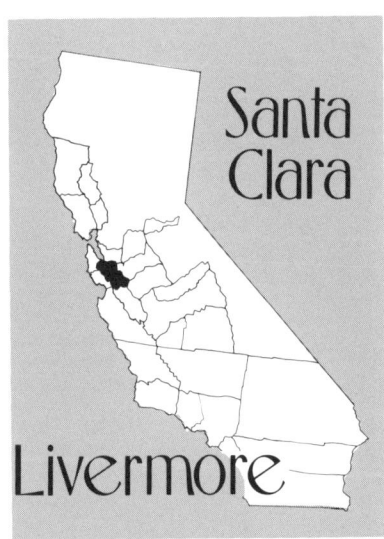

The Livermore Valley, the most famous appellation of Alameda County is famous for its Sauvignon Blanc and Semillon wines. Grey Riesling is also widely planted, and Petite Sirah and Zinfandel are grown in the valley as well. Livermore Valley wines tend to be ripe and subtle in their fruitiness and frequently resemble those made from the Napa Valley floor.

Nearby are Santa Clara and Santa Cruz Counties. Santa Clara produces many table wines. Paul Masson and Almaden have bottling and visitor facilities in San Jose and the large San Martin winery is based in the town of the same name. While there isn't much acreage in Santa Cruz, it houses several wineries.

Ridge Winery

One of the most prestigious of these is Ridge, which sits on a mountain *ridge* called Montebello, overlooking the famous Silicon Valley on one side and the infamous San Andreas Fault on the other.

The winery is a mountain house, built 100 years ago by an Italian immigrant who dug the cellars underground from solid limestone.

The present winery began in 1959, when 4 electronics engineers from Silicon Valley bought the place as a weekend getaway house. One of the partners, David Bennion, began making wine from grapes in the old vineyards, which had been planted by the original owner in the 1880's. The results were so good that David left engineering and went to work full time at the winery. He later brought in winemaker Paul Draper as another partner.

When I arrived at Ridge, after a harrowing drive straight up a curving mountain road, Paul Draper was there to meet me, along with his sales director, Don Reisen.

Paul showed us around the old place, which reminded me of wineries back in Italy because the cellar *smelled* of wine. (Most California wineries are so modern and clean they're as antiseptic as a hospital.)

Although Ridge produces prize wine from their 50 acres of vineyards at the winery (which are the highest elevated vineyards in the state), they buy most of their grapes from other growers.

They send their own trucks down the mountain to pick up the grapes. That way they will know the fruit has not been left sitting anywhere after being picked.

At Ridge, everything is done the old-fashioned, *natural* way — from racking sediment from barrels by hand every few months, to letting the wine ferment only with the grapes' *natural* yeast, adding no commercial yeast.

It is much more of a risk to make wine this way because you do not have as much control. You are depending on nature to do the work. Paul is convinced it is the way to make wines with more personality: "Wines that let the vintage show through," he says. Ninety-nine percent of their product at Ridge is red wine, but they are making about 1000 gallons of Chardonnay now. They are widely acclaimed for their White Zinfandel, too.

Ridge labels each wine with the name of the vineyard where they buy the grapes, but the most prized comes from their own Montebello vineyard — Ridge Montebello Cabernet Sauvignon. Because of the acclaim of this particular wine, dating back to its first 1962 release, Paul says without hesitation that they consider themselves the only "first growth" wine in the Bay Area.

73 Zinfandel, Geyserville, bottled October 1975
The long Indian summer of '73 allowed the Geyserville vines to go well beyond full maturity. The Lytton Springs vineyard, located on the same hills, produced a small proportion of similar grapes. Together they avoided the raisin quality of many late-picked wines and achieved this clean, rich varietal fruit. Though enjoyable tasting in the spring, it should be laid down for at least three years. PD (10/75)

RIDGE wine is made with an emphasis on quality and naturalness that is rarely attempted. Our grapes are grown in select vineyards (usually identified on the label), where they are left to ripen to peak maturity, often at some loss of quantity. We let the wine settle and age in small barrels, with only rare cellar treatment other than racking. Varieties are not blended unless so indicated on the label. Near Black Mountain on Monte Bello Ridge, our main vineyard is 10 miles south of Palo Alto, 15 miles inland from the ocean, and over 2000 feet in elevation. For requesting information on ordering wines or visiting the winery for tasting, please send us a note or call (408) 867-3233.   DRB (1967)

RIDGE
CALIFORNIA
ZINFANDEL
GEYSERVILLE
1973

LATE PICKED GRAPES FROM TWO HILL VINEYARDS BOTTLED OCT 1975 ALCOHOL 14.3% BY VOLUME PRODUCED AND BOTTLED BY RIDGE VINEYARDS 17100 MONTE BELLO RD, CUPERTINO, CALIFORNIA

Paul Draper, Winemaker of Ridge Winery

SOUTH CENTRAL COAST

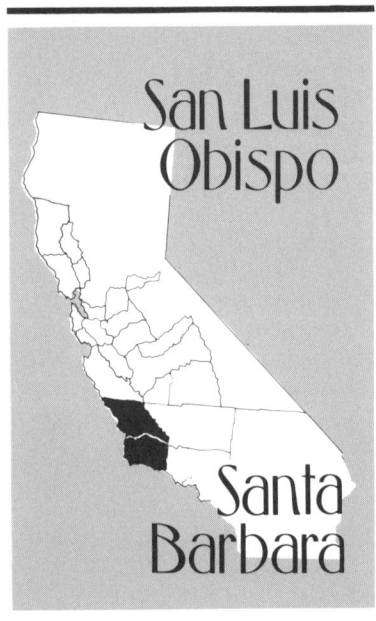

This area, which includes the counties of Santa Barbara and San Luis Obispo, as well as the Santa Ynez Valley, has undergone tremendous growth in the past decade.

During the sixties, there were only about 600 acres planted in vines in San Luis Obispo County. Today, there are over 5,000. There has also been a great deal of growth in the Santa Ynez Valley, and new wineries are springing up all the time around the towns of Santa Barbara and Ojai.

One of the first wineries in the South Central Coastal area to gain national recognition was Firestone. It is also one of my favorite California wineries.

Brooks and Kate Firestone came to the Santa Ynez Valley in the early seventies. Brooks describes himself as the "classic executive drop-out" because after 12 years in the business, he just walked away from his family's multibillion dollar Firestone Tire Company, which was founded by his grandfather in 1900.

"I finally decided my soul wasn't in it," he says, even though at the time he had no clear plans for his future. It wasn't until his father, Leonard, who owned a 300-acre vineyard and cattle ranch near Santa Barbara, asked him to check out the property for investment potential, that Brooks and Kate decided they wanted to go into the wine business.

Kate, who had been a solo ballerina with the London Royal Ballet when they met and married, was equally enthusiastic about starting a winery, even though they were both aware of the hard work that lay ahead.

"I knew it would take 10 years to get the winery in the black," Brooks says. His father and Suntory Ltd., a Japanese whiskey company, became silent partners, helping to provide the necessary operating capital. They planted their first vines in 1973, then began building the winery 2 years later. The building is a four-level, cathedral-like structure of redwood and stained glass with red tile floors. This is a modern winery all the way: enormous temperature-controlled rooms, giant stainless steel tanks and state-of-the-art wine-making equipment.

Allison Green, their young winemaker, doesn't even look old enough to drink wine, much less make it. She grew up in the fermentation rooms, as her father was the owner of the Simi Winery in Healdsburg. She became a protege of the famed oenologist, Andre Tchelistcheff, who recommended her for the job at Firestone in 1976.

I lunched at Firestone, with Kate and the winery's general manager, Allen Russell. We sat in a grass courtyard surrounded by flowers, devouring a lovely picnic under an old olive tree. It reminded me of Italy.

Kate first served a delicious shrimp bisque, with Firestone 1982 Sauvignon Blanc, Alexander Valley. This light, dry, fruity, *crisp* wine was the perfect choice for the rich bisque.

Next Kate brought out a huge platter of croissants filled with turkey, ham and roast beef, and we switched to a 1982 Firestone Chardonnay. It was great with the slightly sweet croissant bread.

Kate Firestone

I asked Kate what wines she and Brooks usually drink at home as their "house wine." She laughed and answered immediately, "Firestone, of course. We usually find ourselves reaching for the Merlot or the Rose of Cabernet Sauvignon." With that, she brought out a bottle of 1979 Merlot, an exceptional wine that everyone agreed made a great match for the roast beef croissant sandwiches.

We finished lunch with fruit, cheese, bread and an *outstanding* dessert wine, the 1982 Santa Ynez Valley Johannisberg Riesling, Ambassador's Vineyard, Selected Harvest.

The grapes have to be attacked by *botrytis* (noble rot) before this wine can be made. As Allen and Kate each pointed out, if you found these grapes in your refrigerator, you would throw them out immediately. They look rotten, but they make a *fabulous* wine.

Allen said while this vintage was fermenting, they kept smelling enticing aromas of apricots, orange blossoms and honey from these tanks. And with one taste you know why. This wine is a dessert in itself, as sweet as a *bacio* (kiss), with a delicious, lingering finish.

That night, I joined Kate and Allen (Brooks was out of town on business) at a local restaurant, where we drank more outstanding Firestone wines: including a 1978 Vintage Reserve Cabernet Sauvignon. This is one of the best California Cabernets I've ever tasted.

After dinner, Kate said she wanted us to try something different, a wine I had never tasted — *Stirrup Cup*. The label read 1978 Firestone Santa Ynez Valley Pinot Noir *Stirrup Cup*.

Allen explained this wine can only be made when there is a second picking of Pinot Noir grapes. This happens only under very specific weather conditions, so they cannot make it every year. They named it *Stirrup Cup* because that is the name of a drink that horsemen like before or after riding on a cold morning. (Brooks is a big polo player.)

The minute I tasted it, I knew I had found the drink I'm taking with me the next time I go duck hunting and have to sit in a cold blind before daylight. This wine is *magnificent!* It has a dry, port-like flavor and because it is 17.2 percent alcohol, it really warms the cockles.

The perfect wine to sip by the fire on a cold winter night!

Brooks Firestone has been determined to achieve excellence in every wine he produces from the day he planted his first vines. So far, he has lived up to his goal, and his wines continue to get better and better. I would heartily recommend any Firestone wine I have ever tasted, and I do not know many other wineries I could say that about. Brooks has said his dream is that some day when people think of Firestone, they will think of wine, not tires. I already do!

THE CENTRAL VALLEY

Due to the fact that this Valley is nearly as big as Tennessee, the wineries range in size and type — from the unbelievably enormous Gallo operation in Modesto, to the small boutique wineries, such as Ficklin Vineyard in Madera. Here they specialize in producing fine vintage port.

The Cribari Winery in Fresno produces a complete line of table, sparkling and dessert wines, as well as Brandy.

This winery was started in the early 1900's, when Beniamino Cribari immigrated from Italy. He settled on 40 acres of land in Santa Clara County, where he made wine for his family and friends. By the time Beniamino died in 1942, his small Santa Clara plot had increased to 5,000 acres, and the winery had grown into one of California's largest. Today, Albert Cribari, one of the founder's grandsons, runs the winery with an emphasis on making table wines that complement food.

In the state of Washington, they believe that California's biggest wine competition isn't going to come from France or Italy, but from their own 100,000 acres suitable for the growth of premium wine grapes. (There are more than 250,000 acres suitable for grape growing. However, most of this is best for the Concord grape, which supplies the fresh grape juice market.)

At present, the Washington wine country comprises about 10,000 acres, concentrated in the Columbia Valley, where the Snake and Yakima Rivers join the Columbia River. Summers in this area are warm and dry with low precipitation and few clouds. The latitude is the same as that of the Bordeaux and Burgundy regions in France, where most of the world's finest wines are made.

Today, Washington State is regarded as one of the great frontiers of American wine making. This region's vineyards are just starting to come into their own.

The winery most responsible

for the state's impact on connoisseurs, both here and abroad, is *Chateau Ste. Michelle.* This winery has pioneered the planting of *vinifera* (European fine-wine grape varieties) and the development of small viticultural zones in Columbia Valley.

As a result, Chateau Ste. Michelle wines have won numerous world awards, causing many experts to predict that 10 years from now, the Pacific Northwest will be the Burgundy, the Bordeaux, the Loire, the Germany and the Northern Italy of the United States.

Chateau Ste. Michelle produces almost 500,000 cases of premium wines under that label, and an additional 100,000 cases of blended (generic) wines under the *Farron Ridge* label. Despite its size, the winery has maintained a quality level that would be a credit to any wine-making region.

Their reds include Cabernet Sauvignon, Merlot and Pinot Noir. Their whites are Chardonnay, Fume Blanc, Johannisberg Riesling, Semillon-Blanc, White Riesling, Semillon and Chenin Blanc. They also make a sparkling wine, Blanc de Noir, and two Roses, Grenache Rose and Rose of Cabernet, plus a delicious dessert wine, Muscat Canelli. All are award winners.

New York is unique among viticultural areas of the world because it produces wine from 3 distinct types of grapes: native American types (mainly lambrusco) vinifera (European), and hybrids of those two.

Of New York's total grape acreage (about 40,000), 90 percent is planted in lambrusco types, of which the Concord is the number one variety. Lambrusco-based wines have little to offer the sophisticated palate. They have intense flavor and usually lack subtlety and complexity. They, more often than not, overpower food.

The vinifera grapes, which make much better wines, are limited to about 1,000 acres. Interest in planting more of these is growing as New York winemakers recognize that an increasingly larger share of the market prefers dry rather than semi-sweet table wines.

The major wine-growing districts of New York are the Hudson River Valley, the Finger Lakes area and the Chatauqua and Niagara districts, near Lake Erie, in the western part of the state. In each case, the proximity to large bodies of water permits grapes to be grown in what would otherwise be very cold latitudes. Even so, the grape growing season is very short, around 150 days.

I am personally not fond of New York wines, generally speaking, but don't take my word for it. To quote an ancient philosopher, Pliny the Elder, "The best kind of wine is that which is most pleasant to him who drinks it."

Oregon is considered by many as the "promised land" for the stubborn Pinot Noir grape, which produces the fine Burgundy of France, but refuses to do well in California.

Oregon's wine industry is still quite small (only about 35 wineries), but sales of their wines were up by 20 percent in 1984. Even so, at 550,000 gallons per year, they were still producing only as much wine as one medium-sized California winery.

What they lack in quantity, however, Oregonians believe they make up for in quality. In addition to the award-winning Pinot Noirs they've produced, several wineries (including Eyrie Vineyards, Ponzi Vineyards and Adelsheim Vineyards, all located near Portland) are now making fine Pinot Gris.

Although popular in Europe, this varietal is virtually unknown in this country. The best European examples of Pinot Gris are the dry Tokay 'd Alsace from France, and the Pinot Grigio (one of my favorite whites) from Italy. In Germany, where it is known as Rulander, the grape is made into Kabinett, Auslese and Spatlese wines.

The Pinot Gris wine is especially suitable for Oregon because it is considered a "match made in heaven" with salmon.

Other varietals produced in Oregon include Chardonnay and White Riesling.

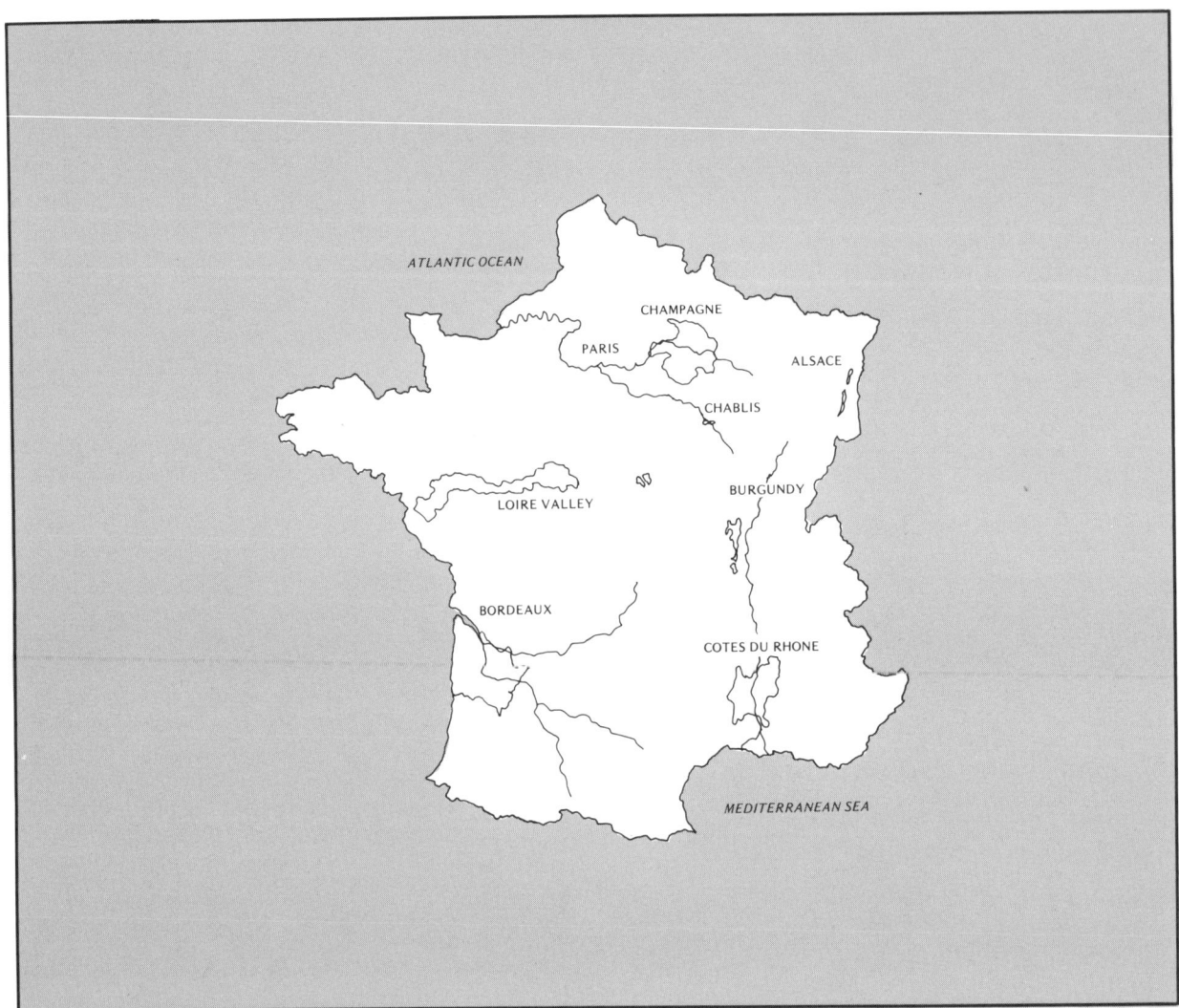

FRANCE

France has been called "the undisputed mistress of the vine" and with good reason. No country in the world produces an *average level* of quality wines as high as those of France. Italy produces more wine, and some of their world-class wines, such as Brunello di Montalcino, can stand up to any of France's best, but their overall level of quality doesn't compare. California, Germany, Spain and Portugal also have their outstanding wines, but again, their proportion of *greats* doesn't measure up to those of France.

There are many reasons for this, including climate, consistency of the soil, years of experience with the vines, and strict laws *(Appellation Controlee)* governing the origin, production method and contents of the wine. But the character of the French people also has much to do with it. The French care intensely about sensual pleasure and certainly no pleasure is more revered than fine wine and food.

Americans tend to believe that all Frenchmen are wine experts simply because they live in the country that produces the best. This is not true. The average Frenchman does know his local wine, just as the average Italian does, and they do drink wine with meals as automatically as we drink water, milk, soda pop or iced tea. But again, like Italians, outside of the few connoisseurs and the world-class winemakers themselves, the average Frenchman would never think to make a *study* of wine. It would be like an American making a *study* of Coke or Pepsi. (When my friends and relatives in Italy first learned that I was writing a weekly wine column they laughed. To them it sounded as silly as it would to us if someone said they were writing an iced tea column!)

Nevertheless, anyone who really wants to know wine, *must* know French wine, since it has set the standard for the rest of the world for centuries. It is especially important for Americans because all of the finest wines in this country are vinified from French grape varieties. Therefore, a knowledge of French wines can lead to a better appreciation of the best American wines.

How to Read a French Wine Label

- The winery coat-of-arms
- Name of the estate on which the wine was grown; also the brand name of the wine.
- Growth classification established in 1855. *Grand* is very good, but the top rating in Bordeaux is *Premier Cru* (First Growth).
- Vintage year — the year the wine was produced.
- Margaux — one of the four *communes* or townships in the Haut-Medoc Subregion of the Bordeaux wine region.
- The wine reaches the quality standards of the Margaux region.
- The wine was bottled at the estate which produced it.
- Identifying number for the bottle and cellar.
- The net contents of the bottle.
- The name and address of the vineyard owner.

How to Read a French Wine Label

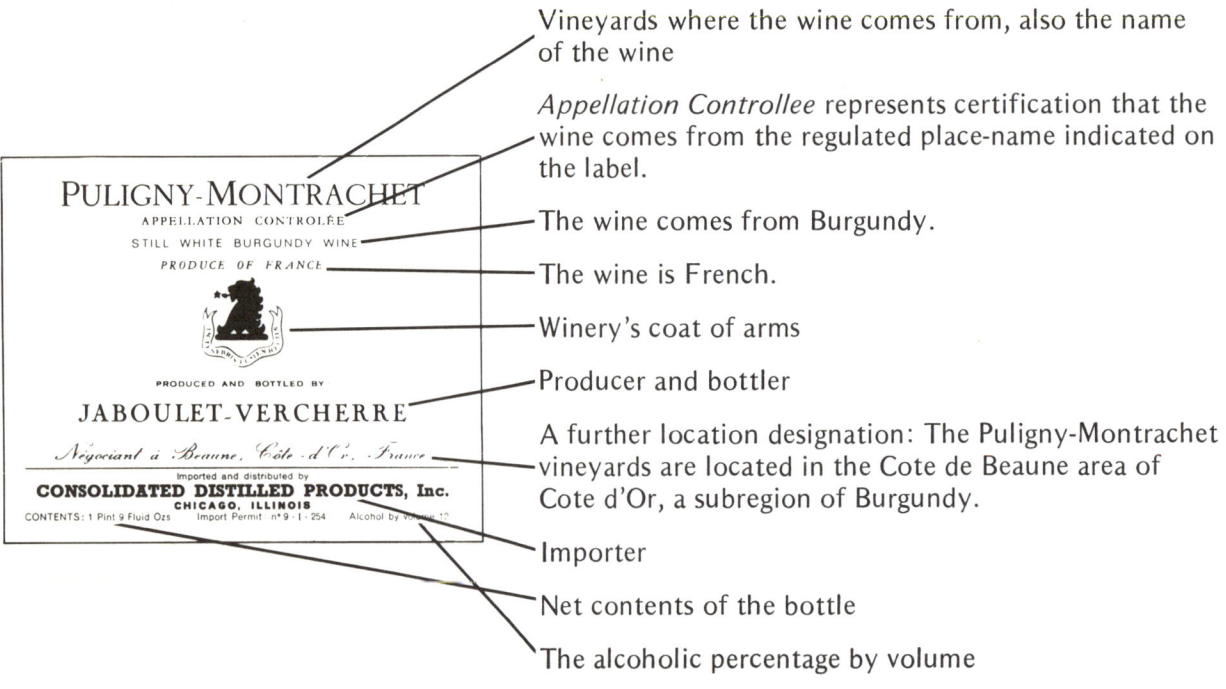

- Vineyards where the wine comes from, also the name of the wine
- *Appellation Controllee* represents certification that the wine comes from the regulated place-name indicated on the label.
- The wine comes from Burgundy.
- The wine is French.
- Winery's coat of arms
- Producer and bottler
- A further location designation: The Puligny-Montrachet vineyards are located in the Cote de Beaune area of Cote d'Or, a subregion of Burgundy.
- Importer
- Net contents of the bottle
- The alcoholic percentage by volume

WINE REGIONS of FRANCE

Some wine is produced in every region of France, but almost all the great French wines come from six areas: *Alsace, Bordeaux, Burgundy, Champagne,* the *Loire Valley* and the *Rhone Valley*.

The major white wine producing regions of France are Alsace, Loire Valley, Bordeaux and Burgundy. Bordeaux and Burgundy also produce the most celebrated reds.

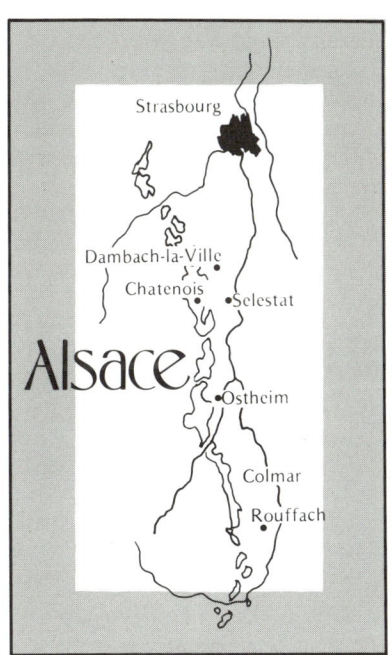

In the far northeastern corner of France, just across the Rhine River from Germany, lies Alsace. These wines are often more German in character than French.

Perhaps because of the German influence, and because the grape varieties are basically not French, the system of naming wines in Alsace is not geographical. *This is the only important region in France where this is true.* Wine names are varietal here, as they are for the best wines of California. This means that the name of the grape variety, rather than the specific vineyard, appears on the label. For this reason, it is especially important to know the names of these varietals. One of the earliest wine regions to decree its own favored grapes, Alsace now allows *seven* varieties to be grown. Four are classified as "Noble Varieties": Riesling (rees-ling); Gewurztraminer (ga-verse-truh-mee-nair); Muscat and Tokay d'Alsace (or Pinot Gris). Sylvaner (sil-vah-ner); and Pinot Blanc (pee-no-blon) follow as "Fine Varieties" with the mild Chasselas (shah-suh-lah) classed as the sole "Standard" grape.

Alsace wines are probably the easiest of all French wines to understand. They're bottled in the slender, easily recognized *flute d'Alsace,* a shape reserved for this region by law. They are easy to enjoy — abundant, and ready to drink young.

The intense floral taste and bouquet of all Alsace wines flatter spicy foods. Served bracingly cold, they're perfect partners for curries, sauerkraut, Mexican food and Chinese cuisine, as well as many types of milder fare.

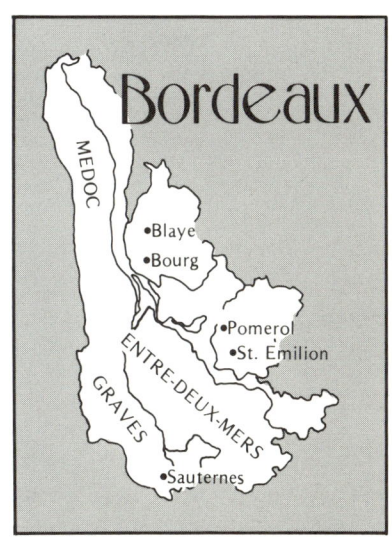

By contrast, Bordeaux is one of the most complicated French wine regions to know well. It is also without question the most important viticultural area of France, and therefore of the world. It produces both red and white wines of extraordinary quality. They have been exported in huge volumes all over the world since 1152. At that time, King Henry II of England married Eleanor of Aquitaine, and received the Bordeaux region as her dowry. With Britain ruling the waves, Bordeaux wines were carried everywhere and their quality became recognized the world over.

Located near the Atlantic coast in southwestern France, the region is ruled by its rivers and the sea. The city of Bordeaux has served as a major seaport for 1,000 years. The vineyard area, entitled to the appellation Bordeaux (about 250,000 acres), produces over 30 million cases annually. The land, spreading out eastward from the seaport, is ideal for cultivating vines. The soil is often coarse and rocky, containing sand, gravel and pebbles. This makes it difficult to grow other agricultural products, but is perfect for growing the Cabernet, Merlot, Malbec, Sauvignon and Semillon grapes used to make the celebrated Bordeaux wines.

Subregions of Bordeaux

The Bordeaux region is broken down into many subregions, the most important being the *Medoc, Graves, St. Emilion, Pomerol, Sauternes/Barsac* and *Entre-Deux-Mers.* These subregions will also be listed on labels. It's important to know them because a bottle of wine labeled Medoc will usually be superior to one labeled Bordeaux alone. *The geographical identity of the wine is narrowed down as the quality rises.*

MEDOC — Within the subregions are individual *communes* or communities. Within the Medoc, for example, are the *communes* of *Margaux, St. Julien, St. Estephe* and *Pauillac;* and bottles labeled with any of these designations are likely to contain wine superior to bottles labeled simply Medoc.

Going one step further, there are specific Bordeaux names of individual vineyards within each *commune*. These vineyards or estates are named after chateaux: Chateau Lafite-Rothschild; Chateau Mouton Rothschild, etc. (Now do you see why Bordeaux is so complicated?)

These wines are the best of Bordeaux and, according to most experts, the best of the world.

Within this category is a group of 65 chateaux that were classified as superior to all others in an exposition in Paris in 1855.

The Classification was broken down into five *crus* or growths. The *Premiers Crus* or First Growths, are considered the best, and the *Cinquiemes Crus* or Fifth Growths are considered the least best. However, a ranking anywhere in the five First Growths sets a chateau high above the thousands of other estates in the Bordeaux region. A Fifth Growth should never be considered a fifth-rate wine, but as one of the most prized wines of Bordeaux.

The only alteration to this *Classification of the Gironde* came in 1973. After 51 years of effort, Baron Phillippe de Rothschild succeeded in having his Medoc chateau, Mouton-Rothschild, upgraded from a Second Growth to a First.

Medoc is the peninsula which extends north of the city of Bordeaux. It is divided into 2 parts: Medoc (may-dok) and Haut-Medoc (oh may-dok), home to the most celebrated chateaux.

GRAVES — (grahv) lies south of Medoc and surrounds the city of Bordeaux. Its name is derived from the valuable gravel in its soil, allowing for better drainage. The gravel also serves as a "leavening agent" which magnifies the character of the soil.

Although Graves is known mostly for its white wines, just as many superb reds are made there. One Graves chateau, *Haut-Brion*, was given a First Growth status in the 1855 classification.

SAINT-EMILION — (a-meel-yone) is the oldest wine district in Bordeaux. Located just east of the city of Bordeaux, it is here — perhaps more than in any part of this aristocratic region — that people exude a passion for making fine wine. The wines are full-bodied and hearty, sharing a characteristic richness.

POMEROL — (pom-er-all) is the smallest of the great Bordeaux districts, producing wine that is treasured for its velvet texture. In the early seventies, it received worldwide attention as the favored wine of rock stars, largely due to Mick Jagger's fondness for it.

SAUTERNES & BARSAC — (saw-tern & bar-zac) are further south where the soil becomes better suited to white grape varieties.

THE OFFICIAL 1855 CLASSIFICATION OF THE MEDOC

The First and Second growths of the 1855 Classifications of the Five Growths of the Medoc of Bordeaux are:

CHATEAU	LOCATION
Premiers Crus (First Growth)	
Chateau Lafite-Rothschild	Pauillac
Chateau Margaux	Margaux
Chateau Latour	Pauillac
Chateau Haut-Brion	Graves
Chateau Mouton Rothschild	Pauillac
Seconds Crus (Second Growth)	
Chateau Rausan-Segla	Margaux
Chateau Rauzan-Gassies	Margaux
Chateau Leoville-Las-Cases	St. Julien
Chateau Leoville-Poyferre	St. Julien
Chateau Leoville-Barton	St. Julien
Chateau Durfort-Vivens	Margaux
Chateau Gruaud-Larose	St. Julien
Chateau Lascombes	Margaux
Chateau Brane-Cantenac	Cantenac-Margaux
Chateau Pichon-Longueville (Baron)	Pauillac
Chateau Pichon-Longueville (Comtesse)	Pauillac
Chateau Ducru-Beaucaillou	St. Julien
Chateau Cos-d'Estournel	St. Estephe
Chateau Montrose	St. Estephe

White grapes are used exclusively here, where they are made into the finest sweet (dessert) wines in the world.

Sauternes is made with painstaking care and expensive procedures. The grapes are left on the vine to ripen until they are affected with "noble rot" (botrytis cinerea), to concentrate their bouquet and sugar. After they are fully shriveled, the grapes are handpicked. The result is a wine so intensely flavorful the taste is an unforgettable experience. The most famous French Sauternes is *Chateau d Y'quem*, the only one designated as a Premier Grand Cru (First Growth) in the 1855 Sauternes classification. It is also one of the world's most expensive wines, selling for as much as $150.00 per half bottle, depending on the vintage.

Barsac wines are similar to Sauternes, though a bit spicier and more flowery.

ENTRE-DEUX-MERS — (on-treh dooh mare) and Premieres Cotes de Bordeaux occupy a wooded, wedge-shaped area formed by the converging Dordogne and Garonne Rivers. Located in the heart of Bordeaux, both produce a variety of wines, from delicate dry whites to fruity clarets (the British word for red Bordeaux wine), red table wines, and even sweet Sauternes-like wine.

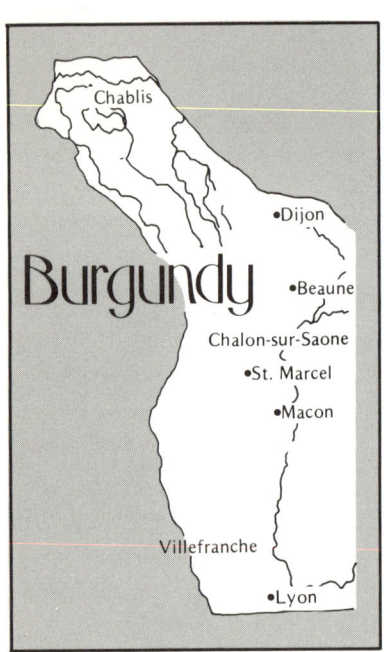

Located at the heart of eastern France, Bourgogne (bore-*goan*-yuh), or Burgundy as we know it, is a region famous for wines that reflect a wholehearted obsession with perfection. Nowhere is wine more a part of everyday life.

The reputation of Burgundy rests on red wines that are velvet-textured, robust and sensuous, and radiant whites that rank among the best in the world. But for all the nobility of its wines, Bourgogne remains a rural, rustic land, home to people of the soil.

This is the only place in the world where *authentic* Burgundy is made. The best reds are made from the Pinot Noir grape; the best whites from the Chardonnay.

The subregion within Burgundy producing the most volume of wine is *Beaujolais,* where huge quantities of light, fresh red wine, meant to be drunk young, is made from the Gamay grape. (A small amount of white Beaujolais, known as Beaujolais Blanc, is produced from the Chardonnay grape.)

The most famous and most copied white wine of Burgundy is *Chablis,* named for the village surrounded by the 10,000 acres of vineyards where it is made.

Just as American wines labeled "Burgundy" have absolutely no resemblance to Burgundy wine, labels in this country reading "Chablis" are equally misleading.

Real Chablis is made from the Chardonnay grape which produces a wine of different flavor there than in the rest of Burgundy. The whites made from the Chardonnay grape in other areas of this region, where the soil is typical limestone, have a soft, rich, full flavor similar to top class California Chardonnays, or Montrachet, the famed Burgundy white. But in the northern vineyards of Chablis, the limestone contains clay which adds a clean, flinty, sometimes smoky edge to the wine, making it what many call the "definitive dry white wine."

Names on Burgundy labels, like nearly all the other important wine regions of France, are strictly geographical. Any wine produced in the region, assuming it meets certain minimal standards, is entitled to the broad appellation Burgundy. But, as in Bordeaux, *the more geographically specific the label, the better the wine.*

Most Burgundies are bottled as commune wines, meaning they are produced in a certain community. Still more specific (and therefore of higher quality) are wines of individual vineyards or estates within each commune. These are the greatest Burgundies that are often as expensive as fine Bordeaux, mainly because they are produced in such small quantities.

The most important subregion of Burgundy is *Cote d'Or* (coat dor), meaning Golden Slope, a 30-mile ridge of vineyards near the villages of Beaune and Nuits-St.-Georges.

The Cote d'Or is subdivided into the *Cote de Beaune* (bone), on the south, and the *Cote de Nuits* (nwee), on the north. Within these 2 categories are the communes

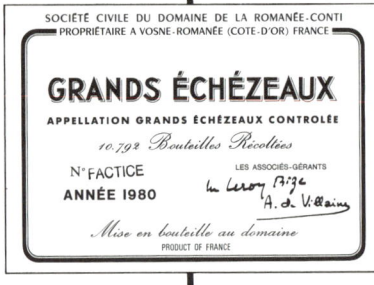

whose names are familiar to Burgundy lovers, but confusing to beginners.

The greatest red Burgundies are produced in the Cote de Nuits and are made nearly exclusively from the Pinot Noir grape. There are 24 Grand Crus from Cote de Nuits seen in the export market. Look for names like Romanee-Conti, Chambertin, Bonnes-Mares, La Tache, and Echezaux, to cite a few.

The wines of Cote de Beaune are softer, more suave and subtle than those of Cote de Nuits. They produce the greatest of the white Burgundies, the Montrachets.

Unlike Bordeaux, in Burgundy there is no one classification that has been around since the 19th century. The wines were ranked when the *Appellation Controlee* was enacted in the mid-30's, and often wines with similar names will be from entirely different ranks. The top rank is *Grand Cru,* and all of the Grand Crus are from specific vineyards. Then there are *Premier Crus* that also come from specific vineyards, followed by the *Commune* wines that come from much larger, more general areas surrounding the villages that bear their names. (Note: This can be confusing because in Bordeaux, the *top* rank is Premier Crus, meaning First Growth.)

I realize how complicated this sounds, and it *is!* Unfortunately, the only way to know exactly what to expect from a bottle of French wine is to know the hundreds of villages and communes by name so that one glance at the label tells the story. Only those who have made a lifelong study of French wines are this well versed, and I am quick to admit that I am not among them.

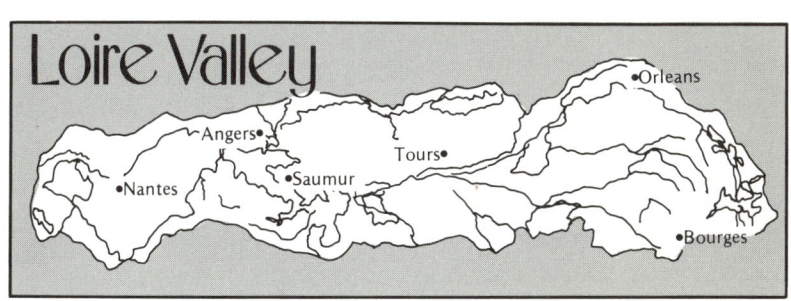

No area of France is more romantic than the valley of the Loire (lwahr) River. Its wide, shallow waters wind westward over gently rolling hills, flowing 350 miles to the Atlantic. Majestic medieval castles crown the valley, rimmed with vineyards and orchards.

The wine it inspires is as pastel-light and lyrical as the landscape. Where Cotes du Rhone wines are hearty and full-bodied, those from the Loire Valley are of spring and summer. They're fresh, grapey, appetizing and unpretentious. And there is a great variety that ranges from crisp whites and golden sweet dessert wines to fine sparkling wines and superb Roses.

Five key districts dominate this region. Both the oceanside district and the wine it produces are called *Muscadet* (mus-kuh-day). Pale, dry and sprightly, Muscadet is a classic match for seafood.

Two large central districts, *Anjou-Saumur* (ahn-ajoo so-mure) and *Touraine,* comprise the middle Loire. Both produce a profusion of wine types, though many have the white Chenin Blanc grape in common. Much of the valley's abundance of Rose is made here — romantic, raspberry-scented wines that range from sweet to dry. There are enchanting *Anjou* dessert wines, and east of Anjou, in *Touraine* the Valley's best reds are made. The vineyards of *Chinon* (sheen-non) and *Bourgueil* (boor-goye) produce soft, light Beaujolais-like wines. Touraine's famous white *Vouvray* (voo-vray) is perhaps the best of all Chenin Blancs.

In the eastern Upper Loire are *Sancerre* (san-sair) and the equally picturesque *Pouilly* (poo-yee), not to be confused with the Pouilly of Southern Burgundy where Pouilly-Fuisse and Pouilly-Fume are made. Sancerre is touched with the same smoky note as Pouilly-Fume, however.

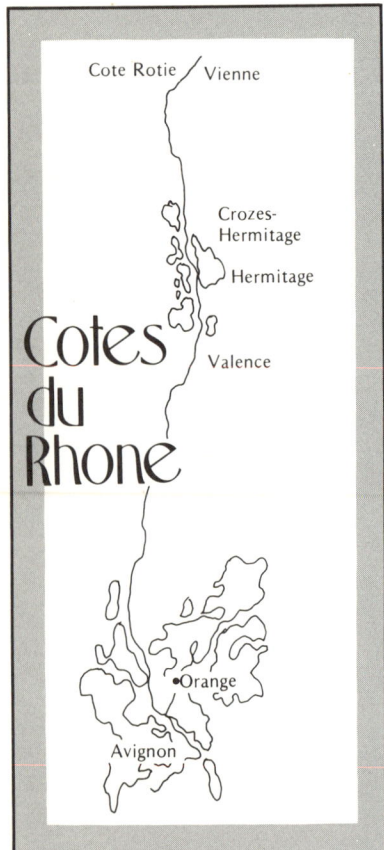

exclusively hearty red wines, while the South has a highly diversified output, ranging from table wines and noble reds to world-famous Roses. Virtually all northern Rhone wines are made solely from the *Syrah* (seer-ah) grape, while in the South, they're often a blend of more than a dozen grape varieties.

Both North and South share the prestige of producing some of the world's most respected wines.

The North treasures its *Hermitage,* one of the oldest vineyards in France where the "manliest of wines" is made. The South boasts *Chateauneuf-du-Pape* (shat-o-nuf-doo-pahp) which means "new home of the Pope." A widely popular wine, Chateauneuf-du-Pape is made from 13 grape varieties.

Tavel and *Lirac* (leer-ack) are The Rhone Valley's famous Roses. Dry, delicate and dependably good, they round out the pride of the South.

Champagne!
The word alone is exciting. It makes us think of celebrations and amore! Yes, *love,* because Champagne is the most romantic of all wines.

Actually, Champagne is more than a wine. It is also a place and a process.

Sun-drenched and dominated by a long, intensely hot growing season, the Rhone River valley produces wines that are generally red, robust and high in alcohol content. They are rich, hearty wines that mature to full-bodied warmth, and often to great softness and depth. The hot climate here is more constant from year to year than in most wine regions of France; therefore, vintages vary little. The vintage year is important to note, however, since most Rhone wines need to age a few years.

Cotes du Rhone is divided into Northern and Southern sections. Production in the North is almost

60

The place is 52,500 acres of vineyards in northeastern France, known as the Champagne district. The process, *methode champenoise,* was discovered in the late 1600's by Dom Perignon, a blind Benedictine monk, who found the secret of capturing fermentation gases through a special aging process using tightly corked bottles.

At that time, there were no cork stoppers. Wine bottles were stopped with wooden plugs that never fit very well, or with oily rags that didn't do much for the taste of the wine.

In order to capture and hold the sparkle his wines developed naturally, the good Monk needed a substance that would fit very tightly, last for a long time, and withstand the pressure from the buildup of carbon dioxide bubbles, a natural by-product of the process of fermentation.

It took him 20 years to find it, but eventually he came up with the idea of using the bark of the cork oak tree.

But that only solved half his problem. Having captured the bubbles, how could he keep the glass bottles from exploding? Legend tells us that Dom Perignon lost nearly half his wine every year from exploding bottles. (He must have had a cellar that sounded like Fourth of July fireworks!) Then he got word that the English had invented a way to make thicker, stronger glass. So, the Monk finally had corks to capture his bubbles and glass strong enough to withstand the 90 pounds pressure that builds up in a bottle of Champagne. But he didn't stop there.

Dom Perignon kept experimenting to make this wonderful wine even better. He learned that by blending grapes from as many as 30 different vineyards, he could make a wine better than any from a single vineyard.

Through the use of his nose and his palate, which were undoubtedly more highly developed due to his blindness, Dom Perignon became France's first master blender. Before this, French winemakers had thought it was sacrilege to blend juice from different vineyards. Even today, Champagne is still one of the few noble wines of France that is almost always a blend. In fact, the talent of the blender is what distinguishes one fine Champagne from another.

All Champagne is sparkling wine (they do make a small amount of still wine in the Champagne district, but it is rarely seen outside of France because the government discourages its export.) However, all sparkling wine is definitely *not* Champagne. Only the sparklers that come from the Champagne district can rightfully be called by that name. Sparklers made in other parts of France are known as *Vins Mousseux* (van-moo-soh). There are some great ones from the Loire Valley, Jura, and Limoux.

Today, every wine-making country in the world makes sparkling wines. In Italy, we call it "Spumante," but in America as well as in other countries, sparkling wine is often wrongly labeled "Champagne."

61

Unlike other French wines, Champagne is known by the name of the shipper, not the vineyard or vintner. The shippers buy wine from surrounding vineyards, then use their own blend, or *cuvee,* to make their brand, which is fermented in their own cellars.

Nonvintage Champagne is a blend of wines from several different years. *Vintage* Champagne is blended entirely of wines pressed in the same year, and only from a year when the grape is exceptionally good.

Most Champagne is made from a blend of dark and white grapes. Dark grapes give body and firmness. White grapes give softness and delicacy. When only white grapes are used, the Champagne will be very light and delicate, known as *Blanc de Blancs.*

The process for making Champagne is long and involved. After the blending of the *cuvee,* the wine is bottled and put into cellars carved out of the chalky subsoil of the Champagne District, with the bottles lying on their sides. The fermentation switches on and off, depending on the activity of the yeasts, and sediment is produced. To prevent it from sticking to the sides of the bottles, they must be moved periodically. At this point, the bottles have temporary corks or caps. They are left in the cellars for two or more years. Toward the end of their aging period, the bottles are hand-turned daily by experts known as *remueurs* until the bottles tilt downward and the sediment rests against the cork.

The bottles are then disgorged by placing the necks of the bottles in a brine solution below the freezing point of water. The sediment freezes against the temporary cork, the cork is removed, and a dosage, containing a small amount of wine and a tiny bit of Brandy (to act as a stabilizing agent) is added. Then the bottles receive their final cork.

The bottle label tells you the degree of dryness of Champagne. *Brut* is the driest and usually the best because of the quality of wine used. *Extra-Sec* or Extra Dry is semi-dry. *Sec* is medium dry. *Demi-Sec* is slightly sweet. *Douz* is sweet and generally used as a dessert wine.

Because all growers and producers of Champagne must adhere to strict rules of the Comite Interprofessionel du Champagne, the standards for this wine are among the highest in the world.

THE SEVENTEEN TOP CHAMPAGNE PRODUCING HOUSES

BOLLINGER	G. H. MUMM
CHARLES HEIDSIECK	PERRIER-JOUET
HEIDSIECK MONOPOLE	PIPER-HEIDSIECK
KRUG	POL ROGER
LANSON	POMMERY ET GRENO
LAURENT PERRIER	RUINART
LOUIS ROEDERER	TAITTINGER
MERCIER	VEUVE CLICQUOT-PONSARDIN
MOET ET CHANDON	

ITALY

In Italy, wine is as much a part of everyday life as water.

We don't make a fuss about it; we drink it. And we produce and drink more of it than any country in the world.

There are nearly two million wine farmers in Italy, and they have always made *good* wines, if for no other reason than because of their fierce sense of competition with their wine-making neighbors.

In an Italian village, it is a big thing to be known as the man who makes the best wine in the area. He often becomes the mayor on the strength of his reputation as a winemaker alone. Even if the wine output is small, the man is *important*. On the other hand, it is a very bad thing to be known as a man who makes inferior wine, even if he produces and sells more.

Unfortunately, most Americans never taste the best wines of Italy, because Italians don't export it. They keep it at home and drink it themselves. This is still basically true, even though more fine wines than ever are now being exported from Italy.

But for many years, only mediocre wines left the country and this caused a serious image problem for Italian vino. The wines were not taken seriously by consumers around the world who considered them lower in quality than French, German and even California wines. But anyone who has traveled through Italy, especially Tuscany and Piedmont, sampling local wines knows better! The great Italian reds — *Brunello di Montalcino, Barolo, Gattinara, Barbaresco, Barbera* and *Ghemme* — are second to none in the world. In fact, a man who has Brunello di Montalcino stored in his cellar has a much more valuable wine collection than a man with a cellar full of first growths of the Bordeaux Medoc.

Italian whites are probably not as high in quality as the great white Burgundies, for example, but give me a bottle of dry, crisp Pinot Grigio over a white Bordeaux any day!

No other country produces as many different wines as Italy does (an estimated four thousand) and each region has its own specialties.

In order to regulate the quality of this staggering quantity of wine, the Italian government set up Denominazione di Origine Controllata (DOC) laws in 1963. To get a DOC rating, a wine must be from specified grape varieties, grown in delimited zones, and processed and aged according to set methods to meet prescribed standards of color, odor, flavor, alchohol content, acidity, etc. Only about ten percent of the wines made in Italy are given a DOC rating. All other still, dry wines, no matter what their class or style, must be called *vino da tavola* (table wine). Light bubbly wine is labeled *frizzante;* sparkling, *spumante;* and strongly alcoholic or fortified wines, *liquoroso*.

More recently, Italy has designated a DOCG (Denominazione di Origine Controllata e Garantita) rating, a step above DOC. It is the country's highest possible rating.

How to Read an Italian Wine Label

On Italian wines the vintage year is usually listed on a separate label around the neck of the bottle.

Other words you might see on Italian wine labels:

Abboccato — lightly sweet
Amabile — semisweet
Annata — year of vintage
Asciutto — bone dry
Bianco — white
Cascina — farm or estate, northern Italy
Classico — zones of long-standing within a DOC and the wine from grapes grown there. Denotes high quality.
Dolce — sweet
Fattoria — farm or estate, central Italy
Frizzante — lightly bubbly
Imbottigliato da — bottled by
Invecchiato — aged
Metodo champenois or metodo classico — the classical Champagne method of bottle-fermenting sparkling wines.
Pastoso — off-dry, a hint of sweetness
Produttore — producer
Riserva — DOC or DOCG wines that have undergone specified aging.
Riserva Speciale — aged even longer than Riserva
Rosato — Rose
Rosso — red
Secco — dry
Semisecco — medium sweet
Spumante — sparkling wine
Stravecchio — very old, a term permitted for very few DOC wines.
Superiore — DOC wines that meet standards above the norm (higher alcohol, longer aging, etc.)
Tenuta — farm or estate
Vecchio — old
Vigna, vigneto — vineyard
Vino da pasto — everyday table wine
Vino da tavola — table wine
Vino novello — new wine, usually red, similar to French Beaujolais nouveau
Vitigno — vine or grape variety

WINE REGIONS of ITALY

A region in Italy is a political division similar to a state in the United States. Each region has provinces, which are just like counties in American states. However, the regions of Italy are cultural, as well as political divisions. At one time, each region was independent, with its own culture and customs, and today they still cling to their own identities and traditions.

In discussing the wines of Italy, you have to treat each region individually, progressing from one end of the peninsula to the other.

One of the most prestigious wine zones of Italy, this area is famous for its big red wines — *Barolo*, *Barbaresco*, *Gattinara*, *Ghemme* and *Barbera*.

Dolcetto, *Grignolino* and *Freisa* are other important reds from this region.

Piedmont is also the home of *Asti Spumante*, Italy's most famous sparkling wine.

Still white table wines from the area include *Moscato*, which is semisweet and *Cortese di Gavi*, a DOC dry wine which is the area's most important white.

Piedmont has nearly 40 DOC zones, the most of any region in Italy. Wine is a way of life in this part of the country, with manicured vineyards gracing every mountain slope at the foot of the Italian Alps. Equally well known for their outstanding cuisine, the Piedmontese excel at refined country cooking — game, hams, cheeses and garden vegetables grown on the hillsides.

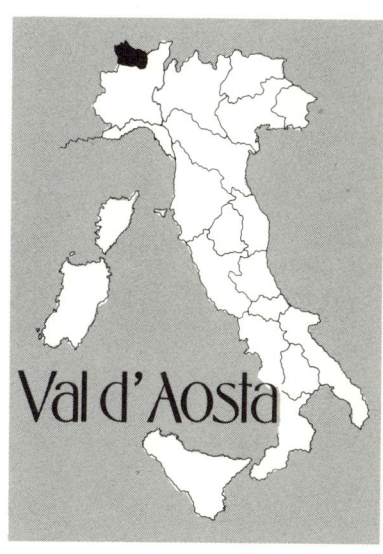

Against a background of snowy Alps, grapes are grown high on hillsides in the Aosta Valley, Italy's smallest region. *Donnaz*, produced from the Nebbiolo grape is the region's best-known wine; it is a smooth, full-bodied red wine, which takes its name from a local town and is a DOC wine. The Petite Rouge grape grown 2,000 feet above sea level produces *Enfer d'Arvier*, the Aosta Valley's only other DOC wine besides Donnaz.

Among the Alps of the *Valtellina*, 2,500 feet above sea level, the Nebbiolo grape is grown to reproduce a hardier red wine than in Piedmont, but one which achieves real delicacy with aging. Sub-districts, e.g. *Sassella, Grumello, Inferno,* often give their names to these Valtellina wines. Also from the Valtellina comes *Sfursat,* a big, robust red wine made from dried grapes.

In the *Oltrepo' Pavese* district, in the Pavia area, fine reds and whites are produced from Pinot and Riesling grapes as well as from a number of native Italian grapes. *Franciacorta Pinot* and *Rosso* are two DOC wines produced in the province of Brescia; the white is made from Pinot Bianco grapes, while the red is a mixture of Cabernet Franc, Barbera, Nebbiolo and Merlot.

From the Lombard bank of Lake Garda, *Chiaretto,* a very pale red wine, has an unusual freshness and charm, and *Lugana,* a light delicate white wine, has a pleasant, fresh taste.

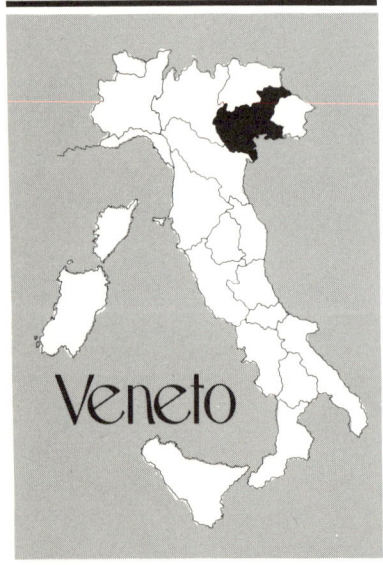

Situated between Lake Garda and the Po and Piave Rivers, Veneto is one of Italy's largest wine producing regions. It is best known for the great trio of Veronese wines, *Valpolicella* and *Bardolino* (reds), and *Soave* (white).

Valpolicella, the largest of the three districts, produces a cherry-red wine, with a gentle sweet fragrance and a nice trace of bitterness in the aftertaste.

Bardolino, from the same grapes grown in lighter soils, is a lighter red with a refreshing touch of sharpness.

Soave, perhaps Italy's most famous white wine, comes from a small hill district, east of Verona. It is dry, pale, very well balanced with a hint of floweriness.

All these wines are also place names. All are best drunk young and cool.

A Veronese specialty is *Recioto,* made from the "recie" (ears) of the grape bunches, which are left to dry before being crushed. Recioto is a rich, sweet wine, often sparkling. *Amarone* is a dry Recioto, an excellent and unusual red table wine.

The hills around the town of Conegliano, north of Venice, pro-

duce an extremely fragrant, clear white wine from the Prosecco grape, in both still and sparkling varieties. Throughout the region, a good deal of wine is made from Cabernet and Merlot grapes, resulting in some excellent reds, and Pinot and Tocai grapes are also widely grown. These will generally have an area name attached to the grape name, e.g. *Cabernet di Pramaggiore, Merlot del Piave, Tocai di Lison.*

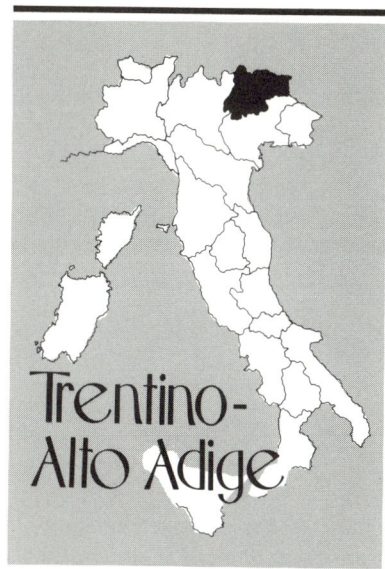

Trentino-Alto Adige

Parts of the Adige Valley from below Trento to Bolzano and Merano are almost carpeted with vines. In the Trentino or lower valley, the *Teroldego* grape gives its name to a quality wine, a big red, full-flavored with a bitter, nutty aftertaste. Other Trentino area wines include *Merlot, Cabernet, Pinot, Moscato* and *Riesling.* A fine full Rose, *Casteller,* is also made around Trento.

In the upper part, as the valley narrows towards Bolzano, the reds are soft and well balanced, with a touch of bitterness. The largest quality red wine area is *Lago di Caldaro* about 30 miles long.

Best known of the other smaller areas is *Santa Maddalena*, east of Bolzano. The village of *Terlano* is a notable producer of white wines such as *Pinot Bianco* and *Riesling*, and Tramin produces a *Gewurztraminer,* somewhat more delicate than its Alsatian namesake.

Friuli-Venezia Giulia

My home town, Trieste, is in this region, which is located in the extreme northeast of Italy, near the Yugoslavia border.

Two of my favorite Italian white wines are made here — *Pinot Grigio* and *Tocia.*

There are six main areas of production in Friuli-Venezia Giulia: Colli Orientali del Friuli (Eastern Friuli Hills); Grave del Friuli (Western Friuli Hills); Collio Goriziano (Gorizia Hills); Isonzo; Latisana and Aquileia.

The white, gray and black Pinot grapes are cultivated in all six areas. The white *(Pinot Bianco)* makes a dry wine, faintly light in texture and color. The gray *(Pinot Grigio)* gives a more deeply colored white, while the black *(Pinot Nero)* makes a smooth red wine of full body and flavor.

Tocai, the local favorite, can match the class of any white in Italy. It should not be confused with Tokays of Hungary and Alsace, an altogether different wine made from a different grape.

Cabernet, Merlot and Riesling grapes are also widely grown in my district. And too, we make *Picolit,* Italy's most fabled dessert wine.

67

Liguria, the narrow coastal strip of the Italian Riviera, produces relatively little wine, but two areas are famous as wine producing centers. One is *Cinqueterre* — or "five villages" — between the cliffs and the sea, west of La Spezia, where some vineyards can be reached only by boat. The dry white wine produced there is full-flavored; a sweet white wine, made from sun-dried grapes, it is luscious but rare. The second area, *Dolceacqua,* is famous for its elegant dry red wine, sometimes called *Rossese.*

Tuscany is the home of Italy's most famous wine, *Chianti,* as well as its most prestigious and expensive, *Brunello di Montalcino.*

Driving through this part of Italy in the spring is a feast for the eyes. This is the land of wine and grape growers — rolling hills crisscrossed by smooth dirt roads that lead to castles, country manors, farms and cottages, and everywhere you look, rows upon rows of vines. Every farmer in Tuscany, no matter how small his plot of land, thinks he makes the best wine in the world, and you'd better not disagree. These men are full of pride and they sincerely believe their wine tastes better than anyone else's.

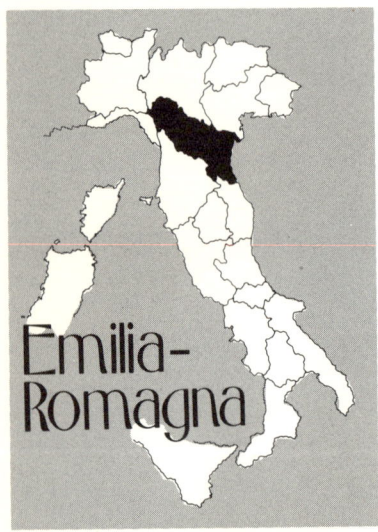

A great center of rich cooking, Emilia-Romagna produces four wines of importance:

Lambrusco, a unique, semi-dry, semi-sparkling red, comes from the grape of the same name, grown in the vicinity of Modena. Fragrant, fresh and clean, its red froth quickly subsides, leaving a pronounced prickle.

Sangiovese, the main grape of Chianti, is used in the Romagna hills to make a full-bodied, well-balanced red wine, whose bouquet is intensified by age. Near Forlì, Ravenna and Bologna, the Trebbiano grape produces a dry well-balanced white wine known as *Trebbiano di Romagna.* On the northern slopes of the Apennines, the *Albana* grape gives its name to a widely popular, light, fresh white wine.

Honorable Vice Counseiller Culinaire, Chaine des Rotisseurs

Chianti

The Chianti zone alone produces about 24 million gallons a year, all from an area about the size of Davidson County.

Most Americans think of Chianti as "Dago Wine," the one that comes in a squat, straw-covered bottle (often recycled as a candle holder). But to assume you know Chianti because you've drunk from one of those straw-covered bottles, is like thinking you know a family of many, many children when you've only seen one of the bambinos.

The Chianti district is located between Florence and Siena where villas, cypresses, vines, woods and olive trees are untouched by time.

This is the land of the Renaissance, of Florenzo d'Medici and Michelangelo, a land so seductive it has attracted more foreign winemakers than anywhere else in Italy.

The central and best portion of the Chianti area lies in hilly country on a line between Florence and Siena, known as the Classico district.

Here winemakers belong to the Chianti Classico Consorzio, a group dedicated to keeping the standards of the wine as high as possible. Their seal of approval is a black rooster (il gallo nero) on a band around the neck of the wine. Most Chianti Classico is good to drink within 2 to 5 years; Classico Riserva within 4 to 8 years, though it will age well beyond a decade from a good vintage year. Vintages 1977

◁ *Collavini Shrimp Crepes, recipe on page 125*

through 1981 were all good and can still improve with further aging.

The formula for making Chianti was set in the 19th century by Baron Bettino Ricasoli. It is 50 to 80 percent Sangiovese grapes; 10 to 30 percent Canaiolo; 10 to 30 percent white Malvasia and Trebiano and 5 percent Colorino.

Today, growers are limiting the amount of white grapes added because in the past many of the wines were too light. This change was due largely to one man, Piero Antinori, who took over the management of his family's 600-year-old winery in the late 1960's.

I had the pleasure of meeting Piero at the 1984 Wine Spectator California Wine Experience in San Francisco.

A proud aristocrat, Piero is totally dedicated to upgrading the quality of all Italian wine and especially those that are exported to other countries.

In 1971 he introduced a new red wine called *Tignanello* that caused great controversy in Tuscany where they've made the wines the same way for centuries. Tignanello is a Chianti-style red which is much more elegant and full-bodied than traditional Chianti. At first, Tuscans dismissed it as too unorthodox. Now, after the wine has had time to become acclaimed all over the world, other Chianti makers have adopted his style, which was to use *malolactic* fermentation instead of white grapes to "soften" the wine.

Tignanello has become very popular in the United States and has made the wine list of many of our finest restaurants, including the Four Seasons and Le Cirque in New York.

Il Gallo Nero (the black rooster) Look for this sign on the neckband of fine Chianti.

Brunello di Montalcino

People are always asking me to name my favorite wine, and I usually say it depends on my mood and the food I'm eating. But if I was forced to choose *one* wine and no other for the rest of my life (what a terrible thought!), I'd have to pick *Brunello di Montalcino*.

This is Italy's finest red wine and one of the most expensive wines in the world. It is big, robusto, rich and fabulous!

In the Brunello section of Tuscany, around the ancient town of Montalcino, there are close to 100 estates where this wine is made, but the most famous and prestigious is Il Greppo, where the fabulous Biondi-Santi family makes their world-renowned vino. This family is so rich and so highly respected in Italy, they are almost like royalty. I visited the estate as the guest of Jacopo Biondi-Santi, the fourth generation to head the Il Greppo wine making estate. Jacopo's great-grandfather, Ferruccio, created Brunello a hundred years ago by developing a clone of the Sangiovese Grosso grape and making wine exclusively from that vine type. Prior to that, wine in this part of Italy had been made by blending the juices of different grapes, the way Chianti is made.

Jacopo took me through the family's fabulous 18th-century villa and then to his wine cellar, where priceless bottles of the first Brunello ever made are stored. The 1888 and the 1891 vintages are called "eternal" wines because they are still perfect after all these years. How do you know? Because every 25 years they uncork the wines, sample them in front of a notary and a small group of experts, then recork. Biondi-Santi Brunello is Italy's longest-lived wine. Some experts say it lives longer than any wine in the world. Like all great aged wines, Brunello is harsh and disagreeable when young. Only with time does it become refined, acquiring a velvet-like harmony that makes it different from other Tuscan wines. As time passes, Brunello's color changes from dark ruby red to garnet. After many years it becomes almost orange. However, its heavenly bouquet, along with its dry, soft and harmonious flavor, do not change.

Jacopo, a tall, dark, handsome man in his thirties, invited me to taste a sample of the 1982 Brunello from the barrel. This wine won't even be released until 1992. Then it will need to age an additional 10 to 15 years before it begins to peak. The young wine was harsh, but you could taste its potential.

Later, Jacopo served homemade bread and cheeses as we sampled the 1964, 1967 and 1970 Brunellos. It was probably the most satisfying wine tasting I've ever experienced. I thought I'd died and gone to heaven!

In Italy, olive trees and grape vines grow side by side, with the trees often used to support the vines. At Il Greppo, there are as many olive groves as vineyards, and Biondi-Santi is as famous for its olive oil as it is for its wine.

Villa Banfi

On this same trip to Italy I visited the new Tuscany facilities of Villa Banfi, the United States' largest wine importer.

Near the village of Santangelo Scala, some 30 miles south of Siena, Villa Banfi has begun one of the most ambitious wine making operations in the world.

More than a million vines have been planted at Poggio d'Oro, as the 7,100-acre estate is called, and the winery itself will be capable of producing some 2.5 million cases of wine a year when it gets into full production in 1986. (That's in addition to Villa Banfi's other Italian vineyards in the Piedmontese towns of Strevi, Acqui and Novi.) The name Poggio d'Oro means "Hill of Gold" which is appropriate considering the 90 million dollars being invested there. A good deal of this money came from the sales of Villa Banfi's *Riunite* in the American market. The owners are now plowing that money back into Italian soil for the purpose of producing world-class wines. Among others, they are making high quality *Brunello di Montalcino* as well as fine *Chardonnay, Cabernet Sauvignon,* and a dry, crisp white *Principessa Gavi,* all aimed toward the United States' market.

On a high hilltop, overlooking the enormous, modern winery, stands a 9th century Tuscan castle which the owners of Villa Banfi have purchased and named Castillo Banfi. The Castle has been restored to house a museum, highlighted by an animated display dramatizing Tuscany's role in the history of wine. There are also guest room accommodations, a gourmet restaurant serving food prepared from the estate's produce, and a wine tasting room for visitors.

Tuscan White Wine

White wines are not big in Tuscany, but one deserves special mention. This is *Vernaccia di San Gimignano,* a dry wine of good quality produced around the small hilltop town famous for its towers. One San Gimignano estate is said to have belonged to Michelangelo's brother.

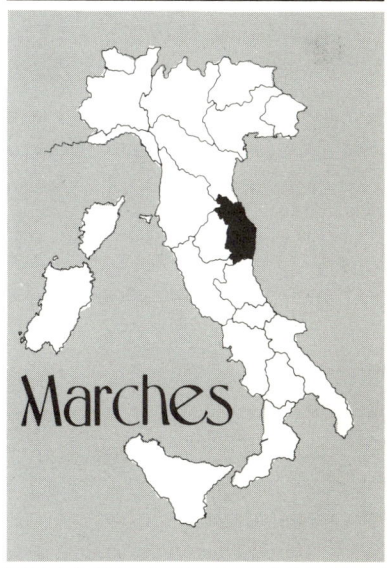

In this Adriatic coastal region, the *Verdicchio* grape and the amphora-shaped bottle have made an admirable dry white wine known wherever Italian food is served. The best known Verdicchio is from the *Castelli di Jesi* area, inland from Ancona. It has a pale straw color and fullness with a touch of austerity. Good Verdicchio is also made in other districts, notably near Matelica.

Conero is a dry, robust red wine which ages nicely; Rosso Piceno is a soft wine of ruby-red color.

Bianchello del Metauro is a dry white wine with an unusual fragrance, produced from the Bianchello grape.

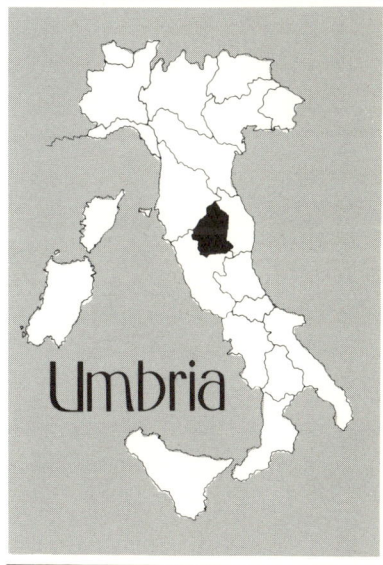

From this, one of the smallest regions, comes a great white wine, *Orvieto*. Its center of production is the city of the same name, perched on its massive rock, out of which are carved the cellars where the wine matures. Orvieto is made both dry and "abboccato" (semi-sweet). The "abboccato" is the area's pride — light and delicate with no hint of cloying. The dry Orvieto is well balanced, with a flowery bouquet.

Near Assisi is the tiny *Torgiano* area, which produces a white and a red. Once of purely local fame, these wines have been developed by an able family firm into wines of national renown. The full red has a pleasant scent and a pronounced flavor, and ages beautifully; the white is quite dry, with a clean, fresh taste.

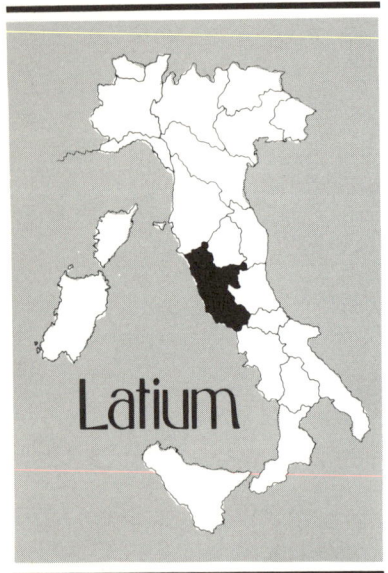

Latium

The area around Rome is known mostly for its white wines.

Frascati has earned an international reputation as a strong, fragrant white with the flavor of golden grape skins. It is made both in dry and abbocato (semi-sweet) styles.

But Frascati is only one of the Castelli Romani wines made among the Roman castles in the Alban hills, southeast of Rome.

Others include *Colli Albani* and *Colli Lanuvini*, whites made from grapes grown on volcanic soil and matured in deep cellars. There's also *Marino*, a very pleasant everyday wine.

Est! Est! Est! resembles the Castelli Romani wines, but comes from the slopes around Lake Bolsena, farther north. It is clear and dry, somewhat lighter than Frascati. The name comes from the steward of a 12th century German bishop travelling to Rome, who was sent ahead of his master to mark the inns where good wine could be found. He was told to chalk "Est" (This is it) on the door of the inns that qualified. At Monteflascone he was so enthusiastic about the wine he chalked "Est! Est! Est!!!"

In the Aprilia district, between the Alban hills and the sea, Trebbiano (white) and Sangiovese and Merlot (red) grapes produce good quality wines which are usually labeled under the grape name: *Merlot di Aprilia*, etc.

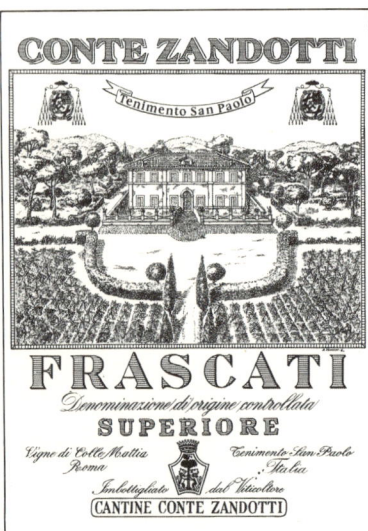

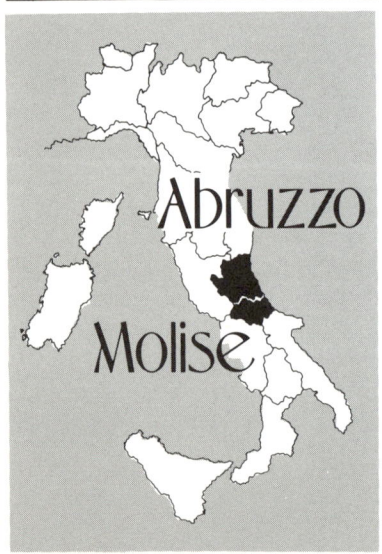

Grapes are grown mainly in the narrow coastal plain of these regions on the Adriatic side of Central Italy. Two grapes, widely cultivated, make pleasant wines. The *Montepulciano d'Abruzzo* is a pale, very drinkable red. The white *Trebbiano d'Abruzzo* is a sharp, medium-bodied wine with a pleasant "nose."

Among the wines for which Campania is famous are the reds and whites of *Ischia*, an island off the coast of this region, and *Lacryma Christi*, grown on the slopes of the volcano Vesuvius and distinguished by the added words "del Vesuvio." The latter wine, meaning "tears of Christ," is made as a red, a white and a Rose, the white being the most well known.

Greco di Tufo is a dry, harmonious white DOC wine made mainly from Greco grapes, and *Taurasi* is a robust red DOC wine which ages very nicely.

Other important wines of Campania are *Fiano*, a dry white wine and *Hirpinia*, which is made in red, white and Rose styles.

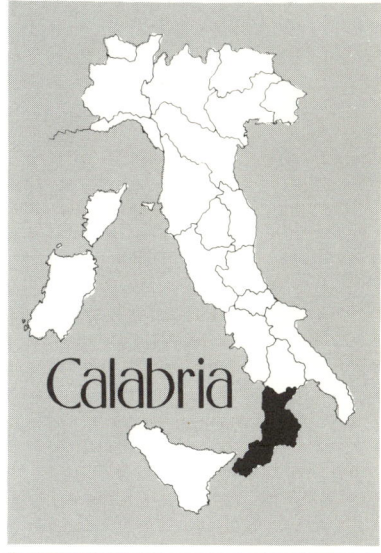

This is one of Italy's largest wine producing regions, once known mainly for its strong wines used for blending. Recent prosperity has brought up-to-date winemaking plants and better care of the vines. Apulia is now fulfilling its promise as a producer of good quality table wines, as are the other two Southern regions, Basilicata and Calabria.

One of the best areas is Castel del Monte, inland between Bari and Foggia, where very enjoyable red, white and Rose wines are produced. The white is fresh and well balanced; the red, dry and velvety; the Rose, fruity and harmonious.

Castel del Monte Rose is often considered Italy's most important Rose wine.

From the north of the region come *San Severo white*, a dry highly alcoholic wine, and *San Severo red*, produced from the reliable Montepulciano grape.

Also, *Torre Quarto* is an excellent red from this area, and *Locorotondo* is a pleasant white from farther south in the region.

Besides this DOC wine, there are several local wines made from this grape, while others are made from the Moscato or the Malvasia grape.

Inland in this region is the extinct volcano, Vulture, on whose slopes grow the unusual Aglianico grape. A dry red, *Aglianico del Vulture,* after a few years in the bottle, can be one of the best wines of Southern Italy.

Here in the "toe" of the Peninsula, the wines of *Ciro'* claim descent from those of the ancient Greek settlers. The red is a big, robust wine. The white is full, flowery and dry. There is also a pleasant Rose.

Calabria produces three additional DOC wines: *Donnici, Pollino* and *Savuto.* All are red wines made from a combination of red and white grapes.

The Service Staff of Special Thousand-Dollar Plate Fund-Raising Dinner for the Community Enhancement Program, featuring the international culinary olympics gold medal chef, Siegfried Eisenberger

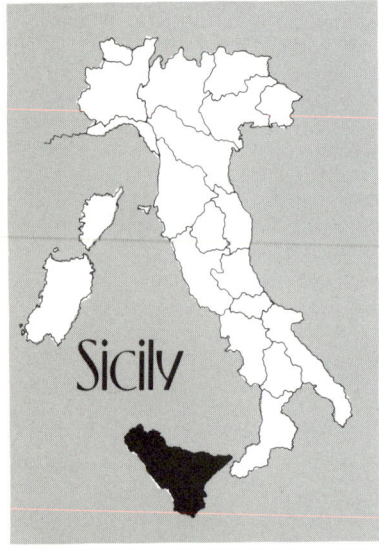

In Sardinia, the Regional authorities have helped co-operatives with new equipment and better cultivation. As a result, this island produces many attractive wines, including:

Vernaccia, a dry, appetizingly bitter aperitif wine is made from the grape of the same name. Sardinians drink it after meals as well.

Cannonau reds and Rose, produced from the most widely grown grape of the Island, are dry, warm and full-bodied.

Torbato is a full harmonious white wine from a Sardinian grape; the dry version doubles as a table wine and an aperitif.

Monica di Sardegna is a red DOC wine produced principally from the Monica grape.

This island has been in the quality wine business for two centuries, with the dessert wine, *Marsala*, as well as table wines.

Marsala is a fortified wine, produced in dry and sweet varieties as well as in specially flavored versions. It is a superior dessert wine which has also achieved fame as an indispensable ingredient in fine cooking and as an unusual aperitif.

Since the war the Sicilian wine industry has moved rapidly towards the production of quality table wines, thanks to a vigorous Regional administration. Sicilian wines are characterized by marked and interesting aromas and are in the 12 to 13 percent alcohol range.

The slopes of Mount Etna, in strictly delimited areas, provide *Etna Red* and *White;* the former is dry, robust and ruby colored, the latter dry and well balanced, with a fragrance of wine and flowers. *Regaleali white* and *red*, produced from grapes grown at a 2,500-foot elevation, are dry, warm and smooth.

Corvo di Salaparuta wines, from near Palermo, have been known outside the island for nearly 150 years. The red is a fine, velvety wine with an interesting aroma. The white is fresh, attractive and full, with the right degree of acidity. Dry red and white table wines named after the ancient Greek city of *Segesta* have proved favorites of many Americans for their well-balanced body and generous taste, while *Draceno, Drepano* and *Saturno* from Southern Sicily, are also popular in parts of the U.S.A.

Pantelleria

The tiny island of Pantelleria, close to Africa, is the home of *Moscato di Pantelleria*. This wine is delightfully sweet, and is made in table wine, sparkling wine and dessert wine versions.

TYPES of ITALIAN WINES

TYPE OF WINE   **SUGGESTED VARIEITIES**

WHITE WINES

Dry, light-bodied whites
- Est! Est!! Est!!!
- Frascati
- Lugana
- Marino
- Pinot Blanco
- Pinot Grigio
- Torgiano Bianco

Dry, medium-bodied whites
- Castel del Monte Bianco
- Corvo Bianco
- Orvieto Secco
- Soave
- Tocai
- Trebbiano di Romagna
- Verdicchio

Mellow whites
- Orvieto Abboccato
- Prosecco
- Moscato d'Asti

RED WINES

Semi-dry reds
- Lambrusco

Dry, light-bodied reds
- Bardolino
- Valpolicella

Dry, medium-bodied reds
- Castel del Monte Rosso
- Cabernet
- Chianti
- Corvo Rosso
- Dolcetto
- Freisa
- Grignolino
- Grumello
- Montepulciano d'Abruzzo
- Meriot
- Nebbiolo
- Sangiovese di Romagna
- Sassella
- Torgiano Rosso

Robust reds
- Amarone
- Barbera d'Asti
- Barolo
- Barbaresco
- Brunello di Montalcino
- Carema
- Chianti Riserva
- Gattinara
- Ghemme
- Inferno
- Spanna
- Vino Nobile di Montepulciano

ROSE, DESSERT & SPARKLING WINES

Rose wines
- Castel del Monte
- Chiaretto

Dessert wines
- Caluso Passito
- Marsala
- Moscato di Pantelleria
- Vin Santo

Sparkling wines
- Asti Spumante
- Nebbiolo Spumante
- Prosecco Spumante
- Spumante Brut

Pronunciation Guide to Italian Wines

Abboccato	*ab-boh-KHAT-oh*
Aglianico del Vulture	*ahl-lee-AH-nee-coh-del vul-TOOR-ay*
Amarone	*ah-mah-ROE-nay*
Asti Spumante	*AHS-tee spoo-MAHN-tay*
Barbaresco	*bar-bar-ESK-coh*
Barbera	*bar-BEHR-rah*
Barbera d'Asti	*bar-BEHR-rah DAHS-tee*
Bardolino	*bar-doh-LEE-noh*
Barolo	*bah-ROH-loh*
Brunello de Montalcino	*brew-NELL-lo-dee mohn-tahl-CHEE-no*
Cannonau	*cahn-noh-NAH-oo*
Castel del Monte	*KAHS-tell dell MON-tay*
Chianti	*kee-YAN-tee*
Chiaretto	*key-ah-RET-toh*
Collio Goriziano	*COLE-lee-oh gore-eet-zee-AH-noh*
Colli Orientali del Friuli	*COLE-lee or-ee-en-TAHL-ee del free-OO-lee*
Corvo Bianco	*Kor-voh-BEEYAN-koh*
Denominazione d'Origine Controllata (D.O.C.)	*day-nom-i-nahtz-ee-O-nay dee or-EE-jee-nay kohn-troll-AH-tah*
Dolcetto	*dole-CHET-toh*
Donnaz	*DONE-natz*
Emilia Romagna	*eh-MEE-lee-ah roe-MAHN-ya*
Enfer d'Arvier	*ahn-FAIR d'AHR-vee-ay*
Frascati	*frah-SKAH-tee*
Freisa	*FRAY-sah*
Friuli-Venezia Giulia	*free-OO-lee vay-NETZ-ee-ah JOO-lee-ah*
Gattinara	*gaht-tee-NAH-rah*
Ghemme	*GEHM-meh*
Grave del Friuli	*GRAH-vay dell free-OO-lee*
Grigio	*GREE-joh*
Grignolino	*grin-yo-LEE-noh*
Ischia	*IS-key-ah*
Liguria	*lee-GORE-ee-ah*
Lugana	*loo-GAH-nah*
Montefiascone	*mohn-tay-fee-ahs-COH-nay*
Montepulciano	*mohn-tay-pull-CHA-no*
Nebbiolo	*nehb-bee-OH-loh*
Oltrepo Pavese	*ohl-tray-PO Pah-VAY-say*
Orvieto	*or-vee-EH-toh*
Prosecco di Conegliano	*pro-SAKE-coh dee co-nell-YAH-noh*
Recioto	*rey-CHO-toh*
Regaleali	*ray-gah-lee-AH-lee*
Sangiovese	*san-jo-VAY-say*
Sassella	*sahs-SELL-ah*
Segesta	*say-JEHS-tah*
Soave	*soh-AH-vay*
Teroldego	*tay-ROHL-day-goh*
Trebbiano	*treh-bee-AH-noh*
Trentino-Alto Adige	*tren-TEE-noh AHL-toe AH-dee-jay*
Valgella	*vall-JELL-ah*
Val d'Aosta	*val-DOSE-tah*
Valpolicella	*val-pol-ee-CHE-lah*
Valtellina	*val-tell-LEE-nah*
Verdicchio	*ver-DEE-kee-oh*

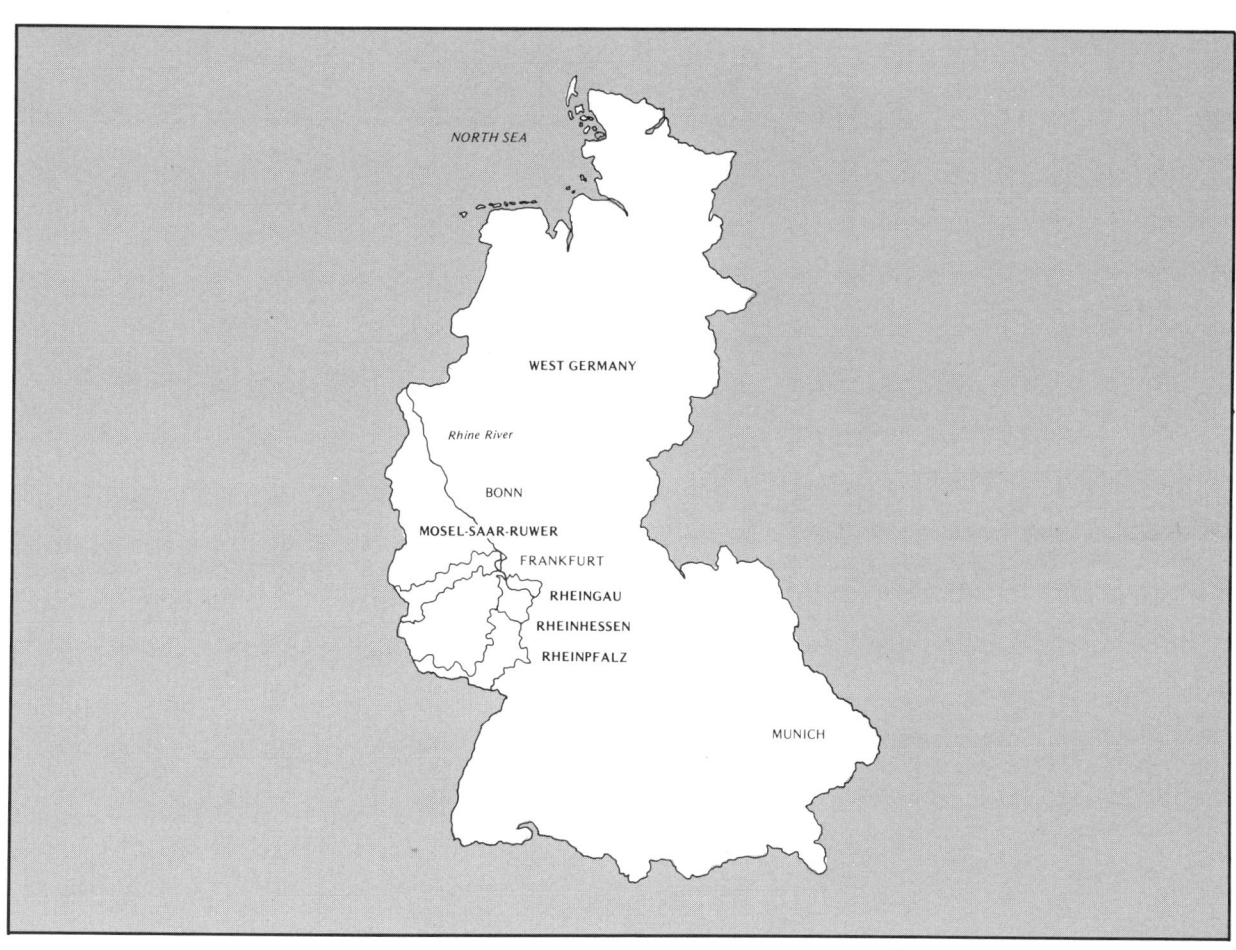

GERMANY

Germany has the strictest wine code of any country in the world. One of the reasons for this is the areas where they can grown grapes are limited. Actually they are too far north to grow vines at all without a great deal of attention and know-how.

The vineyards, located mostly on the steep slopes of the Rhine, the Mosel and other German river banks, do not produce enough grapes to enable German vintners to make large amounts of mediocre bulk wines. When you add this to the German government offering incentives to producers of higher quality wines, and a local government tasting board in every district that must approve each wine before it is released, what you have is a country that produces *only* quality wine. As far as I know this isn't true of any other country.

How to Read a German Wine Label

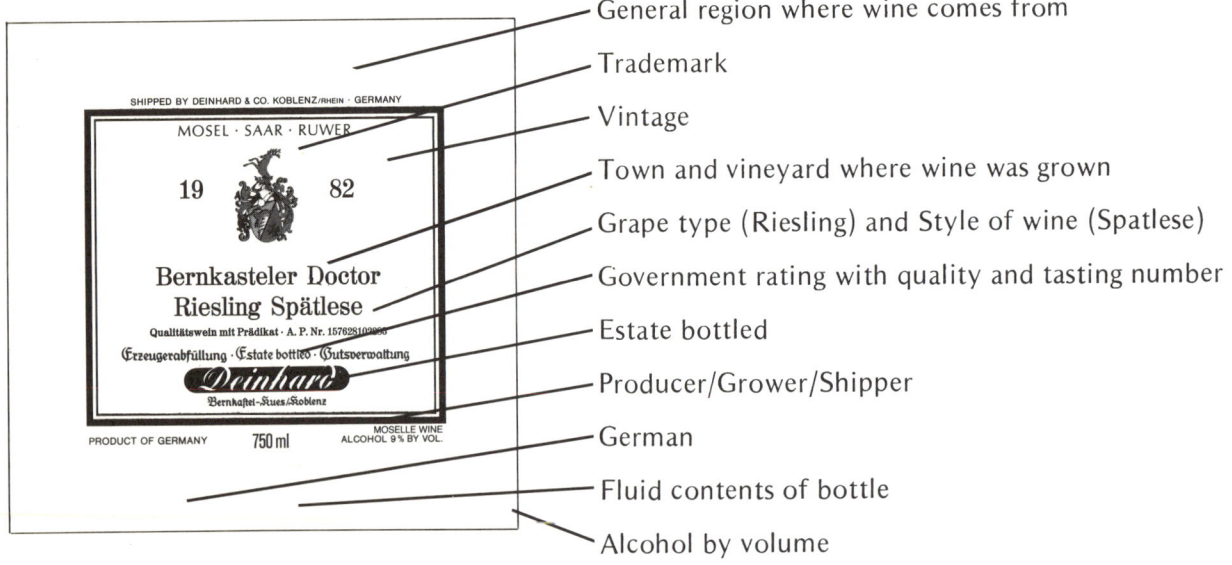

- General region where wine comes from
- Trademark
- Vintage
- Town and vineyard where wine was grown
- Grape type (Riesling) and Style of wine (Spatlese)
- Government rating with quality and tasting number
- Estate bottled
- Producer/Grower/Shipper
- German
- Fluid contents of bottle
- Alcohol by volume

The German wine regions are Rheingau, Rheinpfalz, Rheinhessen, Baden, Franken, Mosel-Saar-Ruwer and Nahe.

Wine produced in the northern regions are generally light, fruity, fragrant and described as being elegant, due to their fresh acidity. The regions further south produce wines with more body, fuller fruitiness and sometimes a powerful flavor.

German wines are 88 percent white and the most noble grape of the country is Riesling. Muller-Thurgau, however, is the most widely planted grape. It contains less acidity than Riesling and has a flowery bouquet and muscat flavor. Other grapes used in German wine making are the Silvaner, Gewurztraminer and Rulander (known as the Pinot Gris in France and the Pinot Grigio in Italy).

Except for Blue Nun, German wines have never enjoyed a popularity in America comparable to other imports, particularly French and Italian.

One of the reasons is that we tend to think of all German wines as sweet, which they're not. Another is those unpronounceable labels nobody except Germans can read. But if you learn just a few things to look for on the label you can know enough to choose which wine to buy.

German wines are rated according to the sugar level in the grapes at the time they were harvested. (This has nothing to do, however, with the sweetness of the wine. I'll explain that later.)

The ratings are:

1. **QbA** (Qualitatswein bestimmter Anbaugebiete — see what I mean by unpronounceable!) Liebfraumilch, of which Blue Nun is the best known in this country, is a QbA wine. The QbA rating is comparable to the Italian DOC, or the French Appellation Controlee.

2. **QmP** (Qualitatswein mit Pradikat — quality wines with special attributes) These are higher class German wines and they fall into five subcategories:

80

- **Kabinett**: wine made from the normal October harvest of grapes. This is the simplest, mildest and least expensive of QmP's.
- **Spatlese**: wine made from grapes harvested at a special picking when the sugar level was a little higher than Kabinett.
- **Auslese**: a selected picking of the ripest grapes that have been affected by botrytis (the "noble rot"). This causes water to evaporate, thereby concentrating the sugar content. These wines are made only in good vintage years.
- **Beerenauslese**: wines made from individual grapes infected with botrytis. The grapes are painstakingly harvested one at a time when they are even riper than the Auslese picking.
- **Trockenbeerenauslese**: a $5 word for wines that cost upwards of five times five a bottle. These wines are among the rarest and the sweetest in the world. They are made from grapes that have dried to raisins.

One of these five words will appear on the label of every German wine in the QmP classification.

The amount of sugar in the grape at the time of harvest is important enough to use as a classification measure, because it determines fermentation, the process by which sugar turns to alcohol.

Left to nature almost all wine would be dry because the fermentation process would continue until all the sugar had turned to alcohol. But winemakers interfere with the natural process to get the sweetness or dryness they want.

This is where the winemakers' art comes in. Knowing how to get the perfect acid/sugar balance into wine is the trick to master. The way you tell whether a German wine in the QmP classification is dry or semi-dry is by the color of the label. **The word Trocken (dry) may not always appear on the label, but the color of the label will always be yellow for dry and green for semi-dry (Halbtrocken).**

Bottle Shapes of German Wines

The color and shape of a bottle of German wine is also important. The delicate, perfumed wines of the Mosel-Saar-Ruwer region are put into tall "hock" bottles made of green glass. The richer, more intense Rhine wines are sold in amber-to-brown bottles. Franconian wines, which tend to be drier, come in short, distinctively flagon-shaped bottles.

Germany's fruity, fresh and light wines are good with many foods. For dishes with delicate flavor and little seasonings: mild, harmonious *QbA* and *Kabinett* wines are a good match. Many vegetables and mild sauces have a slightly sweet taste and call for a semi-dry wine or one with a hint of sweetness. For spicy dishes, lively wines or full, aromatic ones from *Qualitatswein* through *Spatlese* are recommended.

SPAIN and PORTUGAL

SPAIN

Although Sherry is by far the most celebrated wine of Spain, it is by no means the only fine wine made there. Some of the best Spanish table wines rank with the finest in the world, yet few of them reach America. This is a shame since no other country makes good wine so inexpensively.

To say that the Spanish love their wine is an understatement. Only two other countries, Italy and France, produce more wine, and Spain is ranked fifth in terms of per capita consumption (15 gallons per person).

Some of the best Spanish table wines that do get to this country are made by *Torres*. This family has owned vineyards for centuries, and have been bottling and selling wines since 1870. They make a wide variety of whites, red and Rose, and all their wines are wonderfully drinkable, as well as reasonably priced.

There are 3 main wine producing regions in Spain — *Jerez, Rioja* and *Catalonia.*

Jerez

This is the famed Sherry region where 50,000 acres have been defined by the Sherry Control Board as official vineyards. Sherry, which is a *fortified* wine (meaning that Brandy has been added) is made basically from two grape varieties — Palomino and Pedro Ximenez.

There are 5 basic styles of Sherry: *Fino,* dry, light and straw-colored; *Manzanilla,* similar — but drier than Fino; *Amontillado,* moderately dry, medium-bodied, golden; *Oloroso,* gently sweet, full-bodied and golden; *Cream,* sweet, very full-bodied and deep golden brown.

Rioja

The finest wines of Spain come from this region. It is located just 200 miles from Bordeaux. The area is historically rooted in the French wine making style due to the immigration of French wine producers in the 19th century, when disease had devastated French vineyards.

All genuine Rioja must carry a black label on the bottle, specifying the type of wine. These labels define 4 categories: *Garantia de Origen,* wine with little or no cask aging; *Vino de Crianza,* wine which has been matured at least one year in oak with a further period in the bottle; *Riserva,* wine of good vintage matured two years in oak and one in the bottle; and *Gran Reserva,* wine of very good vintage, aged 3 years in oak and two in the bottle, with a minimum of 7 years maturation in the cellar.

The red wines may be labeled *clarete* or *tinto,* depending on whether they are paler in color and lighter-bodied, or darker and more full-bodied.

Claretes go best with less substantial foods; tinto better with stews and roasts.

The whites are of 2 types: the traditional, aged in casks; and the new style made by cold fermentation without aging in oak. These may be dry, semi-dry or sweet.

The cold-fermentation wines are almost white in color and should be drunk as young as possible. They go especially well with delicate white fish and other light foods.

How to Read a Spanish Wine Label

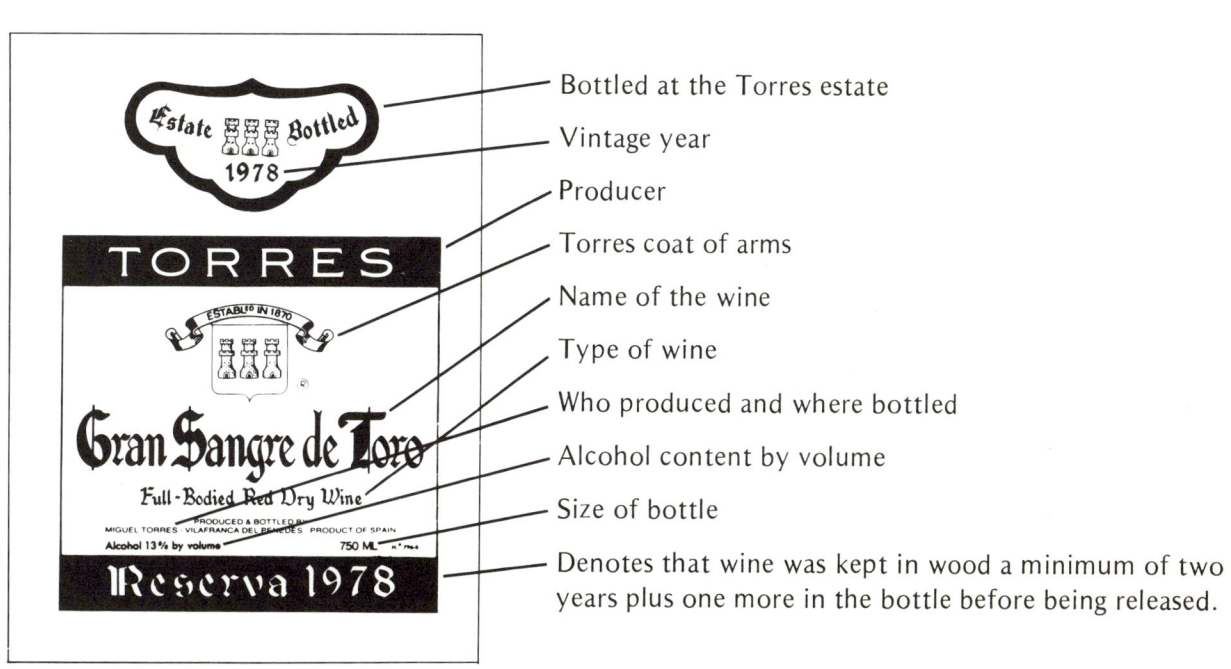

- Bottled at the Torres estate
- Vintage year
- Producer
- Torres coat of arms
- Name of the wine
- Type of wine
- Who produced and where bottled
- Alcohol content by volume
- Size of bottle
- Denotes that wine was kept in wood a minimum of two years plus one more in the bottle before being released.

Catalonia

Besides producing European-style table wines, this area is known for sparkling wines. The process used by most sparkling winemakers here is the same as used in the Champagne district of France, and the wines cost about ¼ as much. Some of the best bargains on the market for sparkling wines come from Spain.

PORTUGAL

Though Portugal is only about the size of Indiana, a large portion of the usable land is in vineyards, and the Portuguese annually consume over three times as much table wine as is *produced* in California. This is especially amazing when you consider their 2 most famous wines — *Port* and *Madeira* — are dessert wines.

Most Americans know Portugal for Mateus and Lancers, but these are not representative of the best the country has to offer.

Douro

Port wine is produced here as well as Douro red and white table wines.

Douro was the first wine region in the world to be demarcated in 1756. All Port exported from Portugal bears a numbered guarantee seal over the neck of the bottle.

Port, a fortified wine, is made from 20 to 30 grape varieties. Fermentation is arrested with grape Brandy. One-fifth of the volume of the wine is Brandy and it must be aged 3 years.

Types of Port are: *Vintage*, from one exceptional year, requiring at least 10 years of aging to achieve full maturity; *Ruby*, a blend of young Ports matured in wood; *Tawny*, made from well-matured Ports and continually refined; *White*, made the same as Port, but with white grapes.

Vinho Verde, an especially youthful and fresh wine is made north of the Douro River, and the vineyards are a strange sight. The vines are trained along wooden or metal jacks that hold them 8 to 10 feet above ground; some vines even grow in trees, and the grapes must be harvested by ladder. White Vinho Verde tends to be slightly sparkling and is very dry, a perfect accompaniment to shellfish. The red is a hard wine and best drunk well chilled.

Dao

Dao wine has an extremely fine bouquet and velvet palate. The reds are lightly aciduous and mature well. The whites are straw-colored and best drunk young.

Bucelas

Growing from loam and limestone soil, the white wine from Bucelas is made from the Arinto grape. The climate of the region prevents the grapes from overmaturing which enables them to retain their acidity and gives the wine a crisp, fresh flavor.

Colares

Some of the best red table wines of Portugal come out of this region located near the Atlantic Ocean. The main type of vine which gives the red wine its distinctive character is the Ramisco. White wine is produced from the Malvasia.

Madeira

An island located 500 miles off the coast of Portugal, Madeira's wine was to America what Porto was to England. It is a wine fortified with Brandy. There are four types of Madeiras: *Sercial*, the palest and driest; *Verdelho*, sweet and round; *Bual* or *Boal*, a pungent soft dessert wine, and *Malmsey*, the sweetest of all the Madeiras.

COOKING WITH WINE

Cooking with wine you wouldn't drink makes as much sense to me as brewing coffee with water you wouldn't drink.

People make the mistake of thinking it doesn't matter if the wine doesn't taste good to drink, that the flavor will somehow improve when it cooks. Wrong. The flavor is the same. Only the alcohol burns off in cooking.

Using good wine not only makes the food taste better, it makes the cook feel better, too. It's a lot more fun to slave over a hot stove if you're sipping the nice white Burgundy you're using in the recipe than if you've opened a bottle of something even a wino wouldn't drink.

The difference the quality of the wine makes in cooking has been proven to me many times in the restaurant business. Usually we use the current house wine, always a very nice French or Italian wine, in the kitchen. But sometimes, when a waiter brings a half bottle of a really fine wine that some customer didn't finish to the kitchen, the chef will use that in cooking. I can't tell you how many times a customer has come to me and said, "The veal I had tonight tasted better than any I've had here before. What did you do different?" Invariably, I'll check in the kitchen and find the wine sauce has been made with some fine *vino* that night, like Montrachet.

I recommend that you use wine whenever it would enhance a dish or a sauce — it can make the difference between an ordinary dish and a great one.

SEASONING WITH WINE

Any meat recipe which requires liquid in the cooking process may be converted to a wine-flavored recipe by simple substitution. For instance, replace ¼ cup water for each pound of meat with an equal amount of red or white table wine. The flavor will be greatly improved. Use red wine for beef, lamb or game, white for veal or pork.

TIPS

■ In long-simmered meaty dishes, such as stews, the acid in the wine helps to tenderize the meat, in addition to adding flavor.

■ A very small amount — ¼ cup or less — of wine added to a soup, stew or braised dish just before the cooking is finished, is a good way to give a final flavor boost.

■ When braising light-colored meats, such as chicken, or poaching white fish, such as sole, many cooks prefer to use white wine to avoid the problem of discolored food. But if you'd like to use red wine, try cooking the meat or fish in a flavorful stock and prepare a red wine sauce separately.

■ Beef is delicious cooked with hearty red wines such as Barolo, Cabernet Sauvignon and Burgundy; chicken with Riesling and Chenin Blanc.

MENUS FROM WINE CONNOISSEURS

DINNER AT JULIAN'S

MENU

Souffle de Cailles, Sauce Madere
DE LADOUCETTE POUILLY-FUME 1983

Vichyssoise

Feuillete de Homard au Safran et Pernod
DOMAINE ROPITEAU PULIGNY-MONTRACHET 1980

*Saddle of Wild Baby Boar
with Armagnac Sauce and Truffles*
GRANDS ECHEZEAUX 1980

Sorbet au Thyme

Filet d'Agneau a la Mandarine
CHATEAU HAUT-BRION 1964

Salade Verte

*Fresh Fruit with Strawberry Coulis
Passionfruit Mousse*
ROEDERER CRISTAL BRUT CHAMPAGNE 1979

JOSE CUERVO 1800 TEQUILA

One night Mike Tomlin and Ronnie Bledsoe, two fellow members of Chaine des Rotisseurs, and I were talking about great restaurants and great meals. Tomlin said he liked Le Francais in Wheeling, Illinois, Bledsoe voted for Lutece in New York.

I decided to make a bet with them. I said, "If I call Sylvain Le Coguic at Julian's and give him a few weeks' notice to get special ingredients, he can make us as good a meal as we could have at either of those restaurants. If I'm wrong, I'll pick up the tab. If I'm right, you pay."

They agreed, and I called Sylvain, who welcomed the challenge. A couple of weeks later, we sat down to a meal fit for a king.

The Quail Souffle with Madeira Sauce was very light with just enough gamy flavor to give it life — a great taste.

Pouilly-Fume is one of the better known white wines from the eastern part of the Loire River Valley. (Zraby says fume refers to morning mists.) Its earthy taste goes well with game. The Ladoucette winery makes the finest example of Pouilly-Fume.

The lobster in pastry was delicious, and the presentation was marvelous. The pastry is shaped like a miniature cup to hold the lobster that had been removed from the shell so carefully that whole claw meat was left intact. The sauce was perfection! Montrachet is the finest example of white Burgundy, and this Puligny was excellent with lobster.

When the rack of wild boar was presented, Hoyt Hill carved it in front of us for another beautiful presentation. He did such a good job, I thought I was standing there using that carving knife like a surgeon! The boar had a mild gamy flavor and was delicious. The **1980 Grands Echezeaux** was a perfect companion. This is a fabulous Grand Cru Burgundy, one of the very best vineyards in that district.

Next, we were served the Thyme Sorbet, the best intermezzo I've had anywhere. Usually sorbets served between courses as a palate cleanser are too sweet for my taste. Even the lemon and lime-flavored ones don't leave my palate really refreshed. But this one, with the pungent flavor of thyme, did the trick.

Chef Sylvain has won awards with his Lamb Napoleon, and deservedly so. It was *outstanding,* and as for the wine, what can you say about Haut-Brion except *fabulous!*

Roederer Cristal is one of my favorite Champagnes, and it made a delicious pairing with the fruit desserts.

Now, are you wondering about the Tequila?

Why not a great Cognac or Port after a meal like this? Because what I really wanted was some Grappa, better known as Italy's firewater.

Grappa is the distillate of pomace, called *vinaccia* in Italy, the leftover skins and stems after the pressing process for table wines. It is not really a Brandy distilled from wine. It is more like the French marc. Water is added, and it is distilled in small pot stills similar to those used in making Cognac. The clear distillate comes out between 100 and 130 proof. It is used in Italy as an after-dinner sipping drink.

Italians believe it is a great digestion aid, especially after you've eaten too much, which is when I like to drink it. But Julian's didn't have Grappa, so I decided to substitute Tequila in hopes it would have the same effect. It did. I woke up the next morning feeling fine.

By the way. Guess who paid for dinner?
It wasn't me!

My compliments to Chef Sylvain for an outstanding meal.

Souffle de Cailles, Sauce Madere
Quail Souffle with Madeira Sauce

4 quail	Salt and pepper
2 eggs, separated	to taste
1/4 cup heavy cream	1/4 cup Madeira

Bone and skin quail, reserving bones. Prepare stock, using reserved quail bones. Press chopped quail meat through fine sieve. Combine with beaten egg yolks, cream, salt and pepper in bowl; mix well. Fold in stiffly beaten egg whites. Spoon into 2 prepared souffle dishes. Bake at 400 degrees for 15 minutes. Prepare Madeira sauce with quail stock and Madeira. Ladle sauce onto serving plates. Unmold souffles; place in sauce. Garnish as desired. Serve immediately.

Feuillete de Homard au Safran et Pernod
Lobster in Pastry with Saffron and Pernod

4 ounces puff pastry	1 cup white wine
1 live lobster	2 cups heavy cream
1 shallot	Saffron, salt and
1 ounce Pernod	pepper to taste

Prepare and bake 2 pastry shells using puff pastry. Cut lobster in half; place in baking pan. Bake at 400 degrees for 10 minutes. Remove meat from shells, reserving shells. Combine lobster shells, shallot, Pernod, wine, cream, saffron, salt and pepper in saucepan. Cook until reduced to desired consistency; strain sauce over lobster meat. Spoon lobster with sauce into pastry shells. Garnish as desired.

Sorbet au Thyme
Thyme Sorbet

1 cup sugar	1 bunch fresh thyme

Combine sugar and 2 cups water in saucepan. Bring to a boil. Cool. Steep thyme in boiling water to cover. Strain. Combine simple syrup and thyme infusion. Freeze. Spoon into chilled tulip glasses. Garnish with fresh thyme.

Filet d'Agneau a la Mandarine
Filet of Lamb Mandarine Napoleon

1 ounce mushrooms, julienned	1 lamb loin
1 ounce ham julienned	1 pound spinach
1 ounce foie gras, julienned	8 ounces puff pastry
1/2 ounce truffles, julienned	3 ounces Mandarine Napoleon liqueur
	1/2 cup butter

Prepare a stuffing of mushrooms, ham, foie gras and truffles. Cut opening in loin; spoon in stuffing. Blanch spinach; wrap around loin. Wrap in puff pastry; place on baking sheet. Bake at 400 degrees for 25 minutes. Prepare a sauce with liqueur. Cook until reduced by half. Whisk in butter. Slice lamb loin in pastry. Serve in sauce. Garnish as desired.

CHEF'S FEAST

On February 3, 1985, I hosted a $1000 a plate benefit dinner for the Community Enhancement Program, a drug and alcohol counseling service for high school students. Some of our top Nashville chefs pitched in and donated their talents to prepare this feast. They were Siegfried Eisenberger of Opryland Hotel, winner of three Culinary Olympic Gold Medals; chef Sylvain Le Coguic of Julian's Four-Star French restaurant; and chef Patrick Raynal from Mario's.

MENU

CHEF'S FEAST
February 3, 1985

ROEDERER CRISTAL BRUT CHAMPAGNE 1979

Ouverture de Perles Noires
STOLICHNAYA VODKA

Symphonie du Jardin
DE LADOUCETTE POUILLY-FUME 1982

Consomme de Gibier Flambe

Fettuccine Verde con Gamberi
PRINCIPESSA GAVI

Filets de Sole Ecossaise
BOUCHARD PULIGNY-MONTRACHET 1982

CAMPARI

Fois Gras de Canard Normand
CHATEAU PETRUS 1980

Agneau a la Mandarine Napoleon
CHATEAU LAFITE-ROTHSCHILD 1970

Salade
Souffle Montrachet
ROMANEE-CONTI 1980

Rose Creme
Chocolate Marquis
Crepe Ricotta
Pineapple and Strawberry Flambe
Cafe Flambe
REMY-MARTIN LOUIS XIII COGNAC

Sylvain Le Coguic's Symphonie du Jardin
Garden Symphony

4 pounds fresh spinach	A small amount of butter
Salt and pepper to taste	2 egg whites, slightly beaten

Saute spinach with salt and pepper in butter in skillet until wilted; drain well. Stir in egg whites; mix well. Set aside.

1 pound carrots, grated	2 egg whites, slightly beaten
A small amount of butter	Salt and pepper to taste

Cook carrots in butter in saucepan over very low heat until moisture evaporates. Puree in food processor. Add egg whites and seasonings; mix well. Set aside.

1 pound celery root, grated	1/2 cup whipping cream
Butter	

Cook celery root in mixture of butter and cream in saucepan until tender. Puree and set aside.

3 large pieces of leek	Flowerets of 1/2 bunch broccoli
Flowerets of 1/2 head cauliflower	1 egg white, slightly beaten

Blanch leeks in boiling salted water in saucepan. Drain; pat dry. Cook cauliflower and broccoli in salted water in separate saucepans until tender-crisp; drain. Line bottom of buttered tureen with half the spinach. Spread half the carrot puree over spinach layer. Arrange cauliflowerets down center of carrot layer; top with remaining carrot puree and leeks. Pour egg white over layers. Spread half the celery root puree over leeks. Arrange broccoli flowerets down center. Cover with remaining celery root and spinach. Place in layer pan half filled with hot water. Bake at 325 degrees for 30 minutes. Cool overnight. Unmold on serving plate. Cut into slices.

Patrick Raynal's Fettuccine Verde con Gamberi
Spinach Pasta with Shrimp

1 1/2 ounces egg fettuccine	1 tomato, chopped
1 1/2 ounces spinach fettuccine	Olive oil
	Butter
3 ounces shrimp, broken	Salt and pepper to taste
1 small clove of garlic, minced	Basil and oregano to taste

Cook fettuccine in boiling water in saucepan with a small amount of salt and oil for 2 minutes; drain. Combine with shrimp, garlic and tomato in bowl. Add olive oil, butter and seasonings to taste; toss lightly. Serve immediately.

Ziggy Eisenberger's Souffle Montrachet
Goat Cheese Souffle

6 tablespoons unsalted butter, melted	Salt, pepper, nutmeg and cayenne pepper to taste
5 tablespoons flour	5 egg yolks, beaten
1 1/2 cups half and half	6 ounces montrachet cheese, shredded
1 cup heavy cream	1 cup egg whites, stiffly beaten
	Thyme

Blend butter and flour in saucepan. Cook until bubbly, stirring constantly. Stir in half and half and cream gradually. Cook until thickened, stirring constantly. Season with salt, pepper, nutmeg and cayenne pepper. Remove from heat. Add a small amount of hot mixture to egg yolks; stir egg yolks into hot mixture. Cook until very thick, stirring constantly. Add 2/3 of the cheese. Stir until melted. Fold 1/3 of the egg whites gently into cheese mixture to lighten. Fold in remaining egg whites gently. Spoon into souffle dish. Sprinkle with remaining cheese and thyme. Bake at 325 degrees for 40 to 50 minutes or until puffed, brown and set.

WISEMAN AND MILAM DINNER

MENU

WISEMAN AND MILAM DINNER

KRUG BRUT CHAMPAGNE

Cream of Asparagus Soup
NOUIROT-CARRIERE MEURSAULT-LES CHARMES 1982

Fillet of Fish Veronique
BOUCHARD CORTON-CHARLEMAGNE 1980

Caesar Salad
BOLLINGER R.D. BRUT CHAMPAGNE 1970

Crown Roast of Lamb
COMTE GEORGES DE VOGUE MUSIGNY 1972

Grand Marnier Souffle

Walnuts
CROFT VINTAGE PORT 1970

I don't often get invited to people's homes for dinner. I'm told that it's because they're intimidated to cook for me. (If they only knew how easy I am to please! I appreciate anything that's been prepared with T.L.C. !) So when I do get an invitation, I really look forward to it, and I haven't been disappointed yet. In a few cases, I've had meals so outstanding that I've asked the hosts and hostesses to promise they'll never open a restaurant in Nashville. If they did, I'd be in a lot of trouble, and so would a few other local restaurateurs I know!

One such meal was prepared for me by Judge Tom Wiseman and his wife Emily, and Tom Milam (whose company, The Southwestern Company, just happens to be publishing this book) and his wife, Carol.

This was one of those occasions when each course complemented the one preceding and following it; every dish was superbly prepared, and the wine chosen to go with it made a perfect pairing.

We started our evening with an aperitif of Krug brut Champagne. Both the Toms are experts on wine, and each wine we drank was chosen from their private cellars to complement the meal in a special way. That's why we started with a clean, crisp, *light* Champagne. It cleanses the palate in addition to being festive and fun to drink.

Our first course was Cream of Asparagus Soup made by Emily Wiseman. She had made a veal stock first, then cooked fresh asparagus, saving the tips, which she later cooked in milk and floated on top of the creamed soup as garnish. It was delicious. With it, we drank 1982 Nouirot-Carriere *Meursault-Les Charmes*, a clean, crisp, white Burgundy with a fragrant nose. It was a pretty golden-green shade which complemented the soup in color as well as flavor.

Next came Fillet of Fish Veronique made by Judge Wiseman.

The judge said he usually makes this dish with sole, but he couldn't find any to suit him, so he used orange roughy, which was excellent. It was firm, flaky meat with no fishy taste. The judge poached it in wine and water with onion and parsley. Then he made a white sauce with the poaching liquid and added seedless white grapes. He peeled the grapes while he was watching a basketball game on television!

For the fish course, Tom opened two Corton-Charlemagne white Burgundies so we could compare the wines. The first, a 1980 Bouchard, had a full, rich, lasting flavor — a magnificent example of a great, white Burgundy.

The second, a 1978 Bonneau du Martray, was different, but equally as good. This one had more of a honey nose compared to the Bouchard's flowery nose, and it was a crisper wine, but also rich and smooth.

We took our time eating and paced ourselves so that by the time Tom Milam got ready to prepare his Caesar Salad, we were ready for it.

I hate to admit it, but Tom makes the best Caesar Salad I've ever tasted. The reason I hate to say it is because I always thought I made a pretty impressive Caesar, but mine couldn't compare.

So I did the only thing a smart restaurateur could do; I stole his recipe and now it's *my* Caesar Salad. The big difference is that Tom uses no vinegar, because vinegar dulls your palate for the wines and other foods. He uses only fresh lemon juice and he uses *no* salt because the Parmesan cheese and the anchovies are salty enough that you don't need it.

He juiced the lemon the right way by rolling the fruit under his hand to loosen the juice before slicing it, then squeezing the juice through a napkin to catch the seeds.

We drank Champagne with the Caesar, and it made a terrific marriage. The bubbly was Bollinger R.D. Brut, 1970, which had been aged for 8 years in the bottle, and it was *outstanding*.

Our main course was a crown roast of lamb prepared by Judge Wiseman. It looked so impressive, I hated to see it carved.

The "crown" had been stuffed with a walnut-bread crumb dressing mounded to look like a head wearing a crown of black jewels. It was a magnificent presentation and tasted as good as it looked.

We again sampled two wines — this time red Burgundies. First came a 1972 Comte Georges de Vogue Musigny. Vogue is considered the best grower in this 25-acre Grand Cru designation, where they say the best wines in Burgundy are made. This one had a nose that was so fabulous you didn't even have to taste it to experience its elegance and full, rich flavor.

The next, a 1961 Patriarche Corton was not as full and rich, but it held up very well for a 24-year-old Burgundy. It had a more delicate nose and surprisingly good color for its age.

Our last course, and the *piece de resistance,* was Emily's Grand Marnier Souffle. It was enough to make a French chef look like a Boy Scout!

This is Robin's favorite dessert, and she orders it anytime she sees it on a restaurant menu. Robin has sampled Grand Marnier souffles in restaurants all across the United States as well as countless places in Europe, and she says Emily's is the best yet. It was cooked absolutely perfectly, soft enough in the middle so that we didn't need a sauce.

We didn't drink anything with this course. We didn't need to. But after the dinner we had some superb Croft 1970 Vintage Port. This rich, plum-like flavored wine was just the right finish for a *superb* five-star meal from four chefs!

I persuaded the Wisemans and the Milams to part with their recipes so I could share them with you. If you really want to impress someone special, prepare this meal. It's a winner all the way!

Cream of Asparagus Soup

2 pounds asparagus	1/4 cup chopped
1/2 cup chopped	onion
celery	8 cups chicken stock

Cut tips from half the asparagus spears; reserve. Combine remaining asparagus and remaining ingredients in saucepan. Simmer for 30 minutes or until tender. Puree in food processor. Put through mesh sieve with wooden spoon.

3 tablespoons butter, melted	Several drops of green food coloring (optional)
3 tablespoons flour	Salt and white pepper to taste
Light cream	Milk

Blend butter and flour in saucepan. Cook until "honeycombed." Do not brown. Add sieved asparagus gradually, stirring constantly. Bring to a boil; reduce heat. Stir in enough cream to make of desired consistency. Add food coloring and seasoning. Cook reserved asparagus tips in a small amount of milk in saucepan until tender-crisp. Ladle soup into soup bowls. Garnish with asparagus tips.
Yield: 6-8 servings.

Fillet of Fish Veronique

2 tablespoons melted butter
6 white peppercorns
2 sprigs of parsley, chopped
1/4 cup flour
2 cups vegetable, veal or chicken stock
3 or 4 mushrooms, sliced
Juice of 1/2 lemon
Salt to taste

Combine butter, peppercorns, parsley and flour in saucepan. Cook until *roux* "honeycombs," stirring constantly. Stir in stock gradually. Add remaining ingredients; mix well. Simmer for 20 minutes. Strain and set Veloute sauce aside.

Sole, scrod or orange roughy fillets
White wine
1 slice onion
1 sprig of parsley
Salt
Heavy cream
Pepper to taste
White seedless grapes

Place fish in deep skillet. Add mixture of half wine and half water or fish stock to cover. Add onion, parsley and 1 teaspoon salt. Poach until fish flakes easily. Place fish on heated serving plate; keep warm. Strain poaching liquid. Boil 2 cups strained liquid in saucepan until reduced by one-half. Stir into Veloute sauce in saucepan. Cook until thickened. Add a small amount of heavy cream and seasonings. Heat 6 to 10 grapes per person in white wine in saucepan. Serve sauce over fish fillets. Garnish with grapes and paprika.

Caesar Salad

2 heads romaine lettuce
5 cloves of garlic, slightly crushed
1 cup light olive oil
4 very thin slices bread, toasted
Anchovy paste
4 eggs
Salt and freshly ground pepper to taste
1 1/3 cups freshly grated Parmesan cheese
1 tablespoon Worcestershire sauce
3 lemons, cut into halves

Wash romaine. Tear into large bite-sized pieces; discard stems. Spin dry. Crisp in refrigerator. Marinate garlic in 1/2 cup olive oil for 30 minutes. Remove garlic; stir in remaining 1/2 cup olive oil. Cut toast into croutons. Brush each crouton with anchovy paste. Boil eggs for 1 minute. Cool under cold running water. Place romaine in large salad bowl. Drizzle with garlic oil. Sprinkle with a small amount of salt and a generous amount of pepper. Sprinkle cheese over romaine. Add soft-boiled eggs, Worcestershire sauce and 2/3 of the croutons. Squeeze lemons through cheesecloth onto salad. Toss lightly and thoroughly until ingredients are well mixed. Serve on individual salad plates. Sprinkle with remaining croutons. Spoon dressing remaining in salad bowl over salads. Yield: 4 generous servings.

Grand Marnier Souffle

Bake souffle during last dinner course, and it will be perfect in time for dessert. Serve at the table for spectacular presentation.

8 egg yolks
1 1/4 cups sugar
Grated zest of 1 orange
1/4 cup Grand Marnier
9 egg whites
Pinch of salt

Beat egg yolks in mixer bowl until lemon colored. Add 1 cup sugar gradually, beating constantly. Beat until mixture forms ribbon when beaters are lifted. Add orange zest and Grand Marnier; mix well. Beat egg whites in copper or mixer bowl until soft peaks form. Add remaining 1/4 cup sugar and salt. Beat until stiff peaks form. Fold 1/3 of the egg whites gently into egg yolks to lighten. Fold in remaining egg whites gently. Do not overmix; mixture will be streaked. Butter 2-quart souffle dish; sprinkle with sugar. Pour in egg mixture. Place on oven rack in center of preheated 375-degree oven. Bake for about 27 minutes or until puffed but slightly runny in center. Spoon some of both crusty outer portion and soft inner portion onto each dessert plate. Serve immediately.

Mayor Richard Fulton (left) and Sylvester Stallone

PEGGY STEINE DINNER

MENU

PEGGY STEINE DINNER

Potage Puree de Potiron

Coquilles Saint Jacques a la Parisienne
POUILLY-FUME 1978

Filet de Boeuf
Aioli Garni
CHATEAU LAFITE-ROTHSCHILD 1962

Fromage

Charlotte Russe
RESERVE BARON PHILLIPPE DE ROTHSCHILD 1973

Another unforgettable meal I had at the home of a friend was when Robin and I were guests at Peggy Steine's Rokeby condominium for dinner. This great lady is not only a gourmet cook, but a wine connoisseur as well.

Peggy's first course was *potage puree de potiron*, a delicious clear (not creamy) soup that I thought was made from potatoes until she told me it was *pumpkin*.

She followed this with *Coquilles Saint Jacques a la Parisienne*, a mixture of shrimp and scallops cooked in white wine and served in a seashell. Magnificent.

With both these dishes, Peggy served a 1978 Pouilly-Fume, a perfect accompaniment for either light soup or seafood. This is a smoky-fragrant, fruity white wine from the upper Loire Valley.

Our main course was a magnificent Chateaubriand which Peggy called Filet of Boeuf with Aioli Garni. The filet was served surrounded by appetizingly fresh vegetables, cooked *al dente*, arranged so attractively the platter looked like a picture from *Gourmet Magazine*.

Peggy chose a 1962 Lafite-Rothschild for the entree, a safe bet since it would be hard to fault a Lafite in a good vintage year . . . and '62 was a very good year!

A great cheese course came next — English Stilton served on a silver tray with Peggy's homemade walnut bread. A superb taste combination. For this, Peggy brought out her *piece de resistance* among the wines of the evening — a 1973 Baron Phillipe de Rothschild private reserve Champagne, which we finished off with a delicious Charlotte Russe for dessert. Exquisite!

Duke and Duchess of Manchester

Potage Puree de Potiron
Pumpkin Soup

4 scallions, chopped	1/2 teaspoon salt
1 small onion, sliced	2 tablespoons flour
4 tablespoons butter	Ginger and nutmeg to taste
1 1/2 pounds pumpkin, peeled, chopped	3/4 cup half and half, heated
4 cups chicken stock	

Saute scallions and onion in 2 tablespoons butter in saucepan until tender. Do not brown. Add pumpkin, chicken stock and salt. Simmer until tender. Combine flour with 1 tablespoon softened butter in small bowl; mix until well blended. Stir into pumpkin mixture. Bring to a boil, stirring constantly. Puree in blender or put through fine sieve. Stir in spices, cream and 1 tablespoon butter. Ladle into bowls. Garnish with lightly salted whipped cream.

Note: May use canned pumpkin.

Aioli Garni
Vegetables with Garlic Sauce

6 to 8 cloves of garlic	Juice of 1 lemon
1 cup homemade mayonnaise	Salt and freshly ground pepper to taste

Crush garlic thoroughly. Garlic cannot be crushed too fine. Combine with mayonnaise, lemon juice, salt and pepper in bowl; mix well. Chill Aioli Garni thoroughly.

Baby limas	Chick peas
Green beans	Tiny green peas
Whole artichoke hearts	Zucchini

Prepare and cook fresh or frozen vegetables. Do not overcook. Serve hot vegetables with chilled Aioli Garni.

Coquilles Saint Jacques a la Parisienne
Scallops and Shrimp Coquilles

1 pound scallops	2 tablespoons finely chopped parsley
1 pound shrimp, shelled	Salt and pepper to taste
2 cups white wine	2 tablespoons flour
3 shallots, finely chopped	2 tablespoons heavy cream
12 mushrooms, sliced	Bread crumbs
3 tablespoons butter	

Combine scallops, shrimp and wine in saucepan. Simmer for 5 minutes. Drain scallops and shrimp, straining and reserving wine. Saute shallots and mushrooms in butter in skillet. Add parsley, salt, pepper and flour; mix well. Stir in reserved wine gradually. Cook until thickened, stirring constantly. Stir in cream. Add shrimp and scallops; mix well. Spoon into ramekins or baking shells. Sprinkle with crumbs; dot with additional butter. Broil until lightly browned and bubbly.

Mayor Richard and Sandra Fulton of Nashville

THE FIRESTONE'S DINNERS

The following menus and recipes were given to me by Kate Firestone of the Firestone Vineyards. Kate, a former solo ballerina with London's Royal Ballet, is also a fabulous cook. One of my fondest memories of my last trip to the California wine country is a picnic lunch I shared with Kate on the grounds of Firestone Vineyards in the Santa Ynez Valley. It was a perfect day, with blue skies and a nice breeze, and we were sitting under an old olive tree that reminded me of Italy. We ate a wonderful lunch Kate had prepared of soup, croissant sandwiches, fruit and cheese, and we drank *great* Firestone wines. What a day!

MENU

TENDERLOIN OF PORK DINNER

Watercress Salad

Tenderloin of Pork en Croute with Rosy Sour Cream Sauce

Baked Parsnips

Green Peas

Cassata Ice Cream

SAUVIGNON BLANC PINOT NOIR

SELECT HARVEST RIESLING

Watercress Salad

Thinly sliced red onion	Orange slices
Lemon juice	Vinaigrette dressing
Watercress	Freshly ground pepper to taste

Marinate onion slices in lemon juice for 1 hour or longer. Drain. Arrange watercress, orange slices and onion on salad plates. Top with vinaigrette dressing and freshly ground pepper.

Tenderloin of Pork en Croute with Rosy Sour Cream Sauce

1 package frozen puff pastry, thawed	1 tablespoon thyme
1 pound ground veal	1 teaspoon each salt and pepper
1 egg	4 ounces ham, sliced
1 tablespoon chopped parsley	Dijon mustard
	2 pork tenderloins
	1 egg, beaten

Roll pastry into 12 x 18-inch rectangle. Combine veal, 1 egg, parsley and seasonings in bowl; mix well. Spread on pastry, leaving 3-inch border on all sides. Arrange ham slices on veal; spread with mustard. Place tenderloins on ham; fold pastry with filling over tenderloins to make long roll. Seal long side and ends. Place seam side down in baking dish. Pierce 5 or 6 times. Brush with beaten egg. Bake at 400 degrees for 10 minutes. Reduce temperature to 350 degrees. Bake for 1 1/2 hours longer. Remove to warm serving dish in warm oven; reserve pan drippings.

3/4 cup Rose or Cabernet	1 cup sour cream
1/4 teaspoon Marmite or meat glaze	

Drain excess drippings from baking pan. Add Rose, stirring to deglaze pan. Add Marmite; mix well. Bring to a boil; remove from heat. Stir in sour cream. Heat to serving temperature. Do not boil. Serve Rosy Sour Cream Sauce with pork tenderloin.

MENU

GRILLED SWORDFISH DINNER

Cream of Spinach Soup
Gougeres

Grilled Swordfish with Scallop Sauce

Patty Pan Squash Filled with Carrot Puree

New Red Potatoes in Parsley Butter

Fruit Salad in Apricot-Honey Sauce

Brandy Snaps

GEWURZTRAMINER   CHARDONNAY

Cream of Spinach Soup

2 pounds fresh spinach	Salt and pepper to taste
6 green onions, chopped	2 cups half and half
4 cups chicken stock	1/2 teaspoon nutmeg
	Crisp-cooked bacon, crumbled

Cook spinach and green onions in stock in saucepan until very tender. Add salt and pepper. Puree in blender. Add half and half and nutmeg. Adjust seasonings. Pour into soup bowls. Top with bacon.

Grilled Swordfish with Scallop Sauce

16 ounces bay scallops	1/4 cup dry Sherry
2 tablespoons butter	1/4 cup heavy cream
2 tablespoons chopped parsley	Salt and pepper to taste
Chopped onion	1/4 pound cooked baby shrimp
1/2 cup dry white wine	Swordfish fillets
	Lemon butter

Saute scallops lightly in butter in skillet. Add parsley and onion. Cook until vegetables are tender. Add white wine and Sherry. Cook for 2 minutes. Puree in blender. Add cream. Puree until very smooth. Add seasonings to taste. Combine with shrimp in saucepan; keep warm. Brush swordfish with lemon butter. Place on rack in broiler pan. Broil until fish flakes easily. Arrange on serving plate. Serve with scallop sauce.

Fruit Salad in Apricot-Honey Sauce

1/4 pound dried apricots	Melon, peeled, chopped
1/2 cup honey	Pears, peeled, sliced
3 tablespoons lemon juice	Fresh pineapple cubes
	Seedless grapes
	Strawberries, sliced

Soak apricots using package directions. Cook in water to cover in saucepan until soft. Add honey. Cook until blended. Stir in lemon juice. Puree in blender. Add about 2 cups water or enough to make of sauce consistency. Combine with fruit in serving bowl; mix well. Chill in refrigerator.

ROBERT MONDAVI'S MENUS

Several years ago the Robert Mondavi Winery held a series of "Great Chefs" cooking schools at the winery in Napa. The following menu and recipes are from this Great Chefs of France series held in 1984.

MENU

GREAT CHEFS OF FRANCE SERIES
1984 LUNCHEON

Medaillons de Homard
aux Poireaux et Champignons
ROBERT MONDAVI 1981 CHARDONNAY RESERVE

Emince de Chevreuil
au Beurre de Genievre et Baies Roses
ROBERT MONDAVI 1974 CABERNET SAUVIGNON RESERVE

Beignets d'Ananas Eventhia
ROBERT MONDAVI 1981 JOHANNISBERG RIESLING BOTRYTIS

Medaillons de Homard
aux Poireaux et Champignons
Lobster Medallions with Leeks and Chanterelles

2/3 pound potatoes
12 baby leeks
1   3 1/4-pound lobster
1/3 pound small firm chanterelles
Vinaigrette
3 tablespoons chopped herbs (parsley, chervil, chives)
5 shallots, minced
1 tablespoon ocetra caviar

Cook potatoes in skins; slice into rounds. Cut leeks into quarters lengthwise. Steam until tender. Steam lobster. Remove shell; cut tail meat into medallions. Trim and brush chanterelles; wash if necessary. Warm lobster in a small amount of Vinaigrette in skillet. Combine potatoes, leeks, a portion of the herbs and shallots and a small amount of Vinaigrette in skillet. Heat until warmed through. Saute chanterelles and remaining herbs and shallots in skillet. Arrange potatoes in circle on serving plates. Alternate leeks and lobster around potatoes; spoon sauteed mushrooms into center. Garnish potatoes with caviar. Serve warm.

Vinaigrette

Combine 1/2 cup olive oil, 1/4 cup peanut oil, 1 tablespoon mustard and 2 tablespoons wine vinegar in bowl; whisk until well blended. Yield: 4 servings.

*Emince de Chvreuil au Beurre
de Genievre et Baies Roses*

Venison with Juniper Berry Butter and Pink Peppercorns

20 juniper berries, finely chopped	1 tablespoons raspberry vinegar
3 1/2 ounces butter	1 1/2 cups red wine
1 1/3 pounds verison filet	Stems from 1 bunch parsley
2 tablespoons lime juice	

Put juniper berries and butter through fine meshed strainer; set aside. Marinate venison in mixture of next 4 ingredients. Drain venison, reserving marinade. Roast venison as desired. Slice; keep warm. Cook reserved marinade in saucepan until reduced. Whisk in juniper butter. Keep warm.

1 red pepper	2 teaspoons pink peppercorns
1 green pepper	Zest of 2 tangerines, chopped
3 leeks, chopped	
1/2 head green cabbage, shredded	Butter

Cut peppers into 1 1/2-inch squares. Blanch the vegetables 1 at a time by steaming briefly. Saute red pepper, green pepper, leeks, cabbage, peppercorns and zest in butter in skillet until glazed. Set aside and keep warm.

1 red pepper, chopped	2 cups whipping cream
1 green pepper, chopped	8 small puff pastry barquettes
1 bunch parsley, chopped	

Blanch the vegetables 1 at a time by steaming briefly. Combine parsley and half the cream in saucepan. Cook until tender. Combine peppers and remaining cream in saucepan. Cook until tender. Spoon parsley mixture into 4 barquettes and pepper mixture into remaining barquettes. Spoon hot juniper sauce onto plates. Arrange hot sauteed vegetables, a barquette of each vegetable and venison slices on each. Serve very hot. Yield: 4 servings.

Beignets d'Ananas Eventhia

Eventhia's Pineapple Fritters

1/2 teaspoon dry yeast or 1/2 package compressed yeast	2 cups beer
	3 cups flour

Mix yeast and beer in bowl. Add flour; mix well. Let stand for 2 hours.

1 cup coconut milk	1 cup confectioners' sugar
9 ounces pineapple pulp	1 1/2 tablespoons rum
2 egg yolks	

Heat coconut milk and pineapple pulp in saucepan to near boiling point. Beat egg yolks with confectioners' sugar in bowl until thick and lemon colored. Stir in hot coconut mixture gradually. Pour into saucepan. Cook until mixture coats spoon, stirring constantly; remove from heat. Add rum; blend well.

1 pineapple	4 scoops pineapple sorbet
Oil for deep frying	
Confectioners' sugar	

Peel pineapple; cut into slices lengthwise. Remove core; cut into 5/8-inch spears. Dip in prepared beer batter to coat. Deep-fry in hot oil until golden brown; drain on paper towel. Place on baking sheet. Sprinkle with confectioners' sugar. Broil until glazed. Spoon warm sauce onto dessert plates. Arrange 3 or 4 pineapple spears on each plate with scoop of sorbet in center. Yield: 4 servings.

Robin and Mario with Alfredo (originator of Fettuccine Alfredo) in Rome

MENU

ROBERT MONDAVI CHARDONNAY BRUNCH

Fresh Orange Juice

Cantaloupe Halves Filled with Fresh Fruit

Chilled Salmon with Basil Mayonnaise

Chilled Fresh Asparagus
ROBERT MONDAVI CHARDONNAY RESERVE

Croissants

Italian Roast Coffee

Chilled Salmon with Basil Mayonnaise

1 egg	1/4 cup melted butter
2 tablespoons lemon juice	1/2 cup olive oil
2 tablespoons sliced green onion	1/4 cup grated Parmesan cheese (optional)
1 cup packed fresh basil leaves or 1/2 cup chopped parsley and 3 tablespoons dry basil	

Combine egg, lemon juice and green onion in blender container. Process at high speed until well blended. Add basil. Process until smooth. Add butter and oil in fine stream, processing constantly until blended. Pour into bowl; mix in cheese. Chill Basil Mayonnaise, covered, in refrigerator.

1/4 cup butter	6 3/4 to 1-inch thick salmon steaks
1/2 cup white wine such as Robert Mondavi White	

Preheat oven to 400 degrees. Heat butter and wine in shallow baking dish until bubbly. Coat salmon on both sides with butter mixture; arrange in baking dish. Cover with lightly buttered parchment. Bake for 5 to 7 minutes or until fish just begins to flake. Do not overcook; center should be slightly creamy. Chill, covered, in refrigerator. Place on serving plate. Garnish with fresh basil or parsley sprigs. Serve with Basil Mayonnaise.

"The Tennessean" publisher John Seigenthaler

MENU

NAPA VALLEY AL FRESCO LUNCHEON

Marinated Scallop Salad

Cold Artichokes with Herbed Mayonnaise

Napa and Sonoma Valley Cheeses

Fresh Napa Valley Bread

ROBERT MONDAVI FUME BLANC

Robert Mondavi and his wife, Margarit Biever, often serve a cool, delicate Marinated Scallop Salad which can be taken on a picnic, or served as a combination first course salad for evening entertaining. It is excellent served with the lively, dry character of Fume Blanc.

To accompany the marinated scallops, cooked and chilled California artichokes are chosen. A homemade mayonnaise, seasoned with fresh herbs from the garden, is offered for dipping. The mayonnaise is made ahead and allowed to mellow overnight with the herbs. Since Napa Valley cooking has a wonderful heritage from old Italian winemaking families, an abundance of oregano and basil are used. The basil is more seasonal, available primarily during the summer months, but the oregano can usually be found throughout the year.

Though the Napa and Sonoma Valleys have long been known for their wines, only recently has the natural counterpart, cheese, become an important product. The Chenel goat cheese comes plain or coated with pepper or herbs. There is also the mild Sonoma Jack and a variety of other cheeses which complement the red and white wines of these grape growing regions.

Long loaves of Napa's Passini bread or the whole wheat Swiss farm bread, made by St. Helena's tiny Sugar House Bakery, are the most popular breads in Napa Valley. Another favorite is the sourdough bread made by the Sonoma French Bakery.

Mario and Robin

Marinated Scallop Salad

1 pound scallops
3 tablespoons lime juice
5 tablespoons lemon juice
1/2 cup olive oil
3 tablespoons Robert Mondavi White or Fume Blanc
1/4 teaspoon orange zest
1 teaspoon orange juice
1/2 teaspoon Dijon mustard
1 small red onion, thinly sliced into rings
1 large avocado, cut into 3/4-inch cubes
Salt and pepper to taste

Cut large scallops in half. Marinate scallops in mixture of lime juice and 3 tablespoons lemon juice for 2 hours. Drain. Slice scallops 1/4 inch thick. Combine olive oil, 2 tablespoons lemon juice, wine, zest, orange juice and mustard. Pour over mixture of scallops, onion and avocado in large bowl; toss lightly. Serve in large shallow lettuce-lined salad bowl or in lettuce cups on salad plates. Sprinkle lightly with salt and pepper. Garnish with orange slices.

Herbed Mayonnaise

Flavorful olive oil can be obtained from the Olive Oil Manufacturing Company in St. Helena to make this Italian-style mayonnaise. This small, family-owned business is located in a white barn on the corner of Charter Oak and McCorkle Avenues in St. Helena; you won't find them in the telephone book.

3 egg yolks
1 tablespoon wine vinegar or lemon juice
Salt and pepper
1/4 teaspoon dry or prepared mustard
1 1/2 cups olive oil
1/4 cup fresh herbs such as oregano, basil, chervil and parsley

Process egg yolks in blender container until thick. Add vinegar, 1/2 teaspoon salt and mustard. Process for 30 seconds. Add olive oil in fine stream, processing constantly until thick and creamy. Pour into bowl. Blanch herbs in boiling water for 1 minute; rinse with cold running water. Pat dry with paper towel. Finely chop herbs; stir into mayonnaise. Season with salt and pepper to taste. Chill, tightly covered, overnight.

ROBERT MONDAVI CABERNET SAUVIGNON DINNER

Green Fettuccine with Gorgonzola and Prosciutto
ROBERT MONDAVI 1980 FUME BLANC RESERVE

Rib Steaks with Sauteed Shallots

Steamed Artichokes
or
Julienned Green Beans
ROBERT MONDAVI CABERNET SAUVIGNON RESERVE

Endive Salad with Toasted Walnuts

Fresh Orange Souffle
ROBERT MONDAVI SPECIAL SELECTION JOHANNISBURG RIESLING

Rib Steaks with Sauteed Shallots

1/4 cup butter
1 tablespoon olive oil
4 boneless rib steaks
1/2 cup chopped shallots
3/4 cup Robert Mondavi Red

Heat 1 tablespoon butter and olive oil in large skillet over medium-high heat. Cook steaks for 3 minutes on each side or to desired degree of doneness. Remove steaks to heated serving plate. Saute shallots in remaining butter and pan drippings until tender but not brown. Add wine; stir to deglaze skillet. Spoon over steaks. Serve immediately.

GOURMET GALA

For the past few years I've been privileged to be one of the judges at the annual March of Dimes Gourmet Gala. This is the event where local celebrity chefs have a cooking competition, and those who attend get to sample their creations.

Each year the food and presentation seems to be more outstanding than the year before, making it difficult for the judges, who have a tough time picking winners. In my book, they're all winners.

The following are some of the recipes from the 1985 Gourmet Gala.

Anne Clayton's Calzone

Prepared by Anne and Ted Clayton.

- 4 ounces montrachet, crumbled
- 7 ounces mozzarella cheese, grated
- 2 ounces prosciutto, shredded
- 2 tablespoons chopped parsley
- 1/2 teaspoon thyme
- 1 teaspoon minced garlic
- Freshly ground pepper to taste
- 1/4 teaspoon each oregano, basil and marjoram
- 2 ounces sliced black olives
- 2 ounces sun-dried tomatoes, chopped, drained

Combine all ingredients in bowl; mix well. Set aside.

- 2 packages dry yeast
- Pinch of sugar
- 5 cups unbleached flour
- 2 teaspoons salt
- 6 tablespoons extra-virgin olive oil

Dissolve yeast and sugar in 1 1/2 cups warm water in bowl. Let stand for 5 to 10 minutes or until foamy. Combine flour, salt and olive oil in bowl or food processor. Mix or process until mixture forms ball, adding a small amount of flour if necessary. Dough should be soft but not sticky. Place in oiled bowl. Let rise for 1 1/2 hours. Shape into 4 balls; roll out each on floured surface. Spoon cheese mixture onto lower half; fold to form turnover. Seal edges. Place on oiled baking sheets. Bake at 450 degrees for 15 to 18 minutes or until golden and crisp. Brush with good olive oil. Serve with green salad and Chianti.
Yield: 4 servings.

Note: Dough may be refrigerated before shaping. May make into 8 to 10 smaller calzone for appetizers.

Corinne's Cold Spinach Soup

Prepared by Corinne Franklin and Carter Andrews.

- 1/2 cup minced shallots
- 3 tablespoons butter
- 2 10-ounce packages frozen chopped spinach
- 3 13-ounce cans chicken broth
- 1 teaspoon salt
- 1/8 teaspoon pepper
- Dash of nutmeg
- 1 8-ounce package cream cheese, cubed

Saute shallots in butter in large skillet until tender. Add spinach. Cook, covered, over low heat for 10 minutes or until spinach is thawed, checking frequently to prevent sticking. Add broth and seasonings. Simmer for 5 minutes; cool slightly. Process in several portions in blender until smooth. Combine with cream cheese in saucepan. Heat until cream cheese melts, stirring constantly with wire whisk. Pour into glass bowl or crock. Chill for 4 hours or longer. Ladle into bowls.

Chicken Dijon, recipe on page 118

Clams New York-New York

Prepared by Mr. and Mrs. Lawrence Lipman.

6 slices pumpernickel bread	2 tablespoons chopped parsley
1 pound Monterey Jack cheese, shredded	2 cloves of garlic, finely chopped
20 ounces chopped clams, drained	Pinch each of black pepper, cayenne pepper

Trim crusts from bread; cut into desired shapes. Toast or saute until crisp. Arrange on baking sheet. Combine cheese, clams, parsley and seasonings in bowl; mix well. Spread over croutons. Broil until brown and bubbly. Place 2 croutons on each plate. Garnish with twist of lemon. Yield: 8 servings.

Poached Norwegian Salmon

Prepared by Mr. and Mrs. Cris Stone.

10 to 12 4-ounce Norwegian salmon fillets	4 sprigs of fresh dill or 2 tablespoons dillweed
2 1/2 cups dry white wine	2 tablespoons minced chives
	6 shallots, minced

Arrange fillets in large baking pan. Combine remaining ingredients in bowl; mix well. Pour over fillets. Cover with plastic wrap. Marinate in refrigerator for 8 hours to overnight, turning fillets over once. Poach, uncovered, at 350 degrees for 8 minutes.

1 cup sour cream	2 tablespoons crushed green peppercorns
2 tablespoons lemon juice	1 small cucumber, seeded, finely chopped
2 tablespoons capers	

Combine sour cream and remaining ingredients in bowl; mix well. Chill until serving time.

20 to 24 asparagus spears	1 head red leaf lettuce
30 to 36 large shrimp	Lemon and lime slices

Steam asparagus spears until tender-crisp. Broil shrimp until pink. Place poached fillets on lettuce-lined plates. Arrange 2 asparagus spears crisscross on top; place 3 shrimp along one side of each fillet. Spoon 2 tablespoons sour cream sauce over top. Garnish with lemon and lime slices.

◁ *Fettuccine Gorgonzola, recipe on page 125*

Chicken Breasts with Tapenade and Tomato-Basil Sauce

Prepared by Mr. and Mrs. George Fehrmann.

8 anchovies	1 tablespoon raspberry vinegar or red wine vinegar
22 Nyons olives or 44 black Nicoise olives, pitted	2/3 cup light olive oil
1 tablespoon Dijon mustard	Freshly ground pepper to taste
1 small clove of garlic	
2 egg yolks	

Soak anchovies in water to cover for 10 minutes. Drain and pat dry. Combine with olives, mustard and garlic in blender container. Process until smooth. Add egg yolks. Process until blended. Add vinegar and olive oil gradually, processing constantly. Blend in pepper. Chill tapenade, tightly covered.

8 whole chicken breasts, skinned boned, split	Salt and freshly ground pepper to taste
1 1/2 tablespoons fresh lemon juice	

Remove small filet from underside of each chicken breast and reserve for another purpose. Sprinkle filets on both sides with next 3 ingredients. Place in single layer on buttered baking sheet. Place tablespoon olive tapenade on each. Chill for 2 hours.

6 pounds Italian plum tomatoes, cored, quartered	1/4 cup Champagne vinegar or white wine vinegar
3 tablespoons olive oil	2 tablespoons minced shallots
1 cup packed fresh basil	3 tablespoons Creme Fraiche (page 141) or whipping cream
Salt and freshly ground pepper to taste	2 sticks chilled unsalted butter, cut into 1-tablespoon pieces
1/4 cup dry vermouth	

Saute tomatoes in olive oil in heavy 6-quart saucepan over medium heat for 15 minutes. Add basil. Simmer for 1 to 1 1/2 hours or until moisture evaporates, stirring frequently. Season with salt and pepper. Puree. Chill for up to 24 hours if desired. Combine vermouth, vinegar and shallots in saucepan. Boil until reduced to 2 tablespoons. Add *creme fraiche*. Boil until reduced to about 2 1/2 tablespoons. Remove from heat. Whisk in 2 tablespoons butter. Return to low heat. Whisk in remaining butter 1 tablespoon at a time. Whisk in tomato mixture. Broil chicken 9 inches from heat source until cooked through. Spoon sauce onto heated plates; arrange chicken on top. Garnish with fresh basil leaves.

Stuffed Onions
Prepared by Mr. and Mrs. Buck Hussung.

6 medium red onions
1 bunch parsley
Tops of 1 bunch green onions
4 stalks celery
1 10-ounce package frozen chopped spinach
1/4 cup unsalted butter
1/4 cup bacon drippings
2 tablespoons Worcestershire sauce
1 teaspoon Tabasco sauce
Salt to taste
1/2 cup bread crumbs
2 eggs, beaten
1/2 cup heavy cream
8 ounces bacon, crisp-fried, crumbled

Cut tops from onions; scoop out centers to form shells. Reserve 1 center; discard remainder. Wrap shells in foil; chill until ready to stuff. Combine reserved onion center, parsley, green onion tops and celery in food processor container; process until finely chopped. Thaw spinach; press out moisture. Melt butter with bacon drippings in skillet. Add finely chopped vegetables. Cook over low heat for 10 to 15 minutes, stirring occasionally. Add spinach and seasonings; mix well. Stir in bread crumbs; remove from heat. Beat eggs with cream; stir into spinach mixture. Add bacon; mix well. Place onion shells in buttered baking dish. Stuff with spinach mixture. Bake at 350 degrees for 45 minutes. Remove to serving plate. Serve with Mornay Sauce.

Mornay Sauce

1/4 cup unsalted butter
1/4 cup flour
1/2 cup heavy cream
1 1/2 cups milk
1/2 cup freshly grated Parmesan cheese
1/2 teaspoon salt
1/4 teaspoon white pepper

Melt butter in saucepan over low heat. Blend in flour. Stir with wire whisk for 2 minutes. Do not brown. Add cream and milk gradually, whisking constantly. Cook until thickened, stirring constantly. Add cheese, salt and pepper. Cook for 4 to 5 minutes longer, stirring constantly. Spoon over onions just before serving.

RASPBERRY CHEESECAKE
Prepared by Mr. and Mrs. Harry Lindhal.

12 egg whites, at room temperature
2 cups sugar
2 tablespoons cornstarch
6 ounces unsalted almonds, toasted, finely ground
6 ounces unsalted hazelnuts, toasted, finely ground

Beat egg whites in mixer bowl until soft peaks form. Combine sugar and cornstarch. Add to egg whites very gradually, beating constantly at high speed until stiff peaks form. Sugar should be completely dissolved. Do not underbeat. Fold in almonds and hazelnuts gently. Pipe or spread into two 9-inch circles on baking parchment-lined baking sheets. Pipe remaining meringue into strips on baking sheet. Strips will be placed around side of assembled cake. Bake at 275 degrees for 1 hour or until dry to the touch. Do not brown. Turn off oven; open oven door. Let stand in oven with door ajar until cool.

3/4 to 1 cup sugar
18 ounces cream cheese, softened
4 eggs
6 to 8 tablespoons raspberry liqueur
1 teaspoon vanilla extract

Line buttered 9-inch cake pan with baking parchment. Butter and flour parchment. Cream sugar and cream cheese in bowl until light and fluffy. Add eggs 1 at a time, beating well after each addition. Blend in liqueur and vanilla. Pour into prepared pan. Rap on counter to spread evenly. Place in shallow baking pan filled with 1/4 to 1/2 inch hot water. Bake in preheated 350-degree oven for 30 to 60 minutes or until knife inserted in center comes out clean. Turn off oven; open door several inches. Let stand in oven with door ajar for 30 to 40 minutes or until cool. Chill for 4 to 6 hours.

3 sticks unsalted butter, softened
12 ounces cream cheese, softened
5 tablespoons sour cream
2 teaspoons vanilla extract
8 ounces semisweet chocolate, melted, cooled
16 ounces frozen raspberries, thawed

Cream butter and cream cheese in mixer bowl until smooth. Add sour cream and vanilla; mix well. Blend in chocolate. Divide in half. Reserve 16 whole raspberries. Fold remaining raspberries into half the frosting. Place 1 meringue shell on silver serving platter. Spread half the chocolate-raspberry frosting on meringue. Remove parchment from cheesecake. Place on frosted meringue. Spread remaining chocolate-raspberry frosting on cheesecake. Top with remaining meringue shell. Spread top and side with thin layer of chocolate frosting. Cut meringue strips to fit side of cake. Press around cake. Score top into 16 wedges. Pipe frosting rosette at edge of each section with star tip. Pipe border between sections. Chill until firm. Top each rosette with reserved raspberry. Cut with warm knife.

SPECIAL CALIFORNIA RECIPES

WINE COUNTRY GARDEN COOKERY

Cooking with wine adds a subtle hint of flavor to garden-fresh vegetable dishes. As alcohol in the wine evaporates while cooking, your dish receives a calorie-free wine essence that has the unique flavor of the grape.

Vicki Sebastiani, author of wine cookery brochures and wife of Sebastiani Vineyards President Sam J. Sebastiani, grows over 100 varieties of herbs and vegetables in her Sonoma garden, including 6 squash and 13 tomato varieties. She combines her vegetables with local ingredients and wine, and has created a culinary collection of great recipes.

For a unique vegetable dish that uses wine, Vicki suggests serving a Green Tomato Pie. Green (unripe) tomatoes have a firm flesh which allows them to cook in a manner that would turn ripe tomatoes into mush.

Zucchini plants bear profusely and offer an opportunity to try many new recipes such as the Zucchini Torta and Stuffed Zucchini Flowers. Don't hesitate to use the zucchini blossoms for the ricotta-stuffed flowers. Try to use the male flowers (ones without fruit developing under them), although it certainly will not harm the plants to use the females.

GREEN TOMATO PIE

Wine: Chenin Blanc.

5 tablespoons flour	3 tablespoons minced
1 recipe 2-crust	dried lemon rind
pie pastry	1/2 teaspoon salt
4 cups sliced	1/4 cup packed
green tomatoes	brown sugar
3 tablespoons	2 tablespoons butter
Chenin Blanc	

Sprinkle 1 tablespoon flour in pastry-lined 9-inch pie plate. Drain tomato slices on paper towels; toss gently with wine in bowl. Add remaining 4 tablespoons flour, lemon rind, salt and brown sugar; toss lightly. Place in prepared pie plate; dot with butter. Top with remaining pastry, sealing to edge and cutting vents. Bake at 375 degrees for 45 minutes or until brown. Serve hot or at room temperature.

RICOTTA-STUFFED ZUCCHINI FLOWERS

Wine: Chilled Sebastiani "Eye of the Swan"
Pinot Noir Blanc or Sebastiani Chardonnay.

These stuffed flowers are very impressive, as well as easy to prepare. The proportions will vary according to the number and sizes of flowers. Use approximately 12 medium zucchini (or any other squash) flowers, freshly picked. Rinse carefully in cold water, if necessary. (Be sure bugs are removed from the center of flowers.)

1 pound ricotta,	1/2 teaspoon pepper
at room temperature	1/2 cup finely
2 tablespoons	grated Italian
Sebastiani "Eye	Asiago (or
of the Swan" Pinot	Parmesan) cheese
Noir Blanc	2 tablespoons minced
1 onion, minced	fresh basil
1/2 cup toasted	2 tablespoons
almonds, finely	minced parsley
chopped	12 medium
1 teaspoon	zucchini flowers
seasoned salt	1/4 cup melted butter

Combine ricotta cheese with next 8 ingredients in bowl; mix well. Stuff into squash flowers using pastry tube. Do not overfill. Arrange stuffed flowers on serving plate; drizzle 1 teaspoon butter over each. Microwave on Medium for 2 to 3 minutes or until just heated through. Do not allow filling to leak out of flowers.

Note: Stuffed flowers may be baked at 350 degrees for 15 minutes.

TOMATOES WITH HERBS

Wine: Cabernet Sauvignon or Barbera.

3 large ripe tomatoes, sliced	1/4 teaspoon seasoned salt
3 tablespoons Cabernet Sauvignon or Barbera	2 tablespoons fresh basil or tarragon
2 tablespoons lemon juice	1 tablespoon minced parsley
5 tablespoons olive oil	1 tablespoon minced chives or shallot
	Freshly ground pepper to taste

Arrange tomato slices in shallow serving dish. Combine remaining ingredients in bowl; mix well. Pour over tomatoes. Let stand at room temperature for 1 hour or longer.
Note: A wedge of imported Parmesan cheese is a tasty complement to this dish.

The following are some delicious recipes I got from the St. Clement winery in Napa.

BEEF BRAISED IN ST. CLEMENT CABERNET

Wine: St. Clement Cabernet Sauvignon, of course!

1 4-pound chuck roast	1 tablespoon butter
1 1/2 cups St. Clement Cabernet	1 cup (or more) beef broth
3 tablespoons chopped yellow onion	1 1/2 tablespoons chopped Italian tomatoes
2 tablespoons chopped carrot	Pinch of thyme
2 tablespoons chopped celery	1/8 teaspoon marjoram
2 tablespoons oil	Salt and freshly ground pepper to taste

Brown roast on all sides in a small amount of hot oil in skillet. Remove roast; drain excess drippings. Add wine. Cook over high heat for about 1 minute, stirring to deglaze skillet; set aside. Saute onion, carrot and celery in mixture of oil and butter in small Dutch oven until tender, stirring frequently. Do not brown. Add roast, broth, tomatoes and seasonings. Add enough additional broth to cover 2/3 of the roast if necessary. Bring to a boil; cover. Bake at 350 degrees for 3 hours, turning and basting roast every 20 minutes. Add several tablespoons water if liquid evaporates. Carve roast; arrange overlapping slices on serving platter. Boil pan juices until reduced to 2/3 cup, stirring to deglaze. Season with salt and pepper. Spoon over roast. Serve immediately.

ST. CLEMENT ICE WITH FRESH FRUIT

4 cups St. Clement Cabernet	3/4 cup sugar
2 tablespoons grated lemon rind	2 tablespoons fresh lemon juice
1 1 1/2-inch cinnamon stick	Ripe melon or pear slices

Combine wine, lemon rind, cinnamon stick, sugar and 2 cups water in saucepan. Bring to a boil. Cook until sugar dissolves, stirring frequently. Reduce heat to medium-low. Simmer for 5 minutes. Cool to room temperature. Stir in lemon juice. Pour into 2 ice cube trays. Freeze overnight. Process 1/2 at a time in food processor until smooth. Freeze until firm. Soften in refrigerator for 15 minutes before serving. Spoon into dessert bowls. Top with melon or pear slices.
Yield: 8 servings.

CRANBERRIES IN ST. CLEMENT CABERNET

1 12-ounce package fresh cranberries	1 1/2 cups sugar
1 cup St. Clement Cabernet	1 3-inch cinnamon stick
	1 7-inch piece of orange zest

Rinse cranberries under cold water; drain. Combine wine and sugar in enamel-lined saucepan. Bring to a boil, stirring constantly. Add cranberries, cinnamon stick and orange zest. Bring to a boil; reduce heat to medium-low. Simmer, covered, for 10 to 15 minutes or until cranberry skins burst. Remove from heat. Discard cinnamon stick. Remove orange zest; cool slightly. Slice zest thinly crosswise; add to cranberries. Cool to room temperature. Spoon into cooled sterilized jars; seal. Store in refrigerator for up to 2 months (if you're lucky enough to have it last that long). Yield: 3 cups.

CAPPELLETTI

Robert Mondavi, the Godfather of the California premium winemakers, loves good food as much as he does good wine. He comes by this naturally. Like most Italian immigrants, his parents considered wine a food rather than an alcoholic beverage and a necessary part of any meal.

Bob has always regarded food and wine as a whole rather than as separate parts. His late mother, Rosa, agreed. Rosa Mondavi was a consummate cook (famous throughout the California wine country) as well as an ardent admirer of good food and wine. She taught her children a solid appreciation of both, and her recipes are still used and enjoyed by members of the Mondavi family and their friends. One of Rosa Mondavi's favorite recipes was for Cappelletti — a variant of ravioli which originated in her home district of Marches, northeast of Rome. Cappelletti is derived from *cappello*, or "hat." They are stuffed pasta shells in the shape of a hat or bonnet. This dish reflects the tastes of the rugged inhabitants of the equally rugged mountains of Marches. Though the current generations of Mondavis enjoy a wide range of cuisines, they still partake regularly of the peasant dishes developed and perfected by their ancestors. The following is Rosa's recipe for Cappelletti. Adjustments according to taste are encouraged. Remember regional Italian cooking always reveals the cook's personal touch; the only real sin is not to experiment.

ROSA MONDAVI'S CAPPELLETTI

Wine: A moderately robust red, such as Mondavi Zinfandel, Napa Gamay or Red Table Wine.

3 cups flour	1/2 teaspoon salt
3 large eggs	

Mound flour on work surface; make a well in center. Beat eggs with salt; pour into well. Mix as much flour as possible into eggs with fork. Knead for 20 minutes or until stiff and satiny, adding 1 to 2 tablespoons of water as necessary to bind dough. Let rest, covered, at room temperature for 45 minutes. Divide into 4 portions. Set pasta machine at thinnest adjustment. Feed each portion of dough through machine; place on floured surface. Cut into small circles using wineglass or cookie cutter.

1/4 cup finely ground salt pork	1 clove of garlic, minced
8 ounces finely ground pork	1/2 teaspoon minced lemon rind
8 ounces finely ground beef	2 eggs, beaten
8 ounces finely ground chicken	1/4 cup grated Parmesan cheese
Dash of nutmeg	Salt and pepper to taste

Saute salt pork in skillet; discard cracklings. Add pork, beef and chicken. Saute until completely cooked. Add remaining ingredients; mix well. Shape into marble-sized balls. Place 1 ball on each dough circle; fold dough over to enclose filling, sealing edges. Fold dumplings over index finger, pressing overlapping ends together to seal; bend edge outward to complete illusion of bonnet. Arrange on tray dusted with flour. Let dry for several hours. Cappelletti may be simmered in light broths or clear soups, served with a variety of sauces from garlic and tomato to pesto, or dressed with butter or olive oil and Parmesan cheese. Yield: 100 Cappelletti.

MARGARIT BIEVER'S SUMMER PASTA SALAD

Robert Mondavi's wife Margarit Biever serves this dish as a summer luncheon entree.

1 8-ounce package corkscrew or shell pasta	1 pound fully ripened tomatoes, peeled, chopped
4 ounces fresh chanterelles, morilles or Japanese mushrooms	1 large shallot, finely chopped
	1 teaspoon balsamic vinegar
1 clove of garlic	1/4 cup light olive oil
1 tablespoon olive oil	1/4 cup finely chopped fresh basil
Salt and pepper to taste	

Cook pasta al dente in boiling salted water in saucepan; drain. Saute mushrooms and garlic in 1 tablespoon olive oil in skillet until tender. Discard garlic. Season with salt and pepper. Combine tomatoes, shallot, vinegar, 1/4 cup light olive oil, salt and pepper in bowl. Add pasta, basil and sauteed vegetables; toss gently. Serve with freshly grated Parmesan cheese.

CAMEMBERT FONDUE

Wine: Bordeaux or Cabernet Sauvignon.

1/2 cup melted butter	1 cup dry white wine
1/2 cup flour	1 cup milk
1 teaspoon instant chicken bouillon	2 or 3 4-ounce packages Camembert cheese, sliced

Blend butter and flour in medium saucepan. Cook over low heat until bubbly, stirring constantly. Stir in 1 cup boiling water, bouillon, wine and milk gradually. Add cheese. Cook until cheese is melted and sauce is thickened, stirring constantly. Strain into fondue pot. Keep warm. Serve with toasted French bread cubes, shrimp, sliced mushrooms, cauliflowerets and carrot sticks. Yield: 3 1/2 cups.

HOMEMADE WINE VINEGAR

Vicki Sebastiani of Sebastiani Vineyards makes her own homemade wine vinegar with leftover table wine. Using her method, the quality of the vinegar is superb and in addition to home use in salads and recipes, it makes a great gift.

To start your own "family reserve" of wine vinegar, Vicki says all you need is table wine and a vinegar culture or "starter." You can make red or white vinegar, or a combination using both red and white. You will need a thoroughly clean crock or wine bottle, at least half-gallon size. An oak barrel can be used instead, and will add oak flavors to the vinegar. You can find "starter" at beer and wine-making supply stores or by writing Beer and Winemaking Supplies, Inc., 154 King Street, Northampton, Massachusetts 01060 or Wine and the People, Inc., 907 University Avenue, Berkeley, California 94710.

Fill your container two-thirds full with the following proportions: two parts wine, one part water, and one part "starter." Lightly cover the container with gauze or cheesecloth. Secure in place with a rubber band or wire.

Place vinegar container near your stove or water heater, as it needs some heat, although over 90°F or under 68°F will slow or stop production. After two to six months you should have vinegar. If you periodically shake it, you will be able to use it sooner.

Vicki periodically draws off some vinegar and replaces it with more red or white wine, keeping a batch going continually. Don't add Port or Sherry, as their high alcohol content inhibits the transformation of wine into vinegar. Remember, better quality wine makes better quality vinegar; and red wines under five years old, because of their fruitiness, make more interesting vinegar than older wines.

When you use your vinegar, be sure to leave sediment deposits at the bottom of the container. You can filter the vinegar through layers of fine gauze or a coffee filter and then store it in airtight bottles.

Vicki steeps herbs in her wine vinegar for flavor subtleties and decoration. Tarragon, dill, rosemary, basil, thyme, garlic and oregano are some of her favorites. Nasturtium and dill flowers also make beautiful additions. Use combinations and quantities of herbs according to your individual taste.

The following is one of the recipes Vicki has created with homemade wine vinegar.

ITALIAN TERIYAKI SAUCE

This sauce can be used on sirloin steak, which has been sliced diagonally into thin slices, boned chicken breasts or fish fillets. These are great to barbecue, grill or broil. Try marinating mushrooms in this teriyaki sauce for an interesting nibble.

1/4 cup Homemade Wine Vinegar
1/2 cup soy sauce
1/2 cup red table wine
1/4 cup olive oil
2 teaspoons Worcestershire sauce
1 tablespoon honey
2 cloves of garlic, minced
1 teaspoon minced fresh gingerroot or 1/2 teaspoon powdered ginger
1/2 teaspoon coarsely ground pepper

Combine all ingredients in jar. Shake to mix well. Pour over meat of your choice in shallow baking dish. Marinate for 1 hour or longer, turning meat occasionally.

FETTUCCINE A LA MYRA

Myra Hoefer, who cooks for the Clos du Bois Dry Creek Vineyard in Sonoma County, contributed this recipe from the delicious luncheon she served me when I visited there.

Greek olives
Sun-dried tomatoes, chopped
Fresh basil, chopped
Fresh watercress, chopped
Red onion, chopped
Cloves of garlic, chopped
Prosciutto, chopped
Sasso olive oil
Fettuccine, cooked
Asiago cheese, grated

Saute olives and next 6 ingredients in olive oil in skillet. Add to hot cooked fettuccine in bowl; toss to mix. Top with cheese. Serve immediately.

ARTICHOKES AND SHRIMP SALAD
Wine: A dry to off-dry full-bodied white, such as Montrachet.

8 large artichokes	1 tablespoon salt
1 lemon, halved	1/4 cup flour

Break stems of each artichoke. Bend leaves back to break. Cut choke even with bottom. Trim bottom. Rub with cut lemon half. Place in mixture of juice of 1/2 lemon and 4 cups cold water in bowl. Bring 2 quarts water to a boil. Stir in salt and mixture of flour and 1/2 cup water. Add drained artichoke bottoms and juice of remaining lemon half. Simmer for 15 to 20 minutes or until tender. Rinse in cool water; drain. Scoop out choke. Chill, covered, in refrigerator.

1/2 cup walnut oil	1/4 teaspoon dried dill
1/4 cup wine vinegar	1 pound cooked
4 teaspoons	shrimp, peeled
lemon juice	2 tablespoons chopped
2 cloves of	chives or parsley
garlic, pressed	Salt and freshly
1/2 pound mushrooms,	ground pepper
very thinly sliced	to taste

Combine walnut oil, vinegar and lemon juice in bowl; mix well. Add garlic and seasonings. Add mushrooms, tossing to coat. Marinate, tightly covered, for 2 hours or longer. Reserve 8 whole shrimp; chop remaining shrimp. Add to mushrooms. Arrange artichokes on salad plates. Mound shrimp mixture in center of each. Garnish each with whole shrimp and chives. Serve chilled.

STUFFED FLANK STEAK ROLL
Wine: A light red, such as Valpolicella, Bardolino or Beaujolais.

This is easy to prepare and tastes great.

1 large flank steak	Salt to taste
1/2 teaspoon tarragon	2 slices
5 slices Thuringer	provolone
or summer sausage	2 tablespoons
1 onion, thickly sliced	butter
1/2 10-ounce	3/4 cup dry
package frozen	white wine
spinach, thawed	

Pound steak to 1/4-inch thickness. Sprinkle with tarragon. Arrange sausage on steak, leaving 1-inch border. Cover with onion. Squeeze spinach dry. Spoon down center of steak. Sprinkle with salt. Place cheese on top. Roll as for jelly roll from long side. Secure in 4 places with string. Brown on all sides in butter in skillet. Place in baking dish. Add wine. Bake, covered, at 350 degrees for 50 minutes. Cut into 12 slices. Yield: 4 servings.

EASY RACK OF LAMB
Wine: A good Bordeaux or Cabernet Sauvignon.

This dish is simple to prepare but elegant enough for company.

3 slices bread,	1 clove of garlic,
crusts trimmed	minced
1/4 cup chopped	2 6-rib racks of lamb
parsley	Olive oil
Salt and freshly	1/2 cup clarified
ground pepper	butter
to taste	

Process bread in blender container to make fine crumbs. Combine crumbs with parsley and seasonings; toss to mix. Trim lamb, removing all fat. Let stand until room temperature. Place bone side up in oiled roasting pan. Brush thoroughly with olive oil. Roast in preheated 500-degree oven for 10 minutes; turn lamb over. Cover with bread crumb mixture. Spoon butter carefully over crumbs. Roast for 5 to 8 minutes or to desired degree of doneness. Place on heated serving platter. Garnish with sprigs of parsley. Serve immediately. Yield: 6 servings.

BOURSIN CHEESE-STUFFED CHICKEN BREASTS
Wine: California Pinot Noir Blanc or Chenin Blanc.

This dish takes a little extra time to slip the cheese under the skin of the breast, but it is well worth it.

4 chicken breast	1/4 cup peanut oil
halves with wings	1 teaspoon
5 ounces Boursin	rosemary
cheese	

Bone chicken breasts, leaving wing bone and skin attached. Place a thin layer of cheese between skin and meat of each breast. Saute chicken breasts 2 at a time in 2 tablespoons oil in skillet over medium-high heat until brown. Place in baking dish. Sprinkle with rosemary. Roast at 350 degrees for 30 minutes or until tender. Yield: 4 servings.

PORK EN CROUTE

Wine: A light red, such as Cabernet del Friuli or Sancerre Rouge.

This is a good party dish; may be made a day ahead, refrigerated, then cooked an hour before serving.

1/4 pound butter, chilled, sliced	1 1/4 cups flour 1/8 teaspoon salt

Cut butter into flour in bowl until crumbly. Add salt and 2 tablespoons cold water. Mix lightly with hands until mixture forms ball. Chill, wrapped, for 1 hour to overnight.

1 3-pound boneless pork tenderloin	1 teaspoon crumbled dried tarragon
1/2 cup Dijon mustard	1 egg, lightly beaten

Brown tenderloin evenly on all sides in large skillet. Cool. Roll pastry into rectangle large enough to enclose tenderloin. Spread mustard on pastry. Sprinkle with tarragon. Place tenderloin in center of pastry; fold to enclose, sealing ends and edges. Place seam side down in baking pan. Brush with egg. Bake at 350 degrees for 1 hour or until golden. Yield: 6 servings.

MEDALLIONS OF VENISON WITH CRANBERRIES

Wine: Jordan 1981, Estate Bottled Cabernet Sauvignon, Alexander Valley.

2 cups cranberries	1 1/2 tablespoons finely chopped shallots
1/4 cup sugar	
Zest of 1 orange, finely chopped	1 cup veal or chicken stock
Pinch of cayenne pepper	1/2 cup Cabernet Sauvignon or dry red wine
1 cinnamon stick	
4 5-ounce venison loin medallions	Salt and pepper to taste
1/2 cup unsalted butter	

Combine cranberries, sugar, orange zest, cayenne pepper, cinnamon stick and 2 cups water in saucepan. Simmer until cranberry skins pop; drain. Remove cinnamon stick. Saute venison medallions in 2 tablespoons butter in skillet until rare. Place in dish in 200-degree oven to keep warm. Saute shallots in pan drippings until tender. Add stock and wine, stirring to deglaze skillet. Cook until liquid is reduced by 2/3. Add cranberries. Season to taste. Bring to a simmer. Add 6 tablespoons butter, a small amount at a time, stirring constantly with wire whisk. Place medallions on serving plates. Spoon sauce over medallions; serve.

CATALINA SAUSAGE ISLE

Wine: Beringer Zinfandel.

This unusual recipe looks as good as it tastes. The contrast in colors makes an eye-appealing dish.

1 1/2 teaspoons salt	1/2 medium green pepper, sliced
1 1/2 cups yellow cornmeal	2 tablespoons peanut oil
1 1/2 cups grated medium Cheddar cheese	2 1/2 cups canned tomatoes
	1/4 cup tomato sauce
10 ounces mild Italian sausage links	1/2 teaspoon thyme
	1/2 bay leaf
	Baby green peas, cooked
1 cup finely chopped onion	
1 clove of garlic, finely minced	Baby onions, cooked

Bring 3 3/4 cups water and salt to a boil in saucepan. Stir in cornmeal mixed with 1 cup water. Cook over low heat for 10 to 15 minutes or until thick and bubbly, stirring constantly. Add cheese; stir until well blended. Spoon into greased 6-cup ring mold. Keep warm. Brown sausage in skillet. Cut into 1/2-inch slices. Saute onion, garlic and green pepper in peanut oil in skillet for 5 minutes. Add tomatoes, tomato sauce, seasonings and sausage. Simmer for 15 minutes. Unmold cornmeal ring on serving plate. Spoon sauce into center. Surround ring with peas and baby onions. Yield: 4-6 servings.

BOUDIN DE FRUITS DE MER
(Seafood Sausage)

Wine: Jordan 1982, Chardonnay, Alexander Valley.

At the Jordan Winery in Sonoma, Chef Franco Dunn prepares sumptuous meals for guests who come to stay at the fabulous "Chateau" winery. I persuaded him to part with this recipe!

Leaves of 2 bunches spinach	1 1/2 teaspoons dried thyme
8 ounces medium shrimp, peeled	2 tablespoons unsalted butter
8 ounces bay scallops	Salt and pepper to taste
1 sweet red pepper, finely diced	
1 carrot, finely diced	10 feet narrow hog sausage casing

Blanch spinach in heavily salted boiling water in saucepan for 2 seconds. Plunge into ice water; drain well. Chop coarsely. Cut shrimp and scallops into quarters. Saute red pepper and carrots with thyme in

112

butter in skillet until tender-crisp. Combine spinach, seafood, sauteed vegetables and seasonings in bowl; mix well. Stuff into sausage casing. Tie with cotton string at 4-inch intervals. Pierce each sausage 5 or 6 times with toothpick. Steam for 4 to 5 minutes. Serve with basic white wine sauce.

Note: Crayfish or lobster may be substituted or added.

LE BERNARDIN'S SHELLFISH STEW

Wine: Sterling Chardonnay.

This is a fabulous shellfish recipe donated by the Sterling Vineyards. It came from Two-Star Chef Gilbert le Coze of the Le Bernardin Restaurant in Paris when he was invited to Napa to prepare a six-course meal for a special banquet at the vineyard.

12 large chowder or razor clams	1 clove of garlic, finely minced
1 1/2 pounds small cherrystone or littleneck clams	1 shallot, finely minced
1 1/2 pounds mussels	1 bunch parsley, finely minced
3/4 cup unsalted butter	1 tablespoon Cognac
1 1/4 cups creme fraiche or heavy cream	Freshly ground pepper to taste
	1 pound shelled bay or sea scallops
4 medium tomatoes, peeled, seeded, chopped	4 freshly opened oysters, in the shell

Scrub clams and mussels in several changes of water. Remove beards from mussels. Combine butter, *creme fraiche*, tomatoes, garlic, shallot and parsley in large skillet. Cook over high heat until butter melts, stirring constantly. Add Cognac and pepper. Bring to a boil. Add large clams. Cook, covered, for about 5 minutes or until shells begin to open. Add mussels. Cook, covered, for 3 to 4 minutes or until all shells are open. Remove clams and mussels with slotted spoon. Place in casserole in 200-degree oven to keep warm. Add small clams. Cook, covered, for 3 to 4 minutes or until shells begin to open. Add scallops. Cook, covered, for 4 minutes. Discard unopened shells. Place clams, mussels and scallops in 4 large heated soup bowls. Place 1 raw oyster in each bowl. Spoon pan juices over shellfish. Serve immediately with empty side dishes for shells. Yield: 4 servings.

Note: If using sea scallops, cut each in half.

GRILLED FISH STEAKS SONOMA-STYLE

Wine: Chilled Sebastiani "Eye of the Swan."

Use either swordfish, sea bass or salmon steaks for grilling. They hold together very well on the grill and are especially moist.

4 3/4 to 1-inch thick fish steaks	1/4 cup white wine vinegar
3/4 cup oil	1/2 cup chopped parsley
1/2 cup olive oil	1/2 cup chopped watercress
1/4 cup Sebastiani "Eye of the Swan" Pinot Noir Blanc	1/2 cup chopped green onion

Place fish steaks in shallow dish. Combine remaining ingredients in bowl; mix well. Pour 2 cups over fish; reserve remaining marinade. Marinate fish, covered, in refrigerator for 1 hour, turning once. Grill fish over medium coals for 3 to 4 minutes on each side or until fish flakes easily. Remove to serving plate. Heat reserved marinade in saucepan. Serve over fish.
Yield: 4 servings.

Photograph for this recipe above.

SAUSALITO SALMON SUPREME
Wine: Beringer Chardonnay.

This recipe came from the Beringer Winery in Napa Valley.

1 cup sour cream	2 pounds 1/2 to
1 tablespoon vinegar	3/4-inch
2 teaspoons	salmon steaks
Dijon mustard	1 tablespoon
2 teaspoons dill	lemon juice
1/8 teaspoon salt	

Combine first 5 ingredients in bowl; blend well. Let stand for 1 hour. Arrange salmon steaks on well-greased rack in broiler pan; brush with lemon juice. Let stand for 10 minutes. Broil 5 inches from heat source for 10 to 12 minutes or until fish flakes easily. Remove to serving plate. Spoon sauce over salmon or serve as dip for salmon. Serve with rice pilaf and fresh broccoli. Yield: 4-6 servings.

SILVERADO GRILLED SEA BASS WITH SALSA

This deliciously different way of preparing sea bass came from the Silverado Winery in Napa. The winery is owned by Walt Disney's widow, Lillian, and his daughter and son-in-law, Diane and Ron Miller. The winery, perched atop a high hill overlooking Napa, is beautiful. There is a terrace where visitors can have lunch. If you can't get there, try this recipe at home. Uncork a bottle of Silverado Sauvignon Blanc and enjoy!

2 tomatoes, peeled,	Juice of 1 lime
seeded, chopped	1 clove of garlic,
1/2 cup chopped	chopped
fresh cilantro	Cumin to taste
Juice of 1 lemon	

Combine tomatoes and next 5 ingredients in bowl; mix well. Set aside.

Juice of 1 lime	1 tablespoon chopped
3 tablespoons mild	fresh cilantro
olive oil	Dash of soy sauce
1/2 sweet red	Fresh sea bass
pepper, sliced	fillets

Combine lime juice, olive oil, red pepper, cilantro and soy sauce in bowl. Add fillets. Marinate for 30 to 60 minutes. Drain fillets, reserving marinade; pat dry. Grill fillets over hot coals in closed grill for 10 minutes. Turn fillets over. Grill for 5 minutes longer or until fish flakes easily. Remove to serving platter. Combine salsa and reserved marinade in blender container. Process for several seconds. Serve over fillets.

Note: Mesquite coals are good but not essential. Brown fillets by cooking on open grill for the first minute on each side.

BASIL-PROSCIUTTO GRILLED SHRIMP
Wine: Same as used for the marinade.

I had this great version of grilled shrimp at a small restaurant in Northern California. I've forgotten the name of the restaurant, but I liked the shrimp so much I came home and figured out the recipe.

24 jumbo shrimp	1/2 cup chopped
1 cup dry white wine	fresh basil
1 cup virgin	Freshly cracked
olive oil	black peppercorns
1/4 cup fresh	24 whole basil leaves
lemon juice	24 thin slices
2 tablespoons	prosciutto,
Dijon mustard	trimmed

Peel and devein shrimp, leaving tails; place in shallow bowl. Pour mixture of wine and next 5 ingredients over shrimp. Marinate in refrigerator for 3 hours or longer, turning shrimp occasionally. Drain shrimp, reserving marinade. Wrap 1 basil leaf and 1 slice prosciutto around middle of each shrimp. Thread 4 shrimp lengthwise on each of 6 metal skewers. Prepare coals with a generous amount of mesquite. Grill shrimp for several minutes on each side, basting frequently with reserved marinade. Serve immediately.

SOLE WITH CAPERS
Wine: Sebastiani Chardonnay, of course.

Capers and lemon add zest to this recipe from Vickie Sebastiani.

4 large fillets	1/2 cup butter
of sole	Juice of 1/2 lemon
2 eggs, beaten	1/4 cup Sebastiani
1/2 cup (about)	Chardonnay
flour	1/4 cup capers

Dip sole fillets in eggs. Coat with flour; shake off excess flour. Brown in 1/4 cup butter in skillet for 2 to 3 minutes on each side, adding additional butter as necessary. Remove sole to heated serving platter; keep warm. Add remaining 1/4 cup butter, lemon juice and wine to pan drippings. Simmer for 2 minutes. Stir in capers. Heat to serving temperature. Pour over sole. Garnish with lemon wedges.
Yield: 4 servings.

PASHKA

I first tasted this in San Francisco. It is like *coeur a la creme*, only richer, and the lemon gives it zest.

1 cup butter, softened	2 teaspoons vanilla extract
32 ounces cream cheese, softened	3/4 cup chopped citron or chopped rind of 1 lemon
3 egg yolks	
2 cups confectioners' sugar	3/4 cup slivered almonds

Cream butter and cream cheese in bowl until light and fluffy. Add egg yolks, confectioners' sugar and vanilla; mix well. Stir in citron and almonds. Line 5 to 7-inch clay flowerpot or mold with hole in bottom with dampened cheesecloth. Pour cream cheese mixture into prepared mold. Place in colander over large dish. Chill for several hours. Mixture will drain. Unmold on serving plate. Remove cheesecloth carefully. Garnish with strawberries or sliced fresh fruit. Yield: 6 servings.

NAPA VALLEY ALMOND TART

Wine: Late Harvest Johannisberg Riesling.

1 cup flour	1 teaspoon vanilla extract
1/2 cup butter	

Combine all ingredients and 1 to 2 tablespoons cold water in food processor. Process until smooth. Dough will be very soft. Roll between waxed paper. Fit into 9-inch tart pan with removable bottom. Line pastry with foil. Fill with dried beans. Bake at 375 degrees for 8 minutes. Remove beans and foil. Bake for 2 minutes longer or until pastry is set, pricking bubbles as necessary. Cool on wire rack for 10 minutes.

3/4 cup heavy cream	3/4 cup sugar
1 tablespoon Late Harvest Johannisberg Riesling	Pinch of salt
	2 cups sliced almonds

Combine cream, wine, sugar and salt in bowl. Let stand in warm place until sugar dissolves, stirring occasionally. Sprinkle almonds in crust. Pour cream mixture over almonds. Bake at 375 degrees for 25 minutes or until golden brown. Cover with foil if tart browns too quickly. Cool on wire rack. Loosen tart; remove from pan. Serve at room temperature. Yield: 8-10 servings.

ROBERT MONDAVI'S KIWI TART

Wine: Mondavi's Moscato d'Oro (a great wine served with any fresh fruit or as a dressing for mixed fresh fruit salad).

3 eggs	1/2 cup sugar
1 cup whipping cream	6 kiwis, peeled, sliced
1/4 cup packed brown sugar	1 baked pie shell

Combine eggs, cream and sugars in food processor or blender container. Process until blended. Arrange kiwi slices in pie shell, overlapping slices. Pour cream mixture over fruit. Bake at 350 degrees for 45 minutes. Yield: 8 servings.

Note: May substitute other fresh fruit for kiwis.

MRS. FETZER'S COCOA-NUT ROUNDS

With 11 kids, Mrs. Fetzer would have gone broke buying cookies, so she learned early to bake her own. Her children say they're the best in the world!

1 cup margarine, softened	2 teaspoons baking powder
1 1/2 cups plus 2 tablespoons sugar	2 tablespoons vanilla extract
2 eggs	3 cups flour
5 tablespoons cocoa	2 cups chopped walnuts
1/4 cup milk	
1/2 teaspoon salt	

Cream margarine, 1 1/2 cups sugar, 1 whole egg and 1 egg yolk in bowl until smooth. Add cocoa, milk, salt, baking powder and vanilla; mix well. Add flour and 2/3 cup walnuts; mix well. Chill until dough can be shaped easily. Shape into 2 logs. Brush with mixture of 1 beaten egg white and 2 tablespoons sugar. Roll in 1 1/3 cups finely chopped walnuts to coat. Wrap in foil. Freeze for 1 hour. Cut rolls into slices; arrange on baking sheet. Bake at 350 degrees for 7 to 9 minutes or until light brown. Do not overbake.

SPECIAL FRENCH RECIPES

COGNAC PATE

1 pound chicken
   livers, trimmed
1 1/4 cups butter
1 large red onion,
   chopped
1/2 cup sour cream
1 1/2 tablespoons
   Cognac
1 1/2 tablespoons
   heavy cream
3/4 teaspoon allspice
Salt and pepper
   to taste
1 cup chopped
   pistachio nuts

Saute chicken livers in 1/4 cup butter in skillet for 5 minutes or until cooked through. Remove with slotted spoon. Saute onion in pan drippings for 3 minutes or until transparent. Puree livers and onion in food processor or blender. Add sour cream, Cognac, heavy cream, allspice, salt and pepper. Process until smooth. Spread evenly on baking sheet; cover with waxed paper. Chill until firm. Cut 1 cup butter into small pieces; place in food processor container. Process until light and creamy. Add chilled liver mixture. Process for several seconds. Stir in nuts. Spoon into decorative molds; cover. Chill until firm. Unmold onto serving plate; serve with thin, toasted French bread slices. *Pate* may be kept refrigerated for about 1 week. Yield: 3 1/2 cups.

MUSHROOMS A LA BOURGUIGNONNE

Wine: A dry white.

If you love the flavor of the garlic butter that comes with *escargots* but don't like the snails, try this mushroom dish. The flavor is basically the same.

1 cup chopped
   parsley
9 or 10 cloves of
   garlic, peeled
1/4 medium onion,
   chopped
4 teaspoons
   white wine
2 teaspoons fresh
   lemon juice
1 teaspoon nutmeg
Salt and pepper
   to taste
3/4 cup melted butter
36 medium
   mushroom caps

Combine first 9 ingredients in food processor or blender container. Process at high speed for 10 seconds. Arrange mushroom caps in *escargot* dishes or shallow baking dish. Spoon sauce into caps. Bake at 375 degrees for 10 minutes. Broil for 1 minute or until sauce is golden brown. Serve with French bread.

WATERCRESS AND ENDIVE SALAD

The taste combination of watercress and endive is one of the best for waking up your palate when it is served at the end of the meal as it is in France.

1 bunch watercress
6 heads Belgian
   endive
1/2 cup olive oil
3 tablespoons
   wine vinegar
1 teaspoon
   minced onion
1/4 teaspoon salt
Freshly ground
   pepper to taste
1/8 teaspoon paprika

Cut stems from tied watercress bunch to make short sprays; discard stems. Place sprays and endive in ice water for 15 minutes or until crisp. Pat dry with paper towels. Cut endive into halves lengthwise from root end; cut into bite-sized pieces. Place endive and watercress in salad bowl. Sprinkle with mixture of olive oil, vinegar, onion and seasonings; toss lightly.

ESCARGOTS BOURGUIGNONNE

*Wine: A light-bodied red to balance the garlic,
   such as a young Bordeaux, Beaujolais or Napa
   Gamay. Many people like a dry full-bodied
   white, such as French Chablis, Meursault or
   Montrachet.*

The French love *escargot* (snails), and those who love the flavor of garlic butter will agree. If you don't have a special snail dish (one with indentations to keep the shells from rolling over and spilling out the butter mixture), you can line the bottom of a baking pan with rock salt and make indentations in the salt for each shell.

1 1/2 cups unsalted
   butter, softened
2 tablespoons finely
   chopped shallot
1/4 teaspoon salt
Pepper and nutmeg
   to taste
4 dozen snails

1 clove of garlic, mashed	Bread crumbs (optional)
2 tablespoons finely chopped parsley	Dry white wine

Cream butter in bowl. Add shallots, garlic, parsley and seasonings. Mix into smooth green paste. Rinse and drain snails and shells according to can directions. Spoon a small amount of butter mixture into each shell. Add 1 snail then fill shell with butter mixture. Arrange shells open side up in snail dishes. Sprinkle with bread crumbs. Pour 2 tablespoons wine into bottom of each dish. Bake at 400 degrees for 8 minutes. Serve with thick slices of French bread.

PAPILLON MIGNON

8 slices bacon	1/4 teaspoon thyme
4 1-inch thick center-cut filets mignons	1/4 teaspoon salt Pinch each of rosemary and pepper
2 tablespoons minced shallots	2/3 cup Papillon red wine
1 tablespoon chopped parsley	

Cook bacon in skillet over medium-high heat until crisp. Drain, reserving 2 tablespoons bacon drippings. Heat bacon drippings in skillet over medium-high heat. Add steaks. Cook for 2 to 3 minutes on each side for medium rare, or to desired degree of doneness. Remove to serving platter. Add remaining ingredients to skillet. Cook for 1 minute, stirring constantly. Pour over steaks; top with bacon slices.

Photograph for this recipe on page 18.

BEEF BOURGUIGNONNE

This is a wonderful French country stew that makes a happy marriage with Burgundy.

4 ounces salt pork, chopped	Dash of cayenne pepper
1/4 cup Cognac	1/2 cup butter
1/4 cup chopped fresh parsley	4 medium onions, chopped
1/8 teaspoon freshly ground pepper	2 cups (about) beef stock
3 pounds bottom round steak, cut into 1 1/2-inch cubes	1 1/2 cups Burgundy 1/2 teaspoon each thyme, marjoram
1/2 cup flour	1 pound fresh mushrooms
1 1/2 teaspoons salt	16 small white onions, peeled
1/2 teaspoon pepper	

Combine first 4 ingredients in bowl. Marinate for 2 to 3 hours. Coat round steak with mixture of flour, salt, 1/2 teaspoon pepper and cayenne pepper. Brown on all sides in 1/4 cup butter in skillet. Add chopped onions. Cook until brown. Place in 3-quart casserole. Drain salt pork, reserving marinade. Brown salt pork in 1 teaspoon butter in skillet. Add to steak. Deglaze skillet with reserved marinade and 1/4 cup stock. Pour over steak. Add wine, thyme, marjoram and enough remaining stock to cover. Bake, covered, at 375 degrees for 2 hours. Saute mushrooms in 2 tablespoons butter in skillet until just tender. Parboil white onions for 3 minutes; drain. Brown lightly in remaining butter in skillet. Add mushrooms and onions to steak. Bake, covered, for 1 hour, adding additional wine or stock if necessary. Adjust seasonings. Garnish with chopped fresh parsley.

STEAK AU POUIVRE VERT
(Steak with Green Peppercorns)

Wine: A big bold red that won't be overpowered by the peppercorns, such as Bordeaux or Brunello di Montalcino.

This is a popular way to prepare filet mignon in France. The green peppercorns give the steak a great flavor.

6 1/3-pound filet mignon steaks	1 tablespoon fresh lemon juice
6 slices dense white bread	1/2 teaspoon salt 3 tablespoons medium-dry Sherry
2 cups heavy cream	
1/2 cup rendered beef fat	1/4 cup green peppercorns, rinsed, drained
1/2 cup Brandy	
2 beef bouillon cubes	

Tie each steak into round compact shape. Cut bread into rounds to fit steaks; toast evenly on both sides. Place on serving platter. Set aside. Cook cream in heavy saucepan over high heat until reduced to 1 cup, stirring occasionally. Chill in refrigerator. Heat rendered fat to the smoking point in large skillet. Arrange steaks in a single layer in skillet. Cook for 3 to 4 minutes on each side. Place steaks on toast rounds; keep warm. Pour off excess drippings; deglaze with Brandy. Set aside. Add bouillon cubes, lemon juice, salt and Sherry to cream. Bring to a boil, stirring constantly; remove from heat. Stir in peppercorns and deglazing liquid. Heat to serving temperature. Pour a small amount of sauce over each steak. Serve remaining sauce in gravy boat.

ESCALOPE DE VEAU MARSEILLAISE

Wine: Same as used in preparing sauce.

This dish is rich and very impressive when served garnished with asparagus tips.

12 veal scallops
Flour
4 tablespoons butter
1 tablespoon oil
2/3 cup canned
    beef bouillon
1/4 cup Madeira
12 lumps crab meat
Bearnaise Sauce
24 asparagus
    tips, cooked

Pound veal scallops to 1/4-inch thickness; pat dry. Coat lightly with flour. Saute several pieces at a time in mixture of 2 tablespoons butter and oil in skillet over medium-high heat for 4 minutes on each side. Remove veal; keep warm. Pour off drippings. Combine 2 tablespoons butter, bouillon and Madeira in skillet. Boil over high heat until reduced to 1/2 cup. Add veal; reduce heat. Simmer for 10 minutes. Arrange veal scallops on warm serving platter. Place 1 lump warmed crab meat and 2 tablespoons Bearnaise Sauce on each. Garnish with asparagus tips.

Bearnaise Sauce

2 tablespoons chopped
    shallots
1/2 cup tarragon
    vinegar
1/2 cup dry
    white wine
6 egg yolks
1 cup melted butter
Salt and pepper
    to taste
2 tablespoons dried
    tarragon leaves

Simmer shallots in vinegar in saucepan until partially cooked. Add wine. Cook until reduced to 1/3 cup. Strain. Beat egg yolks in heatproof bowl until thick. Add wine mixture; beat well. Add butter, drop by drop, beating constantly. Add seasonings.

VEAL CHOPS WITH COGNAC CREAM SAUCE

Wine: A full-bodied white wine, such as Montrachet.

This Cognac sauce is rich and delicious and goes equally well over chicken.

4 veal loin chops
1/2 teaspoon salt
Freshly ground
    pepper to taste
1/2 teaspoon thyme
1/4 cup butter
2 shallots, minced
1/4 to 1/3 cup Cognac
1 1/2 cups heavy
    cream

Sprinkle veal chops with salt, pepper and thyme. Saute in butter in skillet for 5 minutes on each side. Remove veal to serving plate; keep warm. Drain excess drippings. Saute shallots lightly in pan drippings over medium heat, stirring constantly. Add Cognac, stirring to deglaze skillet. Cook until reduced to 2 tablespoons. Add cream. Cook over high heat for 5 to 8 minutes or until reduced to 1 cup. Sauce will be thick and creamy. Adjust seasonings. Pour over veal. Garnish with chopped chives. Yield: 4 servings.

COQ AU VIN (Chicken with Wine)

Wine: Same as used in cooking.

A classic French dish made with fine Chambertin or a Grand Cru Burgundy; good with any red Burgundy.

1 5-pound chicken,
    cut up
Flour
1/2 cup butter
1 slice raw ham,
    chopped
10 small whole white
    onions, peeled
1 clove of garlic,
    finely chopped
8 whole mushrooms
1/4 teaspoon thyme
1 sprig of parsley
1 bay leaf
Salt and freshly
    ground pepper
    to taste
1/4 cup Cognac,
    warmed
1 cup dry red wine

Coat chicken with flour. Brown on all sides in butter in skillet. Place in earthenware casserole. Add ham, onions, garlic, mushrooms and seasonings. Pour Cognac over chicken; ignite. Let flames die. Add wine. Bake, covered, at 300 degrees for 2 1/2 hours or until chicken is tender.

CHICKEN DIJON

3 tablespoons
    imported mustard
3 tablespoons
    Reine Pedauque
    Macon "Le Grand
    Cristal"
    dry white
    wine
1 teaspoon
    Worcestershire
    sauce
4 whole chicken
    breasts, split,
    boned, skinned
Salt and freshly
    ground pepper
    to taste
2 1/2 cups fine
    fresh bread
    crumbs
Butter
Oil

Combine first 3 ingredients in bowl; mix well. Flatten chicken breasts between layers of waxed paper with meat mallet. Sprinkle with salt and pepper. Brush all sides with mustard mixture. Pat crumbs onto both sides of chicken breasts with heavy knife. Brown in mixture of equal parts butter and oil in skillet for 5 minutes on each side. Serve with mustard-sour cream sauce.

Photograph for this recipe on page 103.

TARRAGON CHICKEN

Wine: Same as used in cooking.

This is one of the best French sauces I've ever tasted. It is great over chicken breasts, as in this recipe, but just as good over veal medallions.

6 boned chicken breasts, skinned	1/4 cup dry white Bordeaux
Salt and freshly ground pepper to taste	1 teaspoon freshly chopped tarragon or 1/2 teaspoon dried tarragon
1/4 cup flour	1/4 cup chicken broth
1/4 cup butter	1/4 cup heavy cream
1 tablespoon chopped shallots	

Sprinkle chicken breasts with salt and pepper. Coat with flour; reserve remaining flour. Brown chicken on both sides in 3 tablespoons butter in skillet. Place on heated platter. Saute shallots in pan drippings. Add wine; deglaze skillet. Add reserved flour; blend well. Stir in tarragon and chicken broth. Arrange chicken breasts in skillet. Cook, covered, for 25 minutes or until chicken is tender. Place on heated serving plate; keep hot. Stir 1 tablespoon butter and cream into sauce; blend well. Heat to serving temperature; pour over chicken.

LES FARCIS A LA PROVENCALE
(Stuffed Vegetables Provence-Style)

Wine: Either red or white French Burgundy.

May be served as an entree.

2 Spanish onions, peeled	3 cloves of garlic, crushed
4 large tomatoes	2 tablespoons chopped mixed parsley, basil, sage and rosemary
4 medium zucchini	
1/4 cup olive oil	
1 pound mixed ground beef and pork	
2 eggs, slightly beaten	Salt and white pepper to taste
1/2 cup grated Gruyere cheese	1/4 cup dry bread crumbs

Blanch onions in boiling water for 2 to 3 minutes; drain. Cut and reserve 1 slice from top of each onion and tomato. Cut zucchini into halves lengthwise. Scoop out centers of onions, tomatoes and zucchini to form shells. Chop centers and reserved vegetable slices fine. Saute chopped vegetables in 1 tablespoon olive oil in skillet; pour into bowl. Saute meat in 2 tablespoons olive oil in skillet until no longer pink, stirring until crumbly. Add sauteed vegetables, eggs, cheese and seasonings; mix well. Spoon into vegetable shells; press gently with back of spoon. Sprinkle with bread crumbs and several drops of olive oil. Arrange on lightly greased baking sheet. Bake for about 45 minutes or until vegetables are tender. Arrange on serving platter. Serve hot or cold. Yield: 4 servings.

SOLE IN RED WINE

Wine: Red French Burgundy.

An unusual and great way to prepare sole or any other delicate white fish fillets.

3 thick slices bacon	2 cups red Burgundy
2 pounds new red potatoes	1 tablespoon fish stock
White part of 18 scallions, cut into 1 1/2-inch pieces	1/2 teaspoon fresh lemon juice
5 tablespoons unsalted butter	3 tablespoons unsalted butter, chilled, cut into 3 pieces
2 pounds sole fillets	
Salt and freshly ground white pepper to taste	Chopped fresh parsley

Cut bacon into 1/8-inch strips crosswise. Cook in skillet until crisp. Remove to drain on paper towels, reserving drippings. Cut potatoes into 1 1/2-inch ovals. Cook in boiling salted water in saucepan for 10 minutes. Drain and pat dry. Saute in reserved bacon drippings in skillet until cooked through and golden, turning frequently. Add scallions. Saute until lightly browned. Remove to heated platter. Keep warm in oven with door ajar. Pour off drippings. Melt 5 tablespoons butter in skillet over medium heat. Let foam subside. Rinse fillets; pat dry. Season with salt and pepper. Arrange fillets shiny side up in butter. Saute over high heat for 1 1/2 minutes on each side. Place on platter with potatoes and scallions. Pour off butter from skillet. Add wine; deglaze skillet. Cook until wine is reduced to 1/2 cup. Add fish stock and lemon juice; reduce heat to low. Whisk in chilled butter. Do not boil. Spoon sauce onto serving plates. Arrange fish, potatoes and scallions on plates. Top with reserved bacon and freshly chopped parsley.

RATATOUILLE

Wine: Light-bodied red.

Ratatouille is a French favorite; it's even better the second or third day, either reheated or served cold.

1 pound eggplant, peeled	4 cloves of garlic, mashed
1 pound zucchini	Salt and pepper to taste
2 teaspoons salt	
1/2 cup olive oil	2 pounds tomatoes, peeled
2 pounds onions, thinly sliced	
4 green peppers, sliced	Minced parsley

Slice eggplant and zucchini as for French-fried potatoes. Toss with salt in bowl. Let stand for 30 minutes. Drain and pat dry. Saute in olive oil in skillet until lightly browned. Set aside. Saute onions and green peppers in skillet for 10 minutes. Stir in garlic and salt and pepper. Cut tomatoes into halves; squeeze to remove seeds and juice. Slice into thin strips; add to skillet. Cook over medium-high heat until almost dry. Spoon 1/3 of the tomato mixture into greased flameproof 3 to 4-quart casserole; sprinkle with parsley. Add half the eggplant and zucchini. Repeat layers, ending with tomato mixture. Sprinkle with salt and pepper. Simmer, covered, for 10 minutes. Adjust seasonings. Simmer, covered, for 15 minutes longer. Serve hot or cold. Yield: 16 servings.

CHOCOLATE DREAM MOUSSE

Wine: Champagne.

This mousse is a dream of chocolate and almonds. Delizioso!

2 12-ounce packages semisweet chocolate chips	1/4 cup sugar
	8 egg whites, at room temperature
1/2 cup brewed espresso	Pinch of salt
	1 cup lightly toasted sliced almonds
1/2 cup Amaretto	
4 egg yolks	
1 cup whipping cream, chilled	1 cup creme fraiche

Melt chocolate chips in heavy saucepan over very low heat, stirring constantly. Add espresso and Amaretto; blend well. Cool to room temperature. Add egg yolks one at a time, beating well after each addition. Whip cream in mixer bowl until thickened. Add sugar gradually, beating until stiff. Beat egg whites with salt until stiff. Fold egg whites gently into whipped cream. Add 1/3 of the cream mixture to chocolate mixture; mix well to lighten. Fold in remaining cream mixture gently. Fold in almonds. Spoon into 8 dessert dishes. Chill, covered, for 2 hours or until set. Pipe *creme fraiche* decoratively over mousse.

GRAND MARNIER POTS DE CREME

Looks as good as it tastes.

9 egg yolks	7 tablespoons Grand Marnier
1/2 cup superfine sugar	
	1/4 cup freshly grated orange rind
3 cups heavy cream	
1/4 teaspoon vanilla extract	

Place baking pan with 1 inch water in 325-degree oven to heat. Beat egg yolks with sugar until thick and creamy. Stir very gradually into cream with wooden spoon. Add vanilla and 6 tablespoons Grand Marnier; blend well. Pour into *pot de creme* cups; place in pan of hot water in oven. Bake for 35 minutes or until knife inserted in center comes out clean. Cool completely. Chill in refrigerator for 2 hours or longer. Top with mixture of orange rind and 1 tablespoon Grand Marnier.

SORBET AU CHAMPAGNE

In Europe we always serve a palate-cleansing intermezzo before the entree of a multi-course meal. This is especially good. Add 1/3 cup sugar if you like it sweeter, but I prefer mine tart.

2 cups sugar	1 bottle of dry Champagne
1 cup fresh lemon juice	

Dissolve sugar in 2 cups water in saucepan. Bring to a boil, stirring constantly. Simmer for 3 to 5 minutes. Cool to room temperature, stirring occasionally. Stir in lemon juice and Champagne. Pour into several loaf pans. Freeze until slushy. Place in blender container; process to break up ice crystals. Return to loaf pans. Freeze for 1 hour. Process in blender; return to loaf pans. Freeze until 45 minutes before serving time. Place in refrigerator. Spoon into chilled glasses or hollowed out fruit shells. Garnish as desired. Yield: 6-8 servings.

Note: *Sorbet* can be frozen in ice cream freezer according to manufacturer's instructions.

SPECIAL ITALIAN RECIPES

PATALA BRODO

This is a different version of potato soup, well flavored by leeks, basil and watercress.

3 cups chicken stock	1/2 cup tightly packed watercress leaves
3 thin-skinned potatoes, chopped	
1 small yellow onion, chopped	1/4 teaspoon allspice
1/4 cup tightly packed fresh basil leaves	Salt and freshly ground pepper to taste
2 leeks, chopped	
1/4 cup unsalted butter	1 cup milk

Combine first 3 ingredients in large saucepan. Cook, loosely covered, over medium heat for 15 to 20 minutes or until potatoes are almost tender. Stir in basil. Saute leeks in butter in skillet for 5 to 10 minutes or until almost tender. Add watercress. Saute for 5 minutes. Stir into potato mixture with seasonings. Puree a portion at a time in food processor fitted with steel blade. Pour into saucepan. Add milk. Heat to serving temperature over low heat. Serve immediately. Yield: 6 servings.

Note: Puree in food mill for finer mixture if desired.

ZUPPA ALLA PAUESE

Wine: A light Italian white, such as Pinot Grigio or Verdicchio.

This is a favorite Italian peasant soup.

4 1-inch slices Italian bread	4 eggs
1 clove of garlic, pressed	1/4 cup grated Parmigiano or Romano cheese
1/2 cup butter	6 cups chicken broth

Cut hole in center of each bread slice, using whiskey glass. Saute garlic in butter in skillet. Add bread slices. Brown on both sides in garlic butter. Place 1 slice in each of 4 soup plates. Break eggs into holes. Sprinkle with cheese. Ladle boiling broth carefully over eggs. Serve piping hot garnished with freshly chopped parsley.

Note: The egg will be cooked by the hot broth.

VENETIAN MUSHROOM SOUP

I found this recipe in the most romantic city in the world — Venice. The addition of tomato paste and sweet Vermouth gives it a deliciously different flavor for a hearty, cold weather soup.

1 medium onion, grated	3 tablespoons tomato paste
1 clove of garlic, split	3 cups chicken stock
1 tablespoon butter	2 tablespoons sweet Italian vermouth
1 tablespoon olive oil	
1 pound mushroom caps, thinly sliced	1/2 teaspoon salt
	Pepper to taste

Saute onion and garlic in butter and olive oil in skillet until brown. Discard garlic. Add mushrooms. Saute for 5 minutes. Mix in tomato paste. Stir in chicken stock, vermouth, salt and pepper. Simmer for 10 minutes.

1-inch thick Italian bread slices, buttered	2 tablespoons finely chopped parsley
4 egg yolks, beaten	2 1/2 tablespoons Parmesan cheese

Broil buttered Italian bread until golden; place in soup bowls. Beat egg yolks with parsley and cheese. Beat into boiling soup. Ladle over bread slices immediately.

PASTA WITH VODKA

The last time I was in Rome this dish was very popular in restaurants. They all had their own versions, and I especially liked this one.

1 pound penne or other tubular pasta	1 16-ounce can Italian plum tomatoes, drained, seeded, pureed
5 tablespoons unsalted butter, melted	3/4 cup heavy cream
2/3 cup Polish or Russian vodka	1/2 teaspoon salt
1/4 teaspoon (or more) hot red pepper flakes	3/4 cup freshly grated Parmesan cheese

Cook penne in boiling salted water for 8 to 10 minutes or until *al dente*. Blend butter, vodka and pepper flakes in skillet. Simmer for 2 minutes. Add tomatoes and cream. Simmer for 5 minutes. Add salt, penne and cheese; mix well. Pour into heated serving bowl. Serve immediately.

PAGLIA E FIENO

This is one of my favorite pasta dishes. We call it *Pagia e Fieno* (Straw and Hay) because of the colors of the green and white fettuccine.

1 cup heavy cream	1/4 teaspoon salt
2 cups cooked peas	1/2 teaspoon pepper
1 cup chopped prosciutto or smoked ham	6 ounces fettuccine
1/2 cup grated Parmesan cheese	6 ounces green fettuccine

Heat cream in saucepan. Do not boil. Stir in peas, prosciutto, cheese, salt and pepper. Cook for 5 minutes or until heated through, stirring occasionally. Cook fettuccine *al dente;* place on heated serving platter. Pour sauce over fettucine; toss gently. Garnish with additional Parmesan cheese. Serve immediately. Yield: 4 servings.

LINGUINE WITH PORCINE CREAM SAUCE

This *Porcini* sauce calls for Cognac instead of wine.

1 1/2 cups dehydrated *porcini* mushrooms	Salt and freshly ground pepper to taste
3 cups heavy cream	1 pound homemade linguine
1/2 cup Cognac	
1/2 cup chopped fresh parsley	1 cup grated Parmesan cheese

Soak mushrooms in hot water to cover for 1 hour. Drain. Cut into slivers. Cook cream in saucepan for about 10 minutes or until reduced to 1 1/2 cups. Stir in Cognac. Simmer for 5 minutes. Add mushrooms and seasonings. Simmer for about 10 minutes or until thick. Cook linguine in boiling salted water until tender but firm. Drain. Combine with *porcini* cream sauce in serving bowl; toss to mix. Add parsley and cheese; toss to mix. Serve immediately.
Yield: 4-6 servings.

PORCINE-TOMATO SAUCE

Another version of *porcini* sauce — this one with tomatoes.

2 ounces *porcini* (dried Italian mushrooms)	4 large tomatoes, peeled, cored, seeded, finely chopped
1 medium onion, finely chopped	1 tablespoon tomato paste
1/4 cup olive oil	Salt and freshly ground pepper to taste
2 medium cloves of garlic, finely chopped	

Soak mushrooms in lukewarm water to cover for 30 minutes. Drain and squeeze dry, reserving liquid. Strain liquid through several layers of cheesecloth. Discard mushroom stems; chop caps. Saute onion in olive oil in covered saucepan for 10 minutes or until pale yellow. Add garlic, tomatoes and mushrooms; mix well. Blend tomato paste with a small amount of mushroom liquid. Stir into mushroom mixture with remaining liquid. Simmer for about 25 minutes or until of sauce consistency, stirring constantly. Season with salt and pepper.

PEPPERONI PASTA

Wine: *Chianti Classico.*

This sauce has all the great flavors of pizza.

16 ounces fettuccine, green noodles or spaghetti	8 ounces pepperoni, thinly sliced
1 large onion, sliced	2 medium green peppers, sliced
2 large cloves of garlic, minced	1/4 cup olive oil

1 15-ounce can whole peeled tomatoes	1/2 teaspoon salt Freshly grated Parmesan cheese
1 teaspoon leaf oregano, crumbled	

Cook pasta *al dente* in boiling water in saucepan. Saute onion, garlic, pepperoni and green peppers in olive oil in skillet for 5 minutes, stirring frequently. Add tomatoes, oregano and salt. Cook, covered, for 5 minutes, stirring several times. Cook, uncovered, for several minutes to thicken slightly. Drain pasta. Serve with hot sauce. Sprinkle with Parmesan cheese.

MY FAVORITE LASAGNE

Wine: Red wine, such as Barbaresco, Chianti, Merlot or Cabernet Sauvignon.

This *lasagne* is worth the extra time it takes. It is a complete meal and a *great* one. Use the beef rump later for sandwiches, stew or hash.

2 cloves of garlic, peeled	1/4 pound mushrooms, sliced
1 Bermuda onion, chopped	1 cup red wine
1/4 cup butter	3 2-pound cans peeled tomatoes, strained
6 tablespoons olive oil	
1 1/2-pound piece of beef rump	Salt and pepper to taste

Brown garlic and onion in mixture of butter and olive oil in skillet. Add beef. Brown for 5 minutes. Add mushrooms. Cook for 5 minutes. Add wine. Cook until wine evaporates. Remove garlic. Add tomatoes, salt and pepper. Simmer for 2 hours or until sauce is rich, dark red and thick. Remove beef.

1 cup dry whole wheat bread cubes	1 teaspoon minced parsley
Milk	1 teaspoon grated Parmesan cheese
1/2 pound ground chuck	1 egg, beaten
1 clove of garlic, pressed	Salt and pepper to taste
	Butter

Soak bread cubes in milk to cover in bowl for several minutes; squeeze dry. Add ground chuck, garlic, parsley, cheese, egg and seasonings; mix well. Shape into almond-sized meatballs. Brown in a small amount of butter in skillet; drain.

1 pound mild Italian sausage	1 tablespoon olive oil
16 ounces *lasagne* noodles	1 cup grated Parmesan cheese
16 ounces mozzarella cheese, thinly sliced	1 1/2 pounds fresh ricotta cheese

Saute sausage in skillet for 15 minutes or until evenly browned. Chop finely. Cook *lasagne* with olive oil in boiling salted water in saucepan for 15 minutes or until just tender. Drain. Add a small amount of cold water to prevent sticking. Drain each noodle before using. Spoon a small amount of sauce into square lasagne pan. Layer noodles, Parmesan cheese, sauce, mozzarella cheese, sausage and meatballs in pan. Spoon mixture of ricotta cheese and a small amount of sauce over top. Repeat layers with remaining ingredients, ending with sauce and Parmesan cheese. Bake in preheated 350-degree oven for 20 minutes. Serve with remaining sauce and additional Parmesan cheese. Yield: 6 servings.

ROAST PORK TUSCANY-STYLE

Wine: Chianti Classico.

Tuscany is Chianti country. It is also the home of my favorite Italian red wine, Biondi-Santi Brunello di Montalcino. With Florence as its crown, Tuscany has an ancient heritage of culture, fine art, food and wine. Sometimes the finest things are the simplest — as in this Tuscan Roast Pork.

15 medium cloves of garlic, peeled	1 1/2 tablespoons freshly ground pepper
1/4 cup fresh or 3 tablespoons dried rosemary	2 tablespoons olive oil
2 tablespoons salt	1 5-pound pork loin, bone in

Combine garlic, rosemary, salt and pepper in food processor or blender container. Process until minced. Add oil gradually, processing constantly to make thick paste. Place pork loin bone side down on rack in roasting pan. Rub with garlic mixture. Let stand at room temperature for 2 to 3 hours. Bake at 325 degrees for 1 1/2 hours or to 150 degrees on meat thermometer. Increase temperature to 400 degrees. Bake for 10 to 15 minutes longer or until light brown. Place on carving board. Let rest, loosely covered with foil, for 20 to 30 minutes before carving. Yield: 6-8 servings.

VEAL WITH PROSCIUTTO AND PEPPERS
Wine: Light Italian red, such as Bardolino.

If you are wondering why there are a lot of veal recipes in this book, it is because I love it. This goes back to my childhood in Italy. We didn't have meat often, but when we did it was veal, not beef; because there isn't enough cattle grazing land in Italy to allow the steers to grown to full size. This is a peasant veal dish similar to one my Mama used to make.

1 pound veal scallops, pounded	1/4 cup dry vermouth
3 tablespoons olive oil	1 tablespoon balsamic or red wine vinegar
1 small red pepper, julienned	2 tablespoons *pignoli* (pine nuts)
1/4 cup chopped prosciutto	2 tablespoons butter
2 tablespoons chopped fresh basil	Salt and pepper to taste
1 clove of garlic, minced	

Saute veal quickly in 2 tablespoons oil in skillet. Place on serving platter; keep warm. Saute red pepper, prosciutto, basil and garlic in pan drippings and remaining 1 tablespoon olive oil for 1 minute. Add 1/4 cup water, stirring to deglaze skillet. Add vermouth and vinegar. Cook until reduced by one-half. Add *pignoli*. Stir in butter a small amount at a time. Season with salt and pepper. Spoon over veal. Yield: 4 servings.

SCALOPPINE IN GRAPPA SAUCE
Wine: Chianti Riserva.

Grappa is the Italian grape Brandy affectionately known as "Italian Fire Water." It is made from leftover skins and stems of grapes after the pressing process for table wines. It comes out between 100 and 130 proof. I like a shot of it after a heavy dinner. It settles my stomach and makes it easier to get to sleep. When I saw this recipe with Grappa, I had to try it, and it is delicious. You can substitute other Brandy, but it will not taste exactly the same.

4 ounces cooked unsmoked ham, finely chopped	4 anchovy fillets, coarsely chopped
5 tablespoons unsalted butter	1 pound thinly sliced veal scallops, pounded
1 1/2 tablespoons capers	1/2 cup flour
	2 tablespoons oil
Salt and freshly ground pepper	3 tablespoons Grappa
	1/4 cup heavy cream

Cook ham in 2 tablespoons butter in saucepan for several seconds until heated through. Rinse, drain and coarsely chop capers. Add to saucepan with anchovies. Cook for several seconds longer, mashing anchovies with wooden spoon to make paste; remove from heat. Coat veal with flour; shake off excess. Heat 3 tablespoons butter with oil in large skillet over medium-high heat until foam subsides. Add veal several pieces at a time. Do not crowd. Cook for 1 minute on each side or until brown, turning once. Place on heated platter; season with salt and pepper. Keep warm. Turn off heat under skillet. Add Grappa, stirring to deglaze skillet. Pour into saucepan with ham; place over medium-high heat. Stir in cream. Cook until thickened, stirring constantly. Pour over veal. Yield: 4 servings.

OSSO BUCCO ALLA MILANESE
Wine: I like Italian red wine with this, even though white wine is used in the recipe.

This dish is a specialty in Milan, and it is one of my favorites.

2 veal shinbones, cut into 3-inch pieces	1 large ripe tomato, peeled, seeded, chopped
Flour	1/2 teaspoon crumbled sage
1/4 cup butter	1/2 teaspoon rosemary
1 teaspoon salt	2 cups white wine
1/2 teaspoon pepper	Grated rind of 1 lemon
1/2 cup finely chopped celery	2 tablespoons chopped parsley
1 medium onion, finely chopped	1 anchovy, mashed
1/2 cup finely chopped carrots	1 clove of garlic, minced
1/2 cup minced mushrooms	

Coat shinbones with flour. Brown on all sides in butter in skillet. Turn shinbones on sides to retain marrow. Add salt, pepper, celery, onion, carrots, mushrooms, tomato, sage and rosemary. Simmer, covered, for 10 minutes. Add wine. Simmer, covered, for 2 hours. Stir in mixture of remaining ingredients just before serving. Serve with *Risotto Alla* Milanese (page 126). Yield: 6 servings.

SCAMPI TRIESTE

Wine: Full-bodied white, such as French Chablis, California Chardonnay or Italian Greco di Tufo which is a fine wine from the Campania zone of Southern Italy.

This is how we make scampi in my home town, Trieste.

3 cloves of garlic, finely minced	1/2 cup chopped scallions
2 tablespoons olive oil	1/4 cup minced fresh parsley
2 tablespoons butter	6 tablespoons bread crumbs
1 1/2 pounds shelled shrimp, deveined	1 tablespoon capers
1 cup dry white wine	1/2 teaspoon salt
1/4 cup lemon juice	1/4 teaspoon pepper

Saute garlic in mixture of olive oil and butter in skillet. Do not brown. Add shrimp. Cook for 3 to 6 minutes or until just firm. Place shrimp on heated platter; keep warm. Add wine, stirring to deglaze skillet. Cook until reduced to about 1/3 cup. Add lemon juice. Cook until liquid is almost evaporated. Add scallions, parsley and shrimp. Sprinkle bread crumbs, capers and seasonings over shrimp; toss to mix well. Broil for 1 minute. Serve immediately.

COLLAVINI SHRIMP CREPES

3/4 cup plus 2 tablespoons milk	1 tablespoon melted butter
3/4 cup flour	1 teaspoon salt
2 eggs	

Combine all ingredients in bowl; beat until smooth. Let stand for 30 minutes. Heat 7-inch skillet over medium-high heat until water drop sizzles when dropped on pan. Brush lightly with oil. Pour scant 1/4 cup batter into pan, tilting to coat bottom. Cook for 1 to 2 minutes or until lightly browned. Turn crepe over. Cook for 1 minute. Stack crepes between waxed paper.

1 cup plus 2 tablespoons Collavini Pinot Gregio	3 tablespoons flour
	2/3 cup plus 1 tablespoon heavy cream
1 bay leaf	1 cup grated Swiss cheese
1/8 teaspoon thyme	
1 1/2 pounds small shrimp, peeled	1 tablespoon chopped parsley
2 cups sliced mushrooms	1/4 teaspoon salt
3 tablespoons butter, melted	1/8 teaspoon pepper

Bring 1 cup wine, 1/2 cup water, bay leaf and thyme to a boil in saucepan. Add shrimp and mushrooms. Simmer for 5 minutes or until shrimp are pink and cooked through. Drain shrimp and mushrooms, reserving 1 cup liquid. Blend butter and flour in saucepan. Stir in reserved liquid and 2/3 cup cream gradually. Bring to a boil, stirring constantly. Add remaining ingredients; stir until cheese melts. Stir in shrimp and mushrooms. Spoon 1/3 cup mixture down center of each crepe; roll to enclose filling. Place on ovenproof serving platter. Add remaining 2 tablespoons wine and 1 tablespoon cream to remaining shrimp mixture. Spoon over crepes. Bake at 350 degrees for 10 minutes. Yield: 4 servings.

Photograph for this recipe on page 69.

FETTUCCINE GORGONZOLA

4 large shallots, chopped	1/4 teaspoon salt
	1/8 teaspoon pepper
1/4 cup butter	2 tablespoons light cream
3/4 cup crumbled Italian Gorgonzola cheese	1 8-ounce package fettuccine, cooked
1/2 cup cherry tomato wedges	2 tablespoons chopped parsley
1/2 cup slivered prosciutto	

Saute shallots in butter in skillet until tender. Add cheese, tomatoes, prosciutto and seasonings; toss lightly. Stir in cream. Combine with hot fettuccine in hot serving dish; toss lightly. Garnish with parsley. Serve immediately. Yield: 6-8 servings.

Photograph for this recipe on page 104.

GORGONZOLA GARLIC SPREAD

1/2 cup butter, softened	1/2 cup Italian Gorgonzola cheese, softened
2 tablespoons chopped Italian parsley	1 loaf Italian bread
1 medium clove of garlic, minced	

Combine butter, parsley and garlic in small bowl; mix well. Add cheese. Mix until smooth. Split bread, cutting to but not through long edge. Spread with cheese mixture. Place on foil-lined baking sheet. Bake at 375 degrees for 15 minutes or until crisp and hot.

Photograph for this recipe on page 104.

MARIO'S POLENTA WITH PORCINE WINE SAUCE

Wine: Angoris Pinot Bianco.

This is my favorite version of polenta.

Porcine mushrooms (in Italian *fungo porcino*, or pig mushrooms, so named because pigs love them so much they root them from the ground) are only grown in Italy and are among the world's most coveted mushrooms for gourmet cooking. They are dehydrated when purchased in specialty food markets and must be revived before used in cooking. You simply cover them in tap water for about 10 minutes until they wake up, then drain them and pat them dry.

If you cannot find porcine mushrooms, substitute dried French mushrooms.

2 cups polenta	2 teaspoons salt

Stir polenta gradually into 6 1/2 cups boiling salted water in saucepan. Simmer for 20 minutes or until very thick, stirring frequently. Pour onto large buttered serving platter; keep warm.

1/4 medium onion, chopped	1 cup dry white wine
1 clove of garlic, finely chopped	2 cups dried porcine mushrooms, rehydrated
2 tablespoons virgin olive oil	1/2 cup heavy cream
1/4 cup butter	Salt and pepper to taste

Saute onion and garlic in mixture of olive oil and butter in skillet until golden. Add wine and mushrooms. Simmer until wine evaporates. Add cream. Cook until reduced by 1/2, stirring constantly. Season with salt and pepper. Serve over polenta.

Note: I take my polenta by the forkful and dip it into the sauce, peasant-style. Ah, magnifico!

POLENTA MARIA

In Northern Italy, we eat polenta the way you eat potatoes in this country — often and in many different versions. Polenta is an Italian dish that dates back to the days of the Roman Empire. Then it was called *puls* or *pulmentum*, and it was the field ration of soldiers.

Each man was issued about 2 pounds of grain a day. He roasted it over his campfire, crushed and stored it in his haversack until they stopped marching for the day. Then he would boil it and eat it, either soft (like thick grits) or hardened into a kind of cake. To this day polenta is eaten both ways in Italy.

I love it, and nothing soothes me more than a big dish of it on a cold winter day. This recipe is my grandmother Maria's version. Polenta is available in food specialty stores. You can substitute yellow cornmeal, but it is not the same.

1 1/4 teaspoons salt	1 cup sliced mushroom caps
1 cup polenta	6 tablespoons cream
2 tablespoons bread crumbs	3 tablespoons grated Parmesan cheese
3 tablespoons (about) butter	

Bring 1 quart water to a boil in top of double boiler over direct heat. Add salt. Stir in polenta very gradually. Cook until thick, stirring constantly. Place over hot water. Cook, covered, for 2 hours. Pour into loaf dish. Chill overnight. Invert polenta on work surface. Slice into 3 horizontal layers. Sprinkle buttered loaf pan with bread crumbs. Layer 1 slice polenta, 1 tablespoon butter pieces, 1/2 cup mushrooms, 3 tablespoons cream and 1 tablespoon cheese over top. Repeat layers. Top with remaining polenta, dots of remaining butter and remaining 1 tablespoon cheese. Bake, covered, at 350 degrees for 1 1/2 hours.

Note: Polenta is delicious chilled in 10 x 15-inch pan, cut into 2-inch strips or squares and deep-fried.

RISOTTO ALLA MILANESE

1 small onion, minced	4 cups chicken stock
1/2 cup butter	2 tablespoons freshly grated Parmesan cheese
1 1/2 cups rice	
1 teaspoon saffron	

Saute onion in 1/4 cup butter in skillet until light brown. Add rice; mix well. Soften saffron in 2 tablespoons stock. Add remaining stock to rice. Bring to a boil. Cook, covered, over low heat for 25 minutes, stirring frequently. Add remaining 1/4 cup butter and saffron. Cook, uncovered, over low heat for 5 minutes longer. Spoon into serving dish. Sprinkle with cheese.

RISOTTO AL TARTUFO

Wine: A dry Italian white or a light red.

In northern Italy we eat as much rice *(risotto)* as we do pasta. This marvelous recipe comes from the Al Tartufo Restaurant in Bologna. There they serve it in a hollowed-out wheel of Parmigiano-Reggiano cheese with shavings of white truffles on top. If you cannot find Reggiano, any good freshly grated Parmigiano will do.

1 cup dry white wine
1 cup chicken broth
1/2 cup chopped onion
1 clove of garlic, minced
1/4 cup butter
1 tablespoon oil
1 1/4 cups arborio rice
2/3 cup grated Parmigiano-Reggiano cheese
Salt and pepper to taste

Bring wine, broth and 2 1/2 cups water to a boil in saucepan. Reduce heat to maintain at simmering point. Saute onion and garlic in mixture of butter and oil in saucepan until tender. Add rice, stirring to coat. Add 1/2 cup simmering liquid. Cook until moisture evaporates, stirring constantly. Add remaining liquid 1/2 cup at a time, cooking until dry and stirring frequently after each addition. Cooking time will be about 30 minutes. Add cheese and seasonings; mix well. Yield: 6 servings.

GALLIANO PIE

Galliano is a favorite Italian liqueur. Combined with pineapple it makes a delicious fruity pie.

2 cups canned crushed pineapple, drained
1/4 cup Galliano
3 tablespoons sugar
1 tablespoon cornstarch
1 tablespoon butter
1 teaspoon lemon juice
2 egg yolks, beaten
1 baked 9-inch pie shell

Combine pineapple, Galliano, sugar, cornstarch, butter and lemon juice in saucepan. Cook until thickened, stirring constantly. Stir a small amount of hot mixture into egg yolks; stir egg yolks into hot mixture. Cook over low heat for 1 minute, stirring constantly. Cool slightly. Pour into pie shell.

3 egg whites
1/8 teaspoon cream of tartar
1/8 teaspoon salt
6 tablespoons superfine sugar

Beat egg whites in mixer bowl until foamy. Add cream of tartar and salt. Add sugar 1 tablespoon at a time, beating until stiff glossy peaks form. Spread over warm filling, sealing to edge and swirling into peaks. Bake at 350 degrees for 15 minutes or until meringue is brown on tips.

MERINGUE TORTA ALLA ROMA

This one is worth the trouble. Must be made a day ahead.

4 egg whites, at room temperature
1/2 teaspoon cream of tartar
1 cup sugar
1 teaspoon vanilla extract

Beat egg whites with cream of tartar in mixer bowl until frothy. Add sugar 1 tablespoon at a time, beating for 1 minute after each addition. Beat until stiff peaks form. Add vanilla. Beat for 2 minutes or until very stiff. Butter and flour 2 baking sheets; trace 8-inch circle on each. Spoon meringue evenly onto circles. Make decorative swirls and puffs on 1 circle with spatula. Bake at 250 degrees for 1 1/2 hours. Color should be pure white to pale amber. Turn off oven. Let stand in closed oven for 3 to 4 hours. Remove from oven; flex baking sheets to release meringues. Let stand on sheets until room temperature.

1 teaspoon instant coffee powder
1/4 cup coffee-flavored liqueur
2 cups whipping cream, whipped
1 10-ounce milk chocolate candy bar, coarsely chopped

Blend coffee powder and liqueur in small bowl. Fold gently into whipped cream. Fold in chopped chocolate gently. Place plain meringue layer on serving platter. Spread evenly with whipped cream. Top with decorative meringue. Chill for 8 hours to overnight. Yield: 8-10 servings.

SORBETTA DI MELONE

This can be used as a light refreshing dessert or as an intermezzo to freshen the palate between courses of a heavy meal.

1 envelope unflavored gelatin
1 medium melon, peeled, chopped
1/4 teaspoon salt
Juice of 1 lemon or lime
1/2 cup sugar
2 egg whites, stiffly beaten

Soften gelatin in 1/2 cup cold water in saucepan. Heat until dissolved, stirring constantly; cool. Combine melon, salt, juice and sugar in food processor or blender container. Process until smooth. Add gelatin; process until mixed. Pour into bowl. Fold in egg whites gently. Pour into freezer tray. Freeze for 2 hours, stirring 3 or more times. Spoon into stemmed glasses. Garnish with fresh mint sprigs.

SPECIAL GERMAN RECIPES

A special note on German food:

Traditionally the heaviness of German food and the sweetness of the wine has made it difficult to come up with complementary pairings. Like any other wine and food pairings, you will need to experiment to find out what best suits your taste. The following are some guidelines.

Every time the sauces are made not with flour but with cream, *creme fraiche* or similar products, a *halbtroken* (medium dry) Riesling will do well. *Halbtrocken* means wine with a residual sugar between 0.4 and 1.6, depending on the acidity. (The higher the acidity, the higher the allowance for the residual sugar.) Very typical German food like *Geselchtes* (i.e. smoked pork meat), *Schlachtplatte* (meat plates) or *Saumagen* (regional potato-pie specialty) go very well with a *trocken* Muller-Thurgau type wine (*trocken*-dry means wine with a residual sugar below 0.4 or 0.9, again depending on the acidity.)

The *halbtrocken* and *trocken* types mentioned should be either QbA *(Qualitatsweine besonderer Anbaugebiete)* or Kabinett as a maximum. Dry Spatlese or even dry Auslese are too "egocentric" in that they suppress the food's proper, natural flavor too much in most cases.

If you use German red wine, it is advisable to handle it as if it were Rose from a Mediterranean wine-producing area. It will be a remarkably successful combination. Pheasant, pigeon, partridge or quail with a Spatburgunder (Pinot Noir) Kabinett from Baden, Wurttemberg, Rheingau or Rheinpfalz match beautifully.

- Heavy food as a rule seems fresher and lighter being accompanied by a fruity German wine.
- Nouvelle Cuisine and its fresh produce retain their proper natural flavor in harmony with the fruity acidity of German Wine.
- If the food is not overly seasoned, *trocken* and *halbtrocken* Rieslings or *trocken* Weissburgunder (Pinot Blanc) are very suitable.
- *trocken* Muller-Thurgau blends very well with sausages, warm or cold, and selections of cold cuts German-style.
- Sweeter Riesling wines combine nicely with desserts made from apple, mango, apricot and peaches.

GERMAN POTATO SALAD

This is a warm potato salad that goes well with pork.

4 medium potatoes, cooked, peeled	1/4 cup chopped celery
8 slices bacon, crisp-fried, crumbled	1 tablespoon chopped pimento
1 small green pepper, chopped	1/4 cup bacon drippings
1 small onion, chopped	1/4 cup sugar
	2 tablespoons flour
	1/3 cup vinegar

Cut potatoes into 1/2-inch cubes. Place in serving bowl. Add bacon and vegetables. Combine bacon drippings, sugar, flour, vinegar and 1/3 cup water in saucepan. Cook until thickened, stirring constantly. Pour over potatoes; toss gently. Yield: 6 servings.

SAUERBRATEN MIT KARTOFFEL KLOSSE
(Pot Roast with Potato Dumplings)

Wine: The Germans drink beer with this dish, and it's probably the best choice because of the vinegar in the marinade. However, if you want wine, try Schloss-Johannisberg, QbA.

This meat must marinate for four days before cooking, so plan ahead.

1 3-pound round steak, 2 1/2 to 3-inches thick	1 stalk celery, chopped
1 tablespoon salt	4 cloves
1/2 teaspoon pepper	4 peppercorns
2 onions, sliced	1/2 cup red wine vinegar
1 carrot, sliced	2 bay leaves

Wipe round steak with damp cloth. Sprinkle with salt and pepper. Place in nonmetallic bowl or dish. Add remaining ingredients and 3 1/2 cups water or enough to cover steak. Marinate, covered, in refrigerator for 4 days. Drain, reserving marinade. Pat steak dry with paper towels; strain marinade.

2 tablespoons oil	5 gingersnaps,
4 tablespoons butter	crushed
3 tablespoons flour	Potato Dumplings
1 tablespoon sugar	

Brown steak in mixture of oil and 1 tablespoon butter in heavy saucepan. Add reserved marinade. Bring to a boil. Simmer, covered, for 3 hours. Blend remaining 3 tablespoons butter, flour and sugar in skillet. Cook until caramel-colored, stirring constantly. Stir into pan juices. Simmer, covered, for 1 hour longer. Place on heated serving plate. Add gingersnaps to pan juices. Cook until thickened, stirring constantly. Strain into sauce boat. Slice steak diagonally. Arrange Potato Dumplings around steak. Spoon gravy over steak and dumplings.

Kartoffel Klosse
(Potato Dumplings)

9 medium potatoes, cooked, mashed	1 teaspoon salt
	1/4 teaspoon nutmeg
3 egg yolks, beaten	2 slices white
3 tablespoons cornstarch	bread, cubed
	2 tablespoons hot
3 tablespoons farina	butter
1/2 teaspoon pepper	Flour

Combine potatoes, egg yolks, cornstarch, farina and seasonings in bowl; mix well. Saute bread in butter in skillet until golden brown; drain on paper towel. Shape potato mixture into golf ball-shaped dumplings around croutons. Roll lightly in flour. Place in 1 1/2 quarts boiling salted water in large skillet; reduce heat. Cook, covered, for 15 to 20 minutes or until cooked through. Water should not boil. Remove with slotted spoon.

WIENER SCHNITZEL
(Vienna-Style Veal Cutlets)

Wine: Piesporter-Goldpropschen or Piesporter-Michelsberg, no sweeter than QbA.

This is probably the most popular veal dish in Germany.

4 veal cutlets	Fine dry bread
Lemon juice	crumbs
to taste	Butter
Salt to taste	4 slices lemon
Flour	4 anchovy fillets
1 egg, beaten	(optional)

Pound cutlets lightly; trim and slash edges. Sprinkle with lemon juice and salt. Coat with flour, mixture of egg and 3 tablespoons water then bread crumbs in order listed. Brown in butter in skillet. Place on heated serving platter. Garnish with lemon slices and anchovies. Serve with potatoes, lettuce slices and tomato wedges.

Note: This method of cooking veal did not originate in Austria but was introduced from Italy about 100 years ago. The Milanese took the idea from the Spanish when the Duchy of Milan formed part of the Spanish-Hapsburg Empire. Despite this, every visitor to Vienna seems to make a special point of ordering a crisp and juicy Wiener Schnitzel, one of the city's specialties.

ROTKOHL MIT APFELN
(Red Cabbage with Apples)

This version of red cabbage is very popular in Frankfurt.

1 2 to 2 1/2-pound head red cabbage	2 tablespoons bacon drippings
	1 whole onion, peeled
2/3 cup red wine vinegar	2 whole cloves
	1 small bay leaf
2 tablespoons sugar	3 tablespoons dry red wine
2 teaspoons salt	
2 medium cooking apples, peeled, cut into wedges	3 tablespoons red currant jelly (optional)
1/2 cup finely chopped onion	

Remove outer leaves from cabbage; cut into quarters. Shred into 1/8-inch strips. Combine with vinegar, sugar and salt in bowl; toss to coat. Saute apples and chopped onion in bacon drippings in large saucepan for 5 minutes, stirring frequently. Stud whole onion with cloves. Add to sauteed mixture with cabbage and bay leaf; mix well. Add 1 cup boiling water. Bring to a boil, stirring occasionally. Simmer, covered, for 1 1/2 to 2 hours or until cabbage is tender, adding water 1 tablespoon at a time if necessary. Cooking liquid should be almost evaporated at end of cooking time. Remove onion and bay leaf. Stir in wine and jelly. Adjust seasoning. Spoon into heated serving bowl. Yield: 4-6 servings.

FRANKFURT GREEN SAUCE

This sauce is especially good served cold with beef, fish or poultry. Goes great with asparagus too.

5 hard-boiled eggs, separated	1/2 teaspoon salt
1/2 cup oil	1/8 teaspoon each garlic salt and white pepper
1/2 cup yogurt	
4 1/2 teaspoons each chopped fresh parsley, chervil, chives, watercress, dill, tarragon, lovage, borage and sorrel	Pinch of ground nutmeg
	2 1/2 teaspoons prepared mild mustard
	1/2 cup sour cream

Mash egg yolks in small bowl. Blend in oil until smooth. Chop egg whites finely. Combine egg whites, yogurt, herbs, seasonings, mustard and sour cream in bowl; mix well. Stir in egg yolk mixture. Spoon into serving bowl. Yield: 6 servings.

SCHWARZWALDER KIRSCHTORTE
(Black Forest Cherry Cake)

1 tablespoon butter, softened	1 teaspoon vanilla extract
6 tablespoons flour	1 cup sugar
10 tablespoons unsalted butter	1/2 cup sifted flour
6 eggs, at room temperature	1/2 cup cocoa

Grease three 7-inch round cake pans with softened butter. Coat each with 2 tablespoons flour; shake out excess flour. Melt unsalted butter in saucepan over low heat. Let stand for 1 minute. Skim foam and discard milk solids to clarify. Beat eggs, vanilla and sugar in mixer bowl at high speed for 10 minutes or until almost tripled in volume. Sift in flour and cocoa gradually, folding in gently after each addition. Add clarified butter 2 tablespoons at a time, blending after each addition. Do not overmix. Pour into prepared pans. Bake in center of preheated 350-degree oven for 10 to 15 minutes or until layers test done. Cool in pans for 5 minutes. Loosen layers and turn onto cake racks to cool completely.

3/4 cup sugar	1/3 cup Kirsch

Combine sugar and 1 cup cold water in saucepan. Boil for 5 minutes. Cool to lukewarm. Stir in Kirsch. Punch cake layers with long fork. Sprinkle evenly with syrup. Let stand for 5 minutes or longer.

3 cups whipping cream, chilled	Fresh sweet or maraschino cherries with stems
1/2 cup confectioners' sugar	
1/4 cup Kirsch	Chocolate curls, frozen
1 cup drained and rinsed canned sour red cherries	

Whip cream in bowl until slightly thickened. Sift in confectioners' sugar, beating constantly until stiff peaks form. Add Kirsch gradually, beating just until blended. Place 1 cake layer on cake plate. Spread with 1/2 inch whipped cream. Pat poached cherries dry with paper towel. Spoon into center of layer, leaving 1/2-inch border. Top with second layer; spread with 1/2 inch whipped cream. Place remaining layer on top. Frost top and side with remaining whipped cream. Decorate with stemmed cherries. Press chocolate curls around side and sprinkle on top of cake. Yield: 8-10 servings.

KARTOFFELPUFFER MIT APFELMUS
(Potato Pancakes with Applesauce)

Potato pancakes are good for brunch.

6 medium baking potatoes	1/2 cup bacon drippings
2 eggs, beaten	Applesauce or imported lingonberry preserves
1/4 cup finely grated onion	
1/3 cup flour	
1 teaspoon salt	

Peel potatoes; place in cold water. Combine eggs and onion. Stir in flour and salt. Grate potatoes 1 at a time into colander. Squeeze out excess moisture and stir each immediately into egg mixture. Heat bacon drippings in 8-inch skillet. Add 1/3 cup potato mixture; flatten into 5-inch circle with spatula. Cook over medium heat for 2 minutes on each side, or until golden. Place on heated ovenproof serving plate in 250-degree oven to keep warm. Repeat with remaining potato mixture, adding additional bacon drippings to maintain 1/4-inch depth if necessary. Serve with applesauce or preserves. Yield: 8 servings.

SPECIAL SPANISH RECIPES

SOPA DE AJO (Garlic Soup)

Wine: A big Spanish red such as Torres Sangre de Toro. This soup will overpower any white wine and most reds.

The Spanish love garlic as much as the Italians do. They even invented a soup of it! The trick of this soup is to use *fresh, fresh* garlic and not to let it burn when sauteing it.

8 cloves of garlic, finely chopped	4 cups beef stock
1/4 cup olive oil	1 teaspoon salt
	Eggs

Saute garlic in olive oil in saucepan until lightly browned. Add beef stock and salt. Bring to a full boil. Break an egg into each heated soup plate. Strain hot soup over egg. Serve immediately. Hot soup will cook the egg.

PIERNA DE CORDERO A LA ALMENDRA (Leg of Lamb in Almond Sauce)

Wine: A hearty wine such as Sangre de Toro or Gran Sangre de Toro.

This is an excellent recipe from Marimar Torres.

1 4 to 5-pound leg of lamb, sliced 3/4 inch thick	2 cups veal stock
1/2 cup (about) flour	4 ounces thinly sliced almonds, toasted
Olive oil	4 grams saffron threads or 1/2 teaspoon powdered saffron
1 small head of garlic, peeled, thinly sliced	3 to 4 tablespoons chopped parsley
2 medium onions, chopped	1 tablespoon fresh thyme or 1/2 teaspoon dried thyme
3 ripe tomatoes, peeled, seeded, chopped	Salt and pepper to taste
1/2 cup Torres Gran Reserva Brandy	
1 cup Vina Sol dry white wine	

Coat lamb slices with flour; shake off excess. Saute lightly in hot olive oil in skillet over medium-high heat to seal in juices. Set lamb aside. Saute garlic and onions in a small amount of olive oil in stove-to-table skillet until translucent. Add tomatoes. Cook for 10 minutes or to sauce consistency. Add Brandy, wine and veal stock. Bring to a boil. Cook for 5 minutes. Chop half the almonds. Add to skillet with mixture of saffron, parsley, thyme, salt and pepper; mix well. Add lamb slices; spoon sauce over top to cover. Simmer, covered, over very low heat for 1 hour or until lamb is tender. Sprinkle with remaining almonds. Serve immediately. Yield: 6-8 servings.

Note: New potatoes, baby carrots and pearl onions may be parboiled and added to skillet just before serving or sauteed lightly in butter with parsley and served as a side dish.

POLLO EN PEPITORIA

Wine: A good light red such as Torres Vina Santa Digna (Pinot Noir) or Gran Coronas.

This is a classic Spanish chicken dish.

1 3 to 4-pound chicken, cut up	1 veal or beef bone
Salt and pepper to taste	1 stalk celery, sliced
Olive oil for frying	1 bay leaf
24 small boiling onions, peeled	1 can chicken broth
2 carrots, peeled, sliced	1/2 cup dry Sherry
	2 egg yolks
	A small amount of fresh lemon juice

Season chicken with salt and pepper. Fry in olive oil in skillet until golden. Place in stockpot. Add onions, carrots, bone, celery and bay leaf. Add broth and enough water to cover. Simmer, covered, for 1 1/2 hours or until chicken is tender. Remove chicken and vegetables to serving dish; keep warm. Cook broth until reduced. Add Sherry; adjust seasonings. Skim and remove from heat. Beat egg yolks and lemon juice with wooden fork. Add to broth, beating constantly. Pour over chicken and vegetables. Serve immediately. Yield: 4 servings.

CASTILIAN ROAST PORK

Wine: The same wine used in cooking such as Torres Gran Vina Sol, green label.

This is one of those simple recipes that tastes so good you would think it took hours of preparation.

1 12 to 14-pound fresh ham	2 tablespoons chopped parsley
1/4 cup butter or shortening	3 tablespoons minced onion
3 bay leaves, crumbled	Juice of 1 lemon
	2/3 cup white wine
3 cloves of garlic, minced	2 tablespoons sweet paprika
1/2 teaspoon dry thyme	2 teaspoons salt

Score ham; place in shallow roasting pan. (In Spain an oval earthenware pan is used.) Rub with butter. Sprinkle with mixture of bay leaves and next 4 ingredients. Sprinkle with lemon juice, 1/3 cup wine, paprika and salt. Roast at 350 degrees for 1 1/2 hours. Pour off drippings. Add 1/3 cup wine and 1 cup water to pan. Roast for 3 1/2 to 4 1/2 hours longer or a total of 25 minutes per pound, basting every 30 minutes with pan juices.

ESCALIBADA
(Mixed Grilled Vegetables)

Wine: A dry white such as Gran Vina Sol when served as first course. Match wine with entree when served as accompaniment, but a light red such as Coronas is always safe.

You can cook these vegetables on the grill or in the oven.

4 small thin young Japanese eggplant	2 white onions, peeled, cut into halves
2 red or green peppers	2 baking potatoes, cut into halves
2 jalapeno peppers (optional)	Olive oil
2 tomatoes, cut into halves	Salt and pepper to taste

Coat all vegetables with olive oil. Bake in 350-degree oven or on charcoal grill as follows: 1 1/4 hours for onions, 1 hour for potatoes, 30 minutes for peppers, 30 to 60 minutes for eggplant, 15 minutes for tomatoes. Cool vegetables completely. Peel and slice eggplant and peppers. Arrange all vegetables on serving platter. Sprinkle with olive oil, salt and pepper to taste. Garnish with chopped fresh parsley. Serve warmed or at room temperature as first course or accompaniment to entree. Yield: 4 servings.

CHOCOLATE CAKE RUM ROLL DE MADRID

The Spanish love this dessert — so will you!

1/4 cup confectioners' sugar, sifted	1/4 cup cocoa
	1 1/4 teaspoons rum extract
5 eggs, separated	1 tablespoon superfine sugar
1/4 cup sugar	
1/4 cup flour	1 cup whipping cream, whipped
1 teaspoon vanilla extract	

Line buttered 8 x 15-inch cake pan with buttered parchment paper. Dust with 2 tablespoons confectioners' sugar. Beat egg yolks and sugar in bowl until thick and smooth. Stir in flour, vanilla and cocoa. Fold in stiffly beaten egg whites gently. Spread in prepared pan. Bake in preheated 350-degree oven for 15 minutes. Cool in pan for 5 minutes. Turn onto cloth. Cool for 10 minutes. Peel off paper. Blend rum and superfine sugar into whipped cream. Spread over cake. Roll as for jelly roll from long side. Sprinkle with remaining 2 tablespoons confectioners' sugar. Cut into slices to serve. Yield: 8 servings.

SANGRIA PUNCH

1 bottle of dry white wine	1 orange, sliced
1 1/2 cups Cointreau	1 lemon, sliced
1/4 cup sugar	
1 10-ounce bottle of club soda, chilled	2 limes, cut into wedges

Combine wine, Cointreau and sugar in pitcher; blend well. Stir in ice cubes and club soda. Add fruit. Serve immediately.

SANGRIA

Hulled strawberries, pitted cherries, sliced pineapple, sliced orange (optional)	Juice of 2 lemons
	1 lemon, sliced
	1/4 cup sugar (or to taste)
1/2 cup Brandy	1 to 2 quarts club soda, chilled
3 bottles of full-bodied red wine	

Place fruits in large pitcher or punch bowl. Pour Brandy over fruit. Let stand, covered, for 1 to 2 hours. Add wine, lemon juice, lemon slices and sugar. Chill in refrigerator. Add enough club soda and ice cubes to dilute to desired strength just before serving.

EXTRA SPECIAL RECIPES

FRIED CANAPE OF MOZZARELLA AND ANCHOVY

Wine: A California sparkling wine.

This tasty canape, (cocktail size sandwich) is satisfying enough to take the edge off your hunger, yet light enough to enable you to enjoy the rest of your meal.

8 thin slices homemade-type white bread, crusts trimmed	8 canned anchovy fillets
	2 eggs, slightly beaten
4 ounces mozzarella cheese, thinly sliced	3/4 cup (about) olive oil

Cut bread slices in half. Place mozzarella and anchovies on half the bread. Top with remaining bread. Dip in eggs. Fry in 1/4 inch hot olive oil in skillet until golden brown on both sides. Yield: 8 servings.

ROASTED GARLIC WITH TOAST POINTS

Roasted garlic is one of my favorites, even if nobody can get near me for the rest of the day. Garlic cooked this way is very sweet, with no trace of bitterness. The cloves slip easily from their papery wrappings as a first course or with cocktails.

30 large heads fresh garlic	1 1/2 cups extra-virgin olive oil
1/4 cup (about) mixed minced fresh marjoram, basil and thyme	Salt and coarsely cracked black pepper to taste

Cut tops from unpeeled garlic heads, exposing cloves. Combine remaining ingredients in baking pan. Arrange garlic cut side down in prepared pan. Let stand for 30 minutes or longer. Turn garlic cut side up. Bake at 200 degrees for 1 1/2 hours or until garlic cloves rise from skins.

30 slices day-old bread, crusts trimmed	1 pound butter, softened
	1 bunch fresh dill leaves, minced

Cut each bread slice diagonally into 4 triangles. Mix butter and dill in bowl. Spread on one side of bread; arrange on baking sheet. Bake at 300 degrees for 45 minutes or until crisp and golden brown. Spread garlic on toast points to serve.

PESTO-STUFFED MUSHROOM CAPS

Wine: Sebastiani "Eye of the Swan" Pinot Noir Blanc if white wine is your preference or Sebastiani Zinfandel if you are a confirmed red wine drinker.

Fresh basil is very easy to grow and is also available in specialty stores and some supermarkets.

1/2 cup chopped walnuts	1/4 cup chopped well-drained cooked spinach
2 tablespoons pine nuts	1 cup freshly grated Parmesan cheese
4 ounces lean prosciutto	
3 cups fresh basil leaves	3/4 cup olive oil
6 cloves of garlic	Salt and freshly ground pepper to taste

Combine first 7 ingredients and 1/4 cup olive oil in blender container. Process until smooth. Add remaining olive oil in fine stream, blending constantly. Add salt and pepper.

24 canned snails, mussels or rolled anchovies with capers (optional)	24 1-inch mushroom caps

Place snail, mussel or anchovy in each mushroom cap; top with pesto. Place on baking sheet. Bake in preheated 500-degree oven for 5 minutes or until pesto is bubbly.

NEW POTATO APPETIZERS

I like these best with good Romanoff red salmon caviar or golden whitefish, but they are also delicious with bacon.

24 tiny new potatoes
1/2 cup sour cream
Chopped chives
Caviar or crumbled crisp-fried bacon

Cook potatoes in skins in boiling salted water in saucepan until tender. Drain; cool. Cut potatoes into halves. Scoop out small cavity with spoon or melon baller. Fill with sour cream. Top with chives and caviar. Yield: 8-10 servings.

Pasta

They say we Italians stole pasta from China, but it isn't true. When Marco Polo first went to the Orient, the Chinese *were* eating noodles, and he probably *did* bring that news back to Italy. But it is a documented fact that they were eating ravioli in Rome in 1284, nearly 20 years before Marco Polo traveled the world. And, history also tells us that *fettuccine* was being eaten by the Romans as early as 1200.

Pasta is actually one of the oldest foods known to man. It was written about in 5,000 B. C., and there was already a cookbook about it in 1485, written by Platina.

It is true that we Italians take our pasta seriously, but we have a sense of humor about it, too. If you don't believe me, see what some of the pasta names mean in English:

cappelletti — little hats
cappelli di pagliaccio — clown's hats
ditali — thimbles
elettrici rigati — grooved electric wire (obviously a later pasta shape)
farfalle — butterflies
lingue di passeri — sparrow's tongues
linguine — small tongues
mostaccioli — small moustaches
occhi di lupo — wolf's eyes
penne — pens or feathers
pulcini — little chickens
rotelle — small wheels
spaghetti — cord
stellini — little stars
stivaletti — little boots,
and one we always loved as kids,
vermicelli — *little worms!*

There are literally hundreds of kinds of pasta made in Italy, but only the shapes are different. The basic pasta dough is flour, water and salt, sometimes with eggs, sometimes without.

We usually use semolina flour in Italy. Making homemade pasta in the United States didn't become popular until they came out with the automatic pasta machines. Now, for a couple of hundred dollars, anyone can make pasta as good as Mama used to make it at home. (Well, almost as good!) The machines come with directions on how to make the pasta and are well worth the investment. If you've never tasted homemade pasta, try it and you'll see what I mean. It's the difference between night and day!

The secret to cooking pasta is NOT to overcook it. Fresh pasta will cook in much less time than dried. If you're using packaged, dried pasta from the supermarket, don't go by the package directions. The directions always tell you to cook it a minute or two longer than it should be cooked if it's going to come out *al dente* which means done through, but still firm, *never* soft and mushy. The best way to tell when it is done is to take a piece from the boiling water and test it with a fork or pinch it between your fingers. You'll know if it's cooked all the way through. Take it out of the boiling water immediately; drain and rinse it in tepid water so it will not continue to cook. When you pour hot sauce over it, it may cook a little bit more anyway.

PASTA PRIMAVERA I

Wine: A crisp dry white.

Pasta Primavera is not actually an Italian dish since it was created in New York by the owner of Le Cirque Restaurant. Originally it was intended as a springtime dish, making use of the earliest, most tender young spring vegetables. But it has become so popular throughout the United States that it is now a year-round pasta specialty on restaurant menus. There are many versions of Pasta Primavera (you can use any vegetables you have — just make sure they are *fresh)*, and this pasta is great.

16 ounces fettuccine or linguine
2 tablespoons salt
2 teaspoons minced garlic
1/4 cup butter
2 large carrots, cut into julienne strips
1 small red or green pepper, cut into julienne strips

1 cup whipping cream
1/2 cup freshly grated Parmesan cheese
1/4 cup chopped fresh dill
1/2 teaspoon salt
1/4 teaspoon freshly ground pepper

Cook pasta *al dente* with salt in boiling water; drain. Saute garlic in butter in large skillet for about 1 minute or until golden. Add carrots and pepper. Stir-fry for 2 minutes. Stir in cream, Parmesan cheese, dill, salt and pepper. Add pasta; toss gently to coat. Place on heated serving plates. Garnish with sprigs of dill. Serve with additional Parmesan cheese.
Yield: 4 servings.

PASTA PRIMAVERA II

4 shallots, minced
7 tablespoons unsalted butter
2 carrots, peeled, chopped
1/2 cup Champagne or dry white wine
1 1/2 cup Creme Fraiche (page 141)
3 tablespoons chopped fresh basil
1 tablespoon chopped fresh tarragon
2 cups 1-inch diagonal slices fresh asparagus
2 leeks
8 ounces fresh shiitake mushrooms, sliced
1 1/2 cups shelled fresh peas
3/4 cup crumbled chevre cheese
Salt and freshly ground black pepper to taste
1 pound linguine or thin spaghetti, cooked

Saute shallots in 5 tablespoons butter in large skillet over medium-high heat for 5 minutes. Add carrots. Cook for 3 minutes. Add Champagne, *Creme Fraiche* and herbs. Cook for 15 minutes or until thickened to desired consistency. Cook asparagus in boiling salted water in saucepan until tender but firm; drain. Rinse leeks and pat dry; cut into thin julienne strips. Blanch in boiling water for 1 minute; drain. Saute mushrooms in 2 tablespoons butter in skillet. Add asparagus, mushrooms, peas and half the leeks to sauce. Add cheese, salt and pepper. Spoon over hot cooked linguine on serving plate. Garnish with remaining leeks. Yield: 4-6 portions.

PASTA WITH MOZZARELLA AND COLD TOMATO SAUCE

Wine: A dry white or light-bodied red.

The combination of hot pasta and cold sauce makes a great main dish salad.

1 small clove of garlic, minced
1/2 teaspoon salt
2 tablespoons red wine vinegar
6 tablespoons olive oil
1/4 teaspoon pepper
1 tablespoon crumbled leaf basil
4 cups chopped tomatoes
1/3 cup chopped red onion
1/2 cup small pitted black olives
1 pound mezzani rigati, rigatoni or linguine
1 8-ounce package whole milk mozzarella cheese finely chopped
1/2 cup freshly grated Parmesan cheese

Mash garlic with salt in bowl. Stir in vinegar, olive oil, pepper and basil. Add tomatoes, onion and olives; toss to mix. Cook pasta according to package directions; drain. Add cheeses. Toss until cheese melts. Add tomato mixture; toss to mix. Serve from kettle with additional Parmesan cheese. Yield: 4 servings.

TRIPLE-CHEESE FETTUCCINE

Wine: A full-bodied dry white or light-bodied red.

If you like cheese, you're gonna love this recipe.

1/2 cup coarsely chopped walnuts
8 ounces fresh egg fettuccine
8 ounces fresh spinach fettuccine
2 cups heavy cream, at room temperature
8 ounces fresh unsalted whole-milk mozzarella cheese, shredded
6 ounces sweet Gorgonzola, crumbled
3 tablespoons freshly grated Parmesan cheese
3 tablespoons finely chopped Italian flat-leaf parsley
2 tablespoons finely chopped fresh basil
1 tablespoon finely chopped fresh oregano
1 tablespoon finely chopped fresh chives

Heat small skillet over medium heat for 1 minute or until drop of water evaporates on contact. Add walnuts. Toast for 2 minutes or until fragrant, stirring constantly. Set aside. Cook *fettuccine al dente* in 3 quarts rapidly boiling salted water in saucepan. Drain in colander; shake well. Pour cream into saucepan in which *fettuccine* was cooked. Bring to a boil over high heat. Boil for 1 minute. Add *fettuccine*, cheeses and herbs. Cook for 2 minutes or until well blended, stirring frequently. Pour onto large warm platter. Sprinkle with walnuts and additional Parmesan cheese. Serve immediately.

Note: Sweet Gorgonzola cheese is young, unaged and milder than the aged variety. If sweet Gorgonzola is not available, substitute 4 ounces of aged.

LINGUINE WITH CLAM SAUCE

1 clove of garlic, cut into halves	1 7 1/2-ounce can minced clams
1/3 cup olive oil	2 tablespoons chopped Italian parsley
1/2 cup clam juice	
1/4 teaspoon salt	
Freshly ground pepper	
1/3 teaspoon dried oregano	16 ounces linguine

Saute garlic in olive oil in skillet until golden. Mash garlic; mix well. Discard garlic pieces. Add clam juice, salt, 3 grindings of pepper and oregano. Simmer for 5 minutes. Add clams and juice. Cook for about 10 minutes or until reduced. Stir in parsley. Cook linguine *al dente;* drain. Add half the clam sauce; toss to mix well. Spoon linguine onto serving plates. Top with remaining sauce. Yield: 4-6 servings.

TORTELLINI PALERMITANA

Wine: A light red.

This is one of the best tortellini dishes I've tried, and I didn't find it in Italy, but at Ernie's Restaurant in San Francisco on my last visit there 20 years ago!

1 clove of garlic, minced	1 tablespoon flour
2 medium onions, chopped	1 cup beef stock
	1/4 teaspoon thyme
2 tablespoons butter	1/2 bay leaf
4 ripe tomatoes, peeled, chopped	1 teaspoon salt
	1/2 teaspoon pepper
1 tablespoon tomato paste	2 medium mushrooms, minced

Saute garlic and onions in butter in skillet over medium heat for 5 minutes. Add remaining ingredients except mushrooms. Simmer for 15 minutes, stirring occasionally. Add mushrooms. Simmer for 5 minutes longer.

8 dozen frozen tortellini	1/4 cup freshly grated Parmesan cheese
3 tablespoons butter	

Cook tortellini *al dente* in rapidly boiling salted water in saucepan. Drain and rinse with hot water. Melt 2 tablespoons butter in shallow flameproof baking dish. Add tortellini. Cook over medium heat for 3 minutes, stirring constantly to coat. Stir in half the cheese. Pour sauce over tortellini. Dot with remaining 1 tablespoon butter; sprinkle with remaining cheese. Bake at 450 degrees for 10 minutes. Serve immediately.

Pasta Sauces

In Italy we put anything over pasta — from cauliflower sauteed in butter, to stale bread sauteed in garlic and olive oil. We also make some very fancy sauces, but I really prefer the simpler ones.

One of my very favorites is a sauce I keep ready to go in my refrigerator at all times. Here's how:

MARIO'S TOMATO SAUCE

Take two large cans of Italian plum tomatoes. Pour the contents into a large glass bowl (don't use metal or plastic, and clear glass is better). Put in about 3/4 cup coarsely chopped *fresh* basil leaves. Cover with about one inch of *good* Italian olive oil. *Don't stir* the oil into the tomatoes. The oil will sit on top of the bowl and act as a preservative. This is the way we kept things in the old days in Italy before refrigeration. This marinade will keep for weeks, even months, in the refrigerator as long as you make sure it's always topped with about an inch of olive oil. It isn't necessary to cover the bowl.

Now, when you're ready to make sauce, all you do is saute chopped fresh garlic cubes (number will depend on how much sauce you're making) with a small amount of chopped onion in a mixture of half butter and half olive oil. When onion is golden, but not brown, add tomatoes with juice and simmer for about 20 minutes. You can put cooked sausage, cooked ground beef or ground veal in the sauce if you like, but I prefer mine plain and simple over *fettuccine.*

The following recipes are from my collection of basic and classic pasta sauces, including some that are unusual and seldom seen in American restaurants.

MARINARA SAUCE

This sauce, the invention of Italian fishermen who make it on board their fishing boats, then drop in pieces of the day's catch, is delicious without any fish in it. With this base you can add any seafood you like, from lobster to any firm-fleshed fish that won't fall apart in the sauce.

2 small white onions, chopped	2 small carrots, chopped

1 clove of garlic,
   minced
2 tablespoons
   olive oil
1 teaspoon salt
Freshly ground
   pepper to taste
18 medium ripe plum
   tomatoes, peeled,
   seeded, chopped
3 tablespoons
   butter, melted
1/4 teaspoon hot
   red pepper

Saute onions, carrots and garlic in olive oil in skillet until onions are tender. Add salt, a generous amount of pepper and tomatoes; mix well. Cook for 20 minutes. Put through food mill. Simmer sauce in butter in saucepan for 15 minutes, stirring frequently. Stir in red pepper. Yield: 7 cups.

NEAPOLITAN SAUCE

This sauce is light and easy to prepare and has one of the best flavors of any Italian tomato sauce.

1/4 cup (heaping)
   minced
   prosciutto fat
2 tablespoons
   premium olive oil
1 tablespoon butter
3 large white onions,
   chopped
4 large fresh
   basil leaves,
   minced
10 very large
   ripe plum
   tomatoes, peeled,
   chopped or 9
   cups canned
   Italian plum
   tomatoes
Freshly ground
   pepper
1/2 teaspoon salt

Saute prosciutto fat in mixture of olive oil and butter in skillet until crisp. Do not overbrown. Add onions and basil. Simmer for 6 minutes. Add tomatoes; mix well. Simmer for 20 minutes, stirring frequently. Add a generous amount of pepper and salt; mix well. Increase heat. Cook until thickened, stirring constantly. Yield: 7 cups.

SALSA ALLA MERETRICE
(Harlot's Sauce)

This sauce was created for prostitutes in Naples by cooks in neighboring restaurants along the "streetwalking" avenues. The women wanted something that could be prepared quickly so they could get back to work. It has since become a Naples classic.

2 cloves of garlic,
   minced
2 tablespoons
   olive oil
8 anchovies, chopped
4 1/2 cups canned
   Italian plum
   tomatoes
8 stuffed green
   olives, sliced
8 pitted black
   olives, sliced
1 teaspoon capers
1 teaspoon dried
   sweet basil
1/4 teaspoon red
   pepper

Saute garlic in olive oil in skillet until soft. Add anchovies. Cook until anchovies are broken, stirring frequently. Put tomatoes through food mill. Add to skillet. Simmer for 10 minutes. Add remaining ingredients. Simmer for 20 minutes or until thickened. Serve on vermicelli or other pastas. Yield: 4 cups.

BASIC PESTO
Wine: Frascati Fontana Candida, a dry white Italian wine.

5 cloves of garlic,
   finely chopped
1/3 cup pine nuts,
   coarsely chopped
1 teaspoon salt
1/2 cup crumbled
   or grated pecorino
   or Romano cheese
1 cup grated
   Parmesan cheese
2 cups packed
   chopped fresh
   basil leaves
1/8 teaspoon
   white pepper
1 cup olive oil

Combine garlic, pine nuts and salt in large mortar, blender or food processor. Process until smooth. Add cheeses, basil and white pepper. Process until smooth. Add olive oil gradually, beating constantly. Serve with hot pasta. Yield: 4 servings.

WALNUT PESTO

2 cups
   fresh basil
   leaves
4 medium cloves
   of garlic,
   chopped
1 cup walnuts
1 cup premium
   olive oil
1 cup freshly grated
   imported
   Parmesan cheese
1 cup freshly grated
   imported Romano
   cheese
Salt and freshly
   ground pepper
   to taste

Combine basil, garlic and walnuts in food processor fitted with steel blade. Process until finely chopped. Add olive oil very gradually, processing constantly. Add cheeses and seasoning. Process for several seconds or until blended. Serve with hot pasta. Yield: 2 cups.

Opryland Hotel Executive Chef Ziggy Eisenberger at "Seafood Feast" at Murio's home

The following are four unusual (and unusually delicious) recipes from my friend Ziggy Eisenberger, executive chef at Opryland Hotel, and winner of three Gold Medals at the 1984 Culinary Olympics in Frankfurt, Germany.

SEA BASS MEDALLIONS WITH GRAPE AND SAFFRON SAUCE

3 pounds sea bass	6 mushroom stems
3 shallots, chopped	Salt to taste

Clean and bone sea bass. Cut fillets into 12 medallions; set aside. Combine bones and trimmings with shallots, mushroom stems, salt and 6 cups cold water in saucepan. Simmer for 30 minutes. Strain broth; set aside.

3 tablespoons chopped shallots	3/4 sweet red pepper, cut into strips
1 1/2 cloves of garlic, finely chopped	Grated rind of 1 1/2 lemons
1 tablespoon olive oil	6 white peppercorns, crushed
3 carrots, peeled, chopped	3 small bay leaves
Sliced white part of 3 small leeks	6 threads saffron
6 mushroom caps	1 1/2 cups heavy cream
3 medium tomatoes, peeled, quartered	Salt and white pepper to taste

Saute shallots and garlic in olive oil in skillet. Add vegetables, lemon rind, peppercorns and bay leaves. Saute until vegetables are tender. Add half the strained fish stock, stirring to deglaze skillet. Add enough water to cover vegetables. Simmer for 30 minutes. Strain. Add saffron and cream. Simmer for 20 minutes to reduce. Season with salt and white pepper.

Salt and white pepper to taste	48 white seedless peeled grapes
Lemon juice to taste	

Season medallions with salt, pepper and lemon juice. Poach in the remaining fish stock at 160 degrees for 4 minutes. Spoon saffron sauce into center of serving plates. Garnish with additional saffron threads. Place 2 medallions on each plate. Arrange grapes around fish.

TOMATO MOUSSE SOUP

1 tablespoon chopped shallot	3 pounds tomatoes, peeled, cut into quarters
1 tablespoon butter	6 or 7 fresh basil leaves
1 1/2 cloves of garlic, minced	Sugar, salt and pepper to taste

Saute shallot in butter in skillet until glazed. Add garlic, tomatoes, basil and seasonings. Simmer for 30 minutes or until tomatoes are very tender. Puree in blender. Chill in refrigerator. Pour into soup cups. Garnish with additional basil leaves. Yield: 6 servings.

CREAM OF CELERY ROOT SOUP

1 1/2 celery roots, peeled, cut into 1/2-inch squares	Nutmeg, salt and pepper to taste
3 cups vegetable stock or clear chicken broth	3/4 cup whipping cream, whipped
3/4 cup heavy cream	6 small celery leaves, chopped

Simmer celery root in stock in saucepan until tender. Remove celery root; reserve stock. Puree celery root in blender. Stir into hot stock. Add heavy cream. Simmer for several minutes. Add seasonings. Fold in whipped cream. Pour into soup cups. Garnish with celery leaves. Yield: 6 servings.

EXOTIC FRUITS WITH PUFF PASTRY RIESLING SABAYON

15 ounces puff pastry	3 kiwifruit, peeled
3 mangos, peeled	3 fresh figs, peeled
1 1/2 papayas, peeled	Lemon juice

Divide puff pastry into 3 portions. Roll each portion 1/4 inch thick. Moisten half the dough; fold over and press firmly. Cut into 2 portions; place on baking sheet. Bake at 350 degrees for 10 minutes. Sprinkle lightly with sugar. Bake until golden brown. Slice fruits at varying angles or into different shapes. Sprinkle with lemon juice.

6 egg yolks	3/4 cup pineapple juice
1 1/2 egg whites	
6 tablespoons sugar	3 cups Riesling

Combine all ingredients in double boiler. Cook over hot water until thickened, beating constantly. Spoon warm Sabayon onto dessert plates. Arrange sliced fruit on top. Place puff pastry in center. Garnish with chopped pistachios or walnuts. Serve immediately. Yield: 6 servings.

TORTELLINI SALAD

Wine: Barolo or Amarone.

This is a delicious main course salad.

1 pound cheese-filled tortellini	2 medium carrots, cut into julienne strips
3/4 cup olive oil	1 large sweet red pepper, cut into julienne strips
8 ounces prosciuttino or other ham, sliced 3/8 inch thick	1/2 cup finely chopped parsley
8 ounces smoked turkey, sliced 3/8 inch thick	2 cloves of garlic, minced
1 cup cooked fresh peas	1 head red leaf lettuce

Cook tortellini in boiling salted water in saucepan until just tender. Drain in colander; rinse with cold water until cool. Drain for 5 to 10 minutes. Combine with 1/4 cup olive oil in bowl; toss to mix. Chill, covered, in refrigerator. Cut prosciuttino and turkey into cubes. Add with peas, carrots and red pepper to tortellini. Chill, covered, for 30 minutes. Combine parsley, garlic and remaining 1/2 cup olive oil in bowl; mix with wire whisk. Pour over salad; toss to mix well. Spoon into lettuce-lined salad bowl.

STEAK DIANE

Wine: A Spanish red such as Torres Coronas because the Madeira is a Spanish wine.

When I opened Mario's in 1965, this dish was one of the most popular on the menu because customers loved to see it flamed at tableside.

1 pound 1/2-inch thick boneless sirloin steak	1 tablespoon Worcestershire sauce
1/4 cup unsalted butter	1 teaspoon Dijon mustard
1/4 cup Brandy	Salt and pepper to taste
2 tablespoons Madeira	1 teaspoon minced fresh parsley

Cut steak in half lengthwise; pound to 1/8-inch thickness between waxed paper. Saute steaks 1 at a time in 2 1/2 tablespoons butter in skillet over medium heat for 30 seconds on each side. Place both steaks in skillet; pour Brandy over top. Remove skillet from heat; ignite. Shake skillet over heat until flames die. Remove steaks to heated platter. Add Madeira, Worcestershire sauce, mustard, salt and pepper to skillet; whisk to mix. Simmer for 1 minute. Swirl in 1 1/2 tablespoons butter. Dip steaks in sauce to coat; place on platter. Sprinkle with parsley.
Yield: 2 servings.

STEAK PIZZAIOLI

Wine: Nothing less than a fine Chianti Classico Riserva.

When I lived in Los Angeles in the fifties, a favorite restaurant for the show biz crowd was Villa Capri in Hollywood. This dish was a special favorite of both Frank Sinatra and Dean Martin.

1 tablespoon minced garlic	1 teaspoon basil
1/4 cup olive oil	2 teaspoons oregano
1 35-ounce can peeled Italian tomatoes	1/2 teaspoon crushed hot red pepper
1 teaspoon salt	4 sirloin strip steaks

Saute garlic in olive oil in saucepan until lightly browned. Add tomatoes with juice. Stir with wooden spoon to break up tomatoes. Simmer for 3 minutes. Add seasonings. Simmer for 45 to 60 minutes. Grill, broil or pan-fry steaks in butter to desired degree of doneness. Serve sauce over steaks. Yield: 4 servings.

ROAST LEG OF LAMB WITH WINE SAUCE

1 leg of lamb	2 cloves of garlic,
1 cup Reine Pedauque	minced
Beaujolais	1/2 teaspoon
red wine	Tabasco
1/4 cup oil	sauce
1 onion, coarsely	Salt to taste
chopped	

Place lamb in small deep glass dish. Pour mixture of remaining ingredients over lamb. Marinate, covered, in refrigerator for 6 hours to overnight. Turn lamb occasionally. Drain, reserving marinade. Pat dry with paper towels. Place on rack in roasting pan. Roast at 325 degrees for about 25 minutes per pound or to desired degree of doneness, basting with reserved marinade occasionally. Do not overcook. Lamb should be pink in center. Yield: 6-8 servings.

Photograph for this recipe on page 35.

ZINFANDEL DUCK WITH WILD MUSHROOMS

Wine: Zinfandel.

Zinfandel and veal stock, slow-simmered to a glaze makes an elegant and rich-tasting sauce. You must use a good Zinfandel for this. I suggest Ridge or Simi.

12 ounces fresh wild	4 cups veal stock
mushrooms, such	Several parsley sprigs
as cepes or shiitake	Salt and freshly
Necks and breasts of	ground pepper
2 large ducklings	1/2 stick butter,
2 shallots, chopped	chilled, chopped
1 750-milliliter	1/4 cup butter
bottle of Zinfandel	

Remove and mince mushroom stems. Brown duck necks in skillet over high heat for 10 minutes. Add minced mushrooms. Saute until pan juices are brown. Add shallots. Saute for 1 minute. Add Zinfandel. Boil vigorously until reduced to a glaze. Add stock, parsley, salt and pepper. Cook over medium heat for 30 minutes or until reduced to a syrupy glaze. Strain through fine strainer into double boiler. Whisk in chilled butter 1 piece at a time. Keep warm over hot, not simmering, water. Do not overheat or sauce will separate. Brown duck breasts in skillet over high heat for 15 to 20 minutes, turning frequently. Duck breasts should be rare inside. Cut into thin slices. Saute mushroom caps in 1/4 cup butter in skillet until just tender. Place on serving platter. Arrange sliced duck breasts over mushrooms. Top with sauce. Yield: 6 servings.

PACIFIC LOBSTER WITH CHAMPAGNE SAUCE

Wine: Champagne, of course!

A whole bottle of Champagne goes into this sauce so this is a real "sparkler" of a dish.

2 10-ounce packages	4 1 1/2-pound
frozen peas or 2	live
pounds fresh	lobsters
peas, shelled	

Bring enough water to a boil to generously cover peas. Add peas. Boil for 2 minutes; plunge peas into cold water. Drain and pat dry. Puree peas in blender or food processor. Spoon into saucepan. Bring water to a full rolling boil in large pot. Add lobsters. Cook for 8 minutes. Remove lobsters, reserving cooking water; plunge lobsters into cold water. Crack shells; remove tail meat and discard shells. Set lobster tails aside. Maintain reserved cooking water at the simmering point.

3 shallots,	3 sticks unsalted
minced	butter, chilled,
1 750-milliliter	cut into
bottle of	1-tablespoon
Champagne	pieces
3 tablespoons	Salt and freshly
heavy	ground black
cream	pepper to taste

Combine shallots and Champagne in large saucepan. Boil until reduced to about 1 cup. Add cream. Cook until reduced and thickened. Swirl in butter gradually until sauce is smooth and creamy. Do not boil. Season with salt and pepper. Strain into double boiler. Keep warm over warm water. Heat lobster tails in simmering cooking liquid. Heat pea puree to serving temperature. Spoon onto center of serving platter. Split lobster tails; arrange over puree. Spoon sauce over lobster. Garnish with snipped fresh chives.

ASPARAGUS-LEEK QUICHE

Wine: Fume-Blanc.

Real men *do* eat quiche, and I'm one of them! I like the onion flavor of leek in this recipe.

1 unbaked 10-inch	1 1/2 teaspoons basil
pie shell	2 teaspoons salt
10 to 16 3-inch	Freshly ground
asparagus tips	pepper to taste
2 cups sliced	1 1/2 cups grated
white leek	Gruyere cheese
1 cup chopped	4 eggs
asparagus stalks	2 cups whipping
1/4 cup butter	cream

Bake pie shell at 400 degrees for 10 minutes. Parboil asparagus tips for 3 minutes; drain and set aside. Saute leek and chopped asparagus in butter in skillet for 8 to 10 minutes or until tender. Add basil, 1 teaspoon salt and pepper. Cook for 1 minute. Place in pie shell. Sprinkle with cheese. Combine eggs, cream and remaining 1 teaspoon salt in blender container. Process until blended. Pour into pie shell. Bake at 400 degrees for 30 minutes. Arrange asparagus tips in spoke pattern on quiche. Bake for 10 minutes longer or until puffed, golden and set in center. Let stand for several minutes before cutting.

EGGPLANT CASSEROLE

Wine: Eggplant is one vegetable that always goes better with red wine.

1 medium eggplant, peeled, sliced 1/2 inch thick	3 tomatoes, peeled, thinly sliced
Olive oil	Salt and sweet basil to taste
1 large onion, thinly sliced	Parmesan cheese
2 cloves of garlic, minced	1/4 cup red table wine
	Butter

Soak eggplant in heavily salted water for 20 minutes. Drain; rinse with cold water. Pat dry with paper towels. Brown lightly in 1/4-inch deep olive oil in skillet; remove eggplant. Add onion and garlic. Saute until translucent. Do not brown. Alternate layers of onion, eggplant, tomatoes, seasonings and Parmesan cheese until all ingredients are used, ending with tomatoes in large casserole. Sprinkle with wine and Parmesan cheese. Dot with butter. Bake at 350 degrees for about 45 minutes or until tender.

MACADAMIA-RUM PIE

I had this pie at a restaurant on Maui, and it was so good, I refused to pay the check until they gave me the recipe!

1 3 1/2-ounce jar unsalted macadamia nuts, chopped	1/4 cup sour cream
1/2 cup sugar	1 1/2 cups milk
1 envelope unflavored gelatin	2 eggs, separated
2 tablespoons cornstarch	3 to 4 tablespoons dark rum
1/4 teaspoon salt	1 cup whipping cream, whipped
1 3-ounce package cream cheese, softened	1 baked 10-inch pie shell

Toast nuts at 350 degrees for 5 minutes or until golden. Set aside. Combine sugar, gelatin, cornstarch, salt, cream cheese and sour cream in blender. Process until smooth. Add milk gradually, processing constantly. Pour into double boiler. Cook over simmering water for about 15 minutes or until thick and smooth. Stir a small amount of hot mixture into egg yolks. Stir egg yolks into hot mixture. Cook for 3 minutes, stirring constantly with wire whisk. Remove pan from hot water; cool slightly. Stir in rum. Fold in stiffly beaten egg whites gently. Chill until partially set. Fold in whipped cream and half the nuts. Pour into pie shell. Chill for 2 hours or longer. Sprinkle with remaining nuts just before serving.

BANANA SAUCE

This is a fabulous dessert sauce I first tasted in New Orleans. Serve it over homemade Haagen-dazs or vanilla ice cream.

2 tablespoons butter	4 bananas, sliced lengthwise
1/2 cup sugar	3 tablespoons 100-proof white rum
2 teaspoons cinnamon	
3 tablespoons banana liqueur	Vanilla ice cream

Heat butter, sugar and cinnamon in chafing dish until melted, stirring constantly. Stir in liqueur. Add bananas, turning to coat. Heat rum; ignite. Pour over bananas. Place scoop of ice cream on each chilled plate. Arrange banana slice on each side; spoon sauce over top. Yield: 4 servings.

CREME FRAICHE

Here are two methods for making *Creme Fraiche*. Both are easy. They will keep 7 to 10 days refrigerated but need a couple of days to develop.

I. Combine 1 cup whipping cream and 1 cup sour cream in bowl. Blend with wire whisk. Pour into jar; cover. Let stand in warm place for 12 hours or until thickened. Stir until well mixed. Chill, covered, for 36 hours before using. May store in refrigerator for 7 to 10 days. Yield: 2 cups.

II. Combine 2 cups whipping cream and 2 teaspoons buttermilk in large glass jar. Shake, covered, for 1 minute. Let stand in warm place for 12 hours or until thickened. Stir until well mixed. Chill for 24 hours before using. May store in refrigerator for 7 to 10 days. Yield: 2 cups.

WINE GLOSSARY

I want to share with you some of the terms most widely used by wine tasters for describing the impressions created by wine on the senses, and other wine terms that may be unfamiliar to you.

ACETIC: Vinegary taste or smell that develops when a wine is overexposed to air.

ACID: The acidic taste dimension in wine is primarily due to the presence of tartaric and malic acids, as well as citric, succinic, lactic and acetic acid. The degree of acidity in a wine is described as flat, sharp or tart, or green.

AGED: Mature, fully developed wines are described as aged, and should possess bouquet. The age of a wine may be roughly determined by careful tasting. A wine's age, like that of a person, is described as young, mature or old.

ALCOHOL: Alcohol is found in concentrations of 9 to 15 percent by volume in table wines. Wines of low alcoholic content are described as light or weak; high in alcohol is heady, strong, or powerful.

APPLES: A fruit smell associated with the presence of malic acid; apparent in a number of white wines.

AROMA: See Bouquet.

ASTRINGENT: A wine of high tannin content has a puckering effect on the mouth and is described as astringent, tannic, rough or harsh. A wine of low tannin content is described as smooth or soft. Wines lose astringency with age.

AUSTERE: Somewhat hard, with restrained fruit and character.

BAKED: The flavor that results from grapes grown in hot climates.

BALANCE: Having proper harmony of acidity, sugar, tannin, fruit and other qualities of a wine. A well-balanced wine possesses the various elements in proper proportion to one another.

BIG: Powerful in aroma and flavor; full-bodied.

BITE: Wines with high acidity.

BITTER: An excessively astringent wine.

BODY: The weight and texture of a wine; it may be light-bodied or full-bodied; often refers to alcohol content.

BOTRYTIZED: Wines made from grapes affected by the beneficent mold Botrytis cinerea ("the noble rot"); have a distinctive, perfumey scent.

BOUQUET: The smell or scent that is one of a wine's most important characteristics; provides an indication of taste.

BREATHE: To let a freshly opened wine have contact with the air before consumption.

BREED: Character and complexity, usually employed to connote high quality.

BRIGHT: Said of a wine's color that is clear.

BRILLIANT: Said of a wine's color that is absolutely clear.

BRUT: Dry; usually applied to Champagne and other sparkling wines; indicates less than 1.5 percent residual sugar by volume in Champagne; connotes greater dryness than the term "extra dry."

CHAPTALIZATION: Sugaring; the addition of sugar to the must to ensure complete fermentation.

CHARACTER: A wine of character has something to notice, whether it be virtues or defects.

CLEAN: Fresh with no discernible defects; refers to aroma, appearance, and flavor.

CLOUDY: A wine that is cloudy in appearance; always suspect and usually bad.

CLOYING: Often used to describe wines with a sweet, heavy and tiresome flavor.

COARSE: Rude or harsh in flavor.

COMPLETE: Mature, with good follow-through to the palate, satisfying mouth-feel, and firm aftertaste.

COMPLEX: The best wines display a fairly broad range of qualities that render their taste complex and challenging.

COOPERAGE: Aging vats for wine (could be wood or glass-lined tanks).

CORKED: The offensive smell of a wine spoiled by a moldy (not merely dried-out) cork; infrequently encountered.

CRISP: Fresh, brisk character, usually with high acidity.

DECANT: Transferring the finished wine from bottle to a carafe or decanter for serving, usually done to separate the clear wine from sediments or deposits, or to aerate the wine.

DELICATE: Light fragrance, flavor, and body.

DEPOSIT: The sediment (mostly precipitated tannin) which is left as a powder or crust on the inside walls of undisturbed bottles of certain aged wines.

DEPTH: Similar to complexity, character and body; a wine of depth will have great texture and full body.

DISTINCTIVE: Recognizable character in a wine. Certain varietal wines are said to be distinctive because they can be distinguished from one another.

DRY: Opposite of sweet.

DULL: Lacking liveliness and proper acidity; uninteresting.

EARTHY: Scents or flavors reminiscent of fresh earth; a virtue in some wines, a defect in others.

ELEGANT: Refined character, distinguished quality; stylish, not heavy.

EXTRA-DRY: Denotes the amount of *dosage* (sugary wine) added to Champagne before final corking. Some *dosage* is added to all, even the dryest Champagne, because fermentation eliminates virtually all of the natural sugar in the wine. *Brut*, the dryest of all Champagne, has approximately 0.5 percent dosage. *Extra-Dry*, the second dryest Champagne, has approximately 1 to 2 percent *dosage*.

FINE: Distinguished.

FINESSE: Showing harmony among the best qualities of a good wine; an extra something that sets a wine apart from others.

FINISH: A term used in wine tasting to describe the end taste. Wine cannot be considered well balanced without a good finish, meaning a firm, crisp, distinctive end.

FIRM: Taut balance of elements; tightly knit structure; distinct flavor.

FLAT: A wine lacking acidity.

FLAVOR: Taste of the wine.

FLOWERY: Aroma of some wines is distinctly floral or expansive.

FRESHY: Fatness of fruit; big, ripe.

FRUITY: Fruity wines have various ripe-fruit scents and/or flavors. A fruity wine is not always simply grapey.

FULL: Wines with substantial body.

GOOD: Better than ordinary wine, but not fine.

GREEN: Young, immature; not ready for drinking.

GRIP: Firmness of flavor and structure.

HARD: Tannic young red wines.

HARMONIOUS: All elements in perfect balance.

HARSH: Excessively astringent and/or acidic wine.

HEADY: Attractively strong wine.

HEAVY: Full-bodied wine.

HERBACEOUS: Aromas and flavors reminiscent of grass or hay; grassy.

HERBY: Reminiscent of herbs, such as mint, sage, thyme, eucalyptus.

HONEST: Without flaws; typical and straightforward; decent but not great.

HONEYED: Flavor quality found in some very fine sweet wines.

INKY: Primarily a color term used to describe red wines so dark and concentrated that they appear slightly opaque rather than brilliantly clear.

INTENSE: Wine with highly concentrated qualities.

INTRICATE: Interweaving of subtle complexities of aroma and flavor.

LEAFY: Vegetative nuance in flavor.

LEES: Heavy sediment which is thrown by young wine in cooperage.

LEGS: The drips apparent on the inner walls of the wine glass which reveal the viscosity of the wine.

LENGTH: Lingering aftertaste.

LIGHT: Lacking in alcoholic strength; unassertive.

LITTLE: Wine with little nose, flavor, or character.

LIVELY: Crisp, fresh; having quality.

LONG: Long finish or aftertaste of fine wines.

LUSCIOUS: Quality of body and flavor of some very fine wines with a particularly rich, attractive deliciousness.

MADERIZED: Wine that has oxidized; has brown or amber color; stale odor.

MATURE: Developed fully with age.

MEATY: Wine with chewy, fleshy fruit taste; sturdy and firm in structure.

MELLOW: Soft, smooth, mature and pleasant; lacking somewhat in complexity and body.

MOLDY: Unpleasant smell and taste from rotten grapes.

MUSCULAR: Vigorous fruit; powerful body and flavor; robust.

MUST: The juice of grapes or other fruit before and during fermentation.

MUSTY: Stale, dusty aromas.

NEUTRAL: Unexceptional, undistinctive wine.

NOBLE: Great; of perfect balance and harmonious expression.

NOSE: Smell of a wine, including bouquet and aroma.

NUANCE: Subtle flavor or odor trace.

NUTTY: Nutlike aromas that develop in certain wines, such as Sherries, or old whites.

OAK: Aroma and flavor derived from aging in oak casks or barrels; should not be overly pronounced.

OFF: Wine that is partially or completely spoiled or defective.

OLD: Wine that is past its peak of development.

OPEN: Revealing full character.

ORDINARY: Sound, drinkable table wine; between poor and good in quality.

OXIDIZED: Flat, stale aroma and flavor; spoiled as the result of overexposure to air.

PEACHES: Fruity quality reminiscent of peaches; sometimes noticeable in Chenin Blanc.

PELURE D'OIGNON: Literally "onion skin" referring to the golden or brownish color visible at the surface edges of a mature red wine.

PETILLANT: Light sparkle.

POOR: Sound but barely drinkable wine; below ordinary in quality.

POWERFUL: Used to indicate strength and bigness.

QUICK FINISH: A poor end taste — watery, flavor not sustained and tailing off inconclusively.

RACKING: Drawing off of wine from one vat to another during wine making, usually for the purpose of separating it from its lees or sediment.

RASPBERRIES: Fruity nuance found in a number of red wines, especially Zinfandel.
RICH: Full, opulent flavor, body and aroma.
RIPE: Full, soft, mature character; also, intense fruit flavor.
ROBUST: Full-bodied, powerful, heady.
ROUGH: Harsh edges, biting, unpleasant.
ROUND: Smooth, well-developed flavor, usually medium to full body.
RUBY: Typical color of many red wines.
SAPPY: Lively, straightforward, refreshingly acidic, grapey character.
SEC: Dry; in Champagne, refers to an unfermented sugar content of 1.5 to 4 percent by volume; sweeter than Brut and similar to Extra Dry.
SEVERE: See Austere.
SHARP: Acidic bite; high tannin content.
SHORT: Wine with a quick finish.
SILKY: Smooth, sinuous texture and finish.
SIMPLY: Wines that are lacking in depth and character.
SMOKY: Aroma and flavor sometimes associated with wood.
SMOOTH: Descriptive of the texture of some wines; also a wine low in tannin.
SOFT: May refer to soft, gentle fruit in delicate wines, or to flabbiness or lack of acidity in wines without proper structure.
SOLID: Sound, well-structured, firm.
SOUND: Soundness is the ideal chemical state of a wine which is properly made and stored so that it does not sour or spoil. It is not a judgement of quality but a necessary condition for a drinkable wine.
SOUR: Sharply acidic or vinegary.
SPARKLING: Wines with bubbles created by trapped carbon dioxide gas, either natural or injected.
SPICE: Quality found particularly in Gewurztraminer.
SPOILED: Wine rendered undrinkable by bacterial action. See Acetic.
STALKY: Leafy-woody scent. Terms "stalky" and "stemmy" are also used to describe the flavor of wines which have been fermented too long in the presence of stems.
STEELY: Certain kind of severe or austere quality. It does not mean metallic. Also descriptive of some aciduous wines.
STIFF: Unyielding; not lively.
STRONG: Robust, powerful.
STRUCTURE: Composition of a wine.
STUFFING: Big, flavorful, full-bodied wines are said to have "stuffing."
STURDY: Bold, vigorous flavor; full-bodied and robust.
SUBTLE: Descriptive of wines with complex, yet elusive nuances.

SULFURY: Scent of burned matches caused by sulphur dioxide, an antioxidant used in making most wines.
SUPPLE: Yielding in flavor; accessible and giving.
SWEET: Opposite of dry. The sensation of sweetness in wines is caused by the presence of glucose and fructose sugars.
TANNIN: Astringent substance found in grape skins, seeds, and stems. Essential component of fine red wines.
TART: Sharp; acceptable if not too acidic.
TEXTURE: The "feel" of wine as it moves in the mouth. Some descriptive terms for various impressions of wine textures are: silky, satiny, grainy, chalky, fat, fleshy, viscous, unctuous, velvety.
THICK: Dense and heavy.
THIN: Watery or lacking in body.
TIRED: Past its peak of flavor development; old.
TOUGH: Astringent or hard.
ULLAGE: Airspace below the cork in the neck of the bottle. Evaporation of the wine over time increases this space, which is then called ullage, and can spoil wine if there is too much air in the bottle.
UNBALANCED: Having an improper proportion of acidity, sugar, tannin, fruit and all other elements of a wine.
UNCTUOUS: An almost oily texture to the body of the wine; found in balanced harmony.
UNRESOLVED: Insufficiently developed for its elements to be in balanced harmony.
UNSOUND: Chemical state of a wine that has been made and stored improperly so that it is soured or spoiled; makes a wine undrinkable.
VANILLA: Scent imparted by aging in oak.
VELVETY: Descriptive of a rich, opulent texture.
VIGOROUS: Firm, lively fruit strong body; assertive flavor.
VINEGARY: Having the smell of vinegar; see Acetic.
VINIFICATION: All stages of wine making.
VITICULTURE: Science and technique of grape growing.
WARMTH: Characteristic flavor of wines made in hot climates.
WATERY: Thin; lacking in flavor and color.
WEAK: Lacking grip; without character.
WEEDY: Aromas or flavors reminiscent of hay or grasses; not necessarily unpleasant unless exaggerated.
WEIGHTY: Strong, powerful, full-bodied.
WOODY: Quality of wines kept too long in wooden cooperage, or too long in new oak casks (in which case the wine may be described as "overly oaky").
YEASTY: Bready smell, characteristic of wines that have undergone a secondary fermentation, notably Champagne.
YOUNG: Fresh, not yet developed.

INDEX

WINES AROUND THE WORLD

FRANCE
  Appellation Controlee, 53
  bottle shapes, 54
  vineyards
    Albert Pic & Fils, 58
    Baron Patrick, 58
    Bouchard Pere et Fils, 58-59
    Bourgueil, 59
    Chateau Brane-Cantenac, 56
    Chateau Cantenac Brown, 57
    Chateau Cos-d'Estournel, 56
    Chateau Ducru-Beaucaillou, 56
    Chateau Dufort-Vivens, 56
    Chateau Gruaud-Larose, 56
    Chateau Haut-Brion, 56
    Chateau Lafite-Rothschild, 56
    Chateau Lascombs, 56
    Chateau Latour, 56
    Chateau Leoville-Barton, 56
    Chateau Leoville-Las-Cases, 56
    Chateau Leoville-Poyferre, 56
    Chateau Margaux, 57
    Chateau Montrose, 56
    Chateau Mouton Rothschild, 56
    Chateau Olivier, 57
    Chateau Pichon-Longueville (Baron), 56
    Chateau Pinchon-Longueville (Comtesse), 56
    Chateau Prieure-Lichine, 53
    Chateau Rausan-Segla, 56
    Chateau Rauzan-Gassies, 56
    Chinon, 59
    Hermitage, 60
    Jaboulet-Vercherre, 54
    Louis Jadot, 59
  wine labels, how to read
    Bordeaux, 53
    Burgundy, 54
  wine regions
    Alsace, 55
    Bordeaux, 55
      Barsac, 57
      Entre-Deux-Mers, 57
      Graves, 56
      Medoc, 56
      Pomerol, 56
      Sauternes, 57
      St. Emilion, 56
    Burgundy
      Beaujolais, 58
      Chablis, 58
      Cote d'Or, 58
    Champagne, 60
      process for making Champagne, 62
      top producing houses
        Bollinger, 62
        Charles Heidsieck, 62
        G. H. Mumm, 62
        Heidsieck Monopole, 62
        Krug, 62
        Lanson, 62
        Laurent Perrier, 62
        Louis Roederer, 62
        Mercier, 62
        Moet et Chandon, 62
        Perrier-Jouet, 62
        Piper-Heidsieck, 62
        Pol Roger, 62
        Pomery et Greno, 62
        Ruinart, 62
        Taittinger, 62
        Veuve Clicquot-Ponsardin, 62
    Cotes du Rhone, 60
    Loire Valley
      Anjou-Saumur, 59
      Muscadet, 59
      Pouilly, 59
      Sancerre, 59
      Touraine, 52
  wines
    Beaujolais, 58
    Beaujolais Blanc, 58
    Beaujolais-Villages, 58
    Bordeaux, 55
    Burgundy, 58-59
      White Burgundy, 59
    Chablis, 58-59
    Champagne, 61-62
    Chateau d Y'quem, 57
    Chateauneuf-du-Pape, 60
    Chenin Blanc, 59
    Eschezeaux, 58
    La Tache, 59
    Margaux, 53, 57
    Meursault, 59
    Montrachet, 59
      Puligny-Montrachet, 54
    Muscadet, 59
    Pavillion Blanc, 57
    Pouilly-Fuisse, 59
    Rose, 59
    Sauternes, 57
    Vouvray, 59
GERMANY
  bottle shapes, 81
  wine label, how to read, 80
  wine ratings, 80
  wine regions
    Baden, 80
    Franken, 80
    Mosel-Saar-Ruwer, 80
    Nahe, 80
    Rheingau, 80
    Rheinhessen, 80
    Rheinpfalz, 80

wineries
   H. Sichel Sohne, 80-81
   Leonard Kreusch, 81
   Schloss Johannisberger, 80
   St. Ursula Weinkellerei, 80
wines
   Auslese, 81
   Beerenauslese, 81
   Blue Nun, 80-81
   Kabinett, 81
   Liebfraumilch, 80
   Mosel, 81
   Piesporter Goldtropfchen, 81
   Piesporter Michelsberg, 80
   Rhine, 81
   Riesling, 80
   Spatlese, 81
   Trockenbeerenauslese, 81
   Zeller Schwarze Katz, 81

ITALY
   Chianti Classico Consorzio, 71
   Denominazione di Origine Controllata, 65
   Denominazione di Origine
      e Controllata Garantita, 65
   types of wines, 77
   wine label, how to read, 64
   wine pronunciation guide, 78
   wine regions
      Abruzzo, 74
      Apulia, 75
      Basilicata, 74
      Calabria, 74
      Campana, 74
      Emilia-Romagna, 68
      Friuli-Venezia-Giulia, 67
      Latium, 74
      Liguria, 68
      Lombardy, 66
      Marches, 73
      Molise, 74
      Pantelleria, 76
      Piedmont, 65
      Sardinia, 76
      Sicily, 76
      Trentino-Alto Adige, 67
      Tuscany, 68
      Umbria, 73
      Val d'Aosta, 65
      Veneto, 66
   wineries
      Biondi-Santi, 72
      Collio, 67
      Conte Zandotti, 74
      Folonari, 66
      Pio Cesare, 65
      Ruffino, 71
      Tignanello, 68
      Villa Antinori, 66
      Villa Banfi, 71, 73
   wines
      Agilianico del Vulture, 75
      Albana, 68
      Amarone, 66
      Asti Spumante, 65
      Barbaresco, 64-65
      Barbera, 64-65
      Bardolino, 66
      Barolo, 64-65
      Bianchello del Metauro, 73
      Brunello di Montalcino, 64, 68, 72-73
      Cabernet, 67
      Cabernet di Pramaggiore, 66
      Cabernet Sauvignon, 73
      Cannonau, 76
      Castel del Monte Rose, 75
      Casteller, 67
      Chardonnay, 73
      Chianti, 68, 71
      Chiaretto, 66
      Ciro, 75
      Colli Albani, 74
      Colli Lanuvini, 74
      Cortese di Gavi, 65
      Corvo di Salaparuta, 76
      Dolcetto, 65
      Donnaz, 65
      Donnici Pollino, 75
      Draceno, 76
      Drepano, 76
      Enfer d'Arvier, 65
      Est! Est! Est!, 74
      Etna Red, 76
      Etna White, 76
      Fiano, 74
      Franciacorta Pinot, 66
      Frascatti, 74
      Freisa, 65
      frizzante, 65
      Gattinara, 64-65
      Gewurztraminer, 67
      Ghemme, 64-65
      Greco di Tufo, 74
      Grignolino, 65
      Hirpinia, 74
      Ischia, 74
      Lacryma Christi, 74
      Lambrusco, 68
      liquoroso, 65
      Locorotondo, 75
      Lugana, 66
      Marino, 74
      Marsala, 76
      Merlot, 67
      Merlot del Piave, 66
      Merlot di Aprilia, 74
      Monica di Sardegna, 76
      Montepulciano d'Abruzzo, 74
      Moscato, 65
      Moscato di Pantelleria, 76
      Orvieto, 73
      Picolit, 67
      Pinot, 67
      Pinot Bianco, 67
      Pinot Grigio, 65, 67
      Principessa Gavi, 73
      Recioto, 66
      Regaliali Red, 76
      Regaliali White, 76
      Riesling, 67
      Riunite, 73
      Rossese, 68
      Rosso, 66
      Rosso Conero, 73
      Rosso Piceno, 73
      Sangiovese, 68
      San Severo Red, 75
      San Severo White, 75
      Saturno, 76

Savuto, 75
Segesta, 76
Sfursat, 66
Soave, 66
spumante, 65
table wine, 65
Taurasi, 74
Teroldego, 67
Tignanello, 68, 71
Tocai, 67
Tocai di Lison, 66
Tocia Friulano, 67
Torbato, 76
Torgiano, 73
Torre Quarto, 75
Trebbiano d'Abruzzo, 74
Trebbiano di Romagna, 68
Valpoticella, 66
Verdicchio, 73
Vernaccia, 76
Vernaccia di San Gimignano, 73

PORTUGAL
wine regions
Bucelas, 84
Colares, 84
Dao, 84
Douro, 84
Madeira, 84
wineries
Lancers, 84
Mateus, 84
wines
Bual or Boal, 84
Madeira, 84
Malmsey, 84
Port
Ruby Port, 84
Tawny Port, 84
Vintage Port, 84
White Port, 84
Sercial, 84
table wines, 84
Verdelha, 84
Vinho Verde, 84

SPAIN
wine label, how to read, 83
wine regions
Catalonia, 83
Jerez, 83
Rioja, 83
wineries
Torres, 83
Vinos Blancos de Castilla, 84
wines
Amontillado, 83
Clarete, 83
Fino, 83
Manzanilla, 83
Marques de Riscal, 84
Oloroso, 83
Rioja, 83
Sherry, 82-83
Cream Sherry, 83
Tinto, 83

UNITED STATES
California
Central Valley, 50
North Central Coast
Livermore County, 46
Monterey County, 45
San Benito County, 45
Santa Clara County, 46
Santa Cruz County, 47
North Coast
Lake County, 44
Mendocino County, 44
Napa Valley, 37
Sonoma County, 40
South Central Coast
San Luis Obispo County, 48
Santa Barbara County, 48
Santa Ynez County, 48
New York, 51
Oregon, 51
Washington, 50
wine label, how to read, 33
wineries
Adelsheim Vineyards, 51
Almaden, 46
Beaulieu, 37
Cain Cellars, 40
Chappellet, 39
Charles Krug, 37
Chateau Ste. Michelle, 51
Chateau St. Jean, 40
Clos du Bois, 40
Clos du Val, 40
Cresta Blanca, 44
Cribari, 50
Domaine, Chandon, 40
Dry Creek Vineyard, 43
Eyrie Vineyards, 51
Far Niente, 40
Fetzer, 44
Ficklin Vineyard, 50
Firestone, 48
Freemark Abbey, 37
Gallo, 50
Grgich Hills, 37-38
Groth, 38-39
Hanns Kornell, 37
Heitz, 37
Jordan, 40
Joseph Phelps, 40
Kenwood, 40
Louis Martini, 37
Mondavi, 37
Monterey Vineyards, 46
Parducci, 44
Paul Masson, 46
Ponzi Vineyards, 51
Raymond, 37
Ridge, 47
San Martin, 47
Schramsberg Vineyards, 40
Sebastiani, 43
Silverado, 39
Stag's Leap, 38
St. Clement, 39
Sterling, 37
Stonegate, 37
Stony Hill, 37
Sutter Home, 37
Weibel, 44
wines
Blanc de Noir, 51
Cabernet Sauvignon, 37, 39-44, 46-47, 49, 51
Chardonnay, 37, 39-43, 45, 47, 49, 51

Chenin Blanc, 39, 46, 51
Fume Blanc, 44, 51
Gewurztraminer, 40
Grenache Rose, 51
Hearty Burgundy, 46
Johannisberg Riesling, 43, 49, 51
jug wine, 34, 44
Marlstone, 43
Merlot, 42-43, 49, 51
Muscat Canelli, 51
Pinot Gris, 51
Pinot Noir, 40, 43-44, 51
Pinot Noir Blanc, 44
Port, 50
Rose of Cabernet, 51
Sauvignon Blanc, 39, 46, 49
Semillion, 46, 51
Semillion-Blanc, 51
Stirrup Cup, 49
White Riesling, 40-41, 45, 50-51
Zinfandel, 40-41, 44, 47
    White Zinfandel, 44, 47

SPECIAL RECIPES

CALIFORNIA
artichokes and shrimp salad, 111
basil-prosciutto grilled shrimp, 114
beef braised in St. Clement Cabernet, 108
boudin de fruits de mer, 112
Boursin cheese-stuffed chicken breasts, 111
Camembert fondue, 109
Catalina sausage isle, 112
cranberries in St. Clement Cabernet, 108
easy rack of lamb, 111
fettuccine a la Myra, 110
green tomato pie, 107
grilled fish steaks Sonoma-style, 113
homemade wine vinegar, 110
Italian teriyaki sauce, 110
Le Bernardin's shellfish stew, 113
Margarit Biever's summer pasta salad, 109
medallions of venison with cranberries, 112
Mrs. Fetzer's cocoa-nut rounds, 115
Napa Valley almond tart, 115
pashka, 115
pork en croute, 112
ricotta-stuffed zucchini flowers, 107
Rosa Mondavi's cappelletti, 109
Sausalito salmon supreme, 114
Silverado grilled sea bass with salsa, 114
sole with capers, 114
St. Clement ice with fresh fruit, 108
stuffed flank steak roll, 111
tomatoes with herbs, 108

FRANCE
beef Bourguignonne, 117
chicken Dijon, 118
chocolate dream mousse, 120
Cognac pate, 116
coq au vin, 118
escalope de veau Marseillaise, 118
escargots Bourguignonne, 116
Grand Marnier pots de creme, 120
les farcis a la provencale, 119
mushrooms a la Bourguignonne, 116
papillon mignon, 117
ratatouille, 120
sole in red wine, 119
sorbet au Champagne, 120
steak au pouivre vert, 117
tarragon chicken, 119
veal chops with Cognac cream sauce, 118
watercress and endive salad, 116

GERMAN
Frankfurt green sauce, 130
German potato salad, 128
kartoffelpuffer mit apfelmus, 130
rotkol mit apfeln, 129
sauerbraten mit kartoffel klosse, 128
Schwarzwalder Kirschtorte, 130
Wiener schnitzel, 129

ITALY
Collavini shrimp crepes, 125
fettuccine Gorgonzola, 125
Galliano pie, 127
Gorgonzolla garlic spread, 125
linguine with porcine cream sauce, 122
Mario's polenta with porcine wine sauce, 126
meringue torta alla Roma, 127
my favorite lasagne, 123
osso bucco alla Milanese, 124
paglia e fieno, 122
pasta with vodka, 122
patala brodo, 121
pepperoni pasta, 122
polenta Maria, 126
porcine-tomato sauce, 122
risotto alla Milanese, 126
risotto Al Tartufo, 126
roast pork Tuscany-style, 123
scaloppine in Grappa sauce, 124
scampi Trieste, 125
sorbetta di melone, 127
veal with prosciutto and peppers, 124
Venetian mushroom soup, 121
zuppa alla Pauese, 121

SPAIN
Castilian roast pork, 132
chocolate cake rum roll de Madrid, 132
escalibada, 132
pierna de cordero a la almendra, 131
pollo en pepitoria, 131
sangria, 132
sangria punch, 132
sopa de ajo, 131

SPECIAL RECIPES
asparagus-leek quiche, 140
banana sauce, 141
basic pesto, 137
cream of celery root soup, 138
creme fraiche, 141
eggplant casserole, 141
exotic fruits with pastry
    Riesling sabayon, 139
fried canape of mozzarella and anchovy, 133
linguine with clam sauce, 136
macadamia-rum pie, 141
marinara sauce, 136
Mario's tomato sauce, 136
Neapolitan sauce, 137
new potato appetizers, 134
Pacific lobster with Champagne sauce, 140
pasta primavera number one, 134

pasta primavera number two, 135
pasta with mozzarella and cold
    tomato sauce, 135
pesto-stuffed mushroom caps, 133
roasted garlic with toast points, 133
roast leg of lamb with wine sauce, 140
salsa alla meretrice, 137
sea bass medallions with grape
    and saffron sauce, 138
steak Diane, 139
steak pizzaioli, 139
tomato mousse soup, 138
tortellini Palermitana, 136
tortellini salad, 139
triple-cheese fettuccine, 135
walnut pesto, 137
Zinfandel duck with wild mushrooms, 140

WINE CONNOISSEUR'S MENU RECIPES
Chef's Feast
    Patrick Raynal's fettuccine verde
        con gamberi, 89
    Sylvain Le Coguic's symphonie du jardin, 89
    Ziggy Eisenberger's souffle Montrachet, 89
Dinner at Julian's
    feuillete de homard au safran et Pernod, 87
    filet d'agneau a la Mandarine, 87
    sorbet au thyme, 87
    souffle de cailles, sauce Madere, 87
Gourmet Gala
    Ann Clayton's calzone, 102
    chicken breasts with tapanade
        and tomato-basil sauce, 105
    clams New York-New York, 105
    Corinne's cold spinach soup, 102
    poached Norwegian salmon, 105
    raspberry cheesecake, 106
    stuffed onions, 106
Mondavi Menus
    Cabernet Sauvignon dinner
        rib steaks with sauteed shallots, 101
    Chardonnay brunch
        chilled salmon with basil mayonnaise, 99
    Great Chef's of France Luncheon
        beignets d'ananas Eventhia, 98
        emince de chevreuil au beurre
            de genievre et baies roses, 98
        medaillons de homard aux
            poireaux et champignons, 97
    Napa Valley Luncheon
        herbed mayonnaise, 101
        marinated scallop salad, 101
Peggy Steine Dinner
    aioli garni, 94
    coquilles Saint Jacques a la Parisienne, 94
    potage puree de potiron, 94
The Firestone Dinners
    Grilled Swordfish Dinner
        cream of spinach soup, 96
        fruit salad in apricot-honey sauce, 96
        grilled swordfish with scallop sauce, 96
    Tenderloin of Pork Dinner
        tenderloin of pork en croute with
            rosy sour cream sauce, 95
        watercress salad, 95
Wiseman and Milam Dinner
    Caesar salad, 92
    cream of asparagus soup, 91
    fillet of fish Veronique, 92
    Grand Marnier souffle, 92

APPETIZERS
    Camembert fondue, 109
    Cognac pate, 116
    escargots Bourguignonne, 116
    fried canape of mozzarella and anchovy, 133
    garlic, roasted, with toast points, 133
    mushrooms
        a la Bourguignonne, 116
        caps, pesto-stuffed, 133
    new potato appetizers, 134
BEEF
    Bourguignonne, 117
    braised in St. Clement Cabernet, 108
    steaks
        Diane, 139
        flank steak roll, stuffed, 111
        papillon mignon, 117
        pizzaioli, 139
        rib steaks with sauteed shallots, 101
        sauerbraten with potato dumplings, 129
        with green peppercorns, 119
Beverages
    sangria, 132
    punch, 132
Cheese
    calzone, Ann Clayton's, 102
    Gorgonzola garlic spread, 125
    souffle, goat cheese, 89
CHICKEN
    breasts
        Dijon, 118
        stuffed, Boursin cheese, 111
        tarragon, 119
        with tapanade and tomato-basil sauce, 105
    en pepitoria, 131
    with wine, 118
Cranberries in St. Clement Cabernet, 108
Creme Fraiche, 141
DESSERTS
    banana sauce, 141
    cakes
        cherry, Black Forest, 130
        chocolate cake rum roll de Madrid, 132
    cheesecake, raspberry, 106
    chocolate dream mousse, 120
    cocoa-nut rounds, Mrs. Fetzer's, 115
    fruits and puff pastry, 139
    ice with fresh fruit, St. Clement, 108
    meringue torta alla Roma, 127
    mousse, chocolate dream, 120
    pashka, 115
    pies
        Galliano pie, 127
        macadamia-rum, 141
    pineapple fritters, Eventhia's, 98
    pots de creme, Grand Marnier, 120
    sorbet
        au Champagne, 120
        au thyme, 87
        melon, 127
    souffle, Grand Marnier, 92
    tart, almond, Napa Valley, 115
Duckling
    Zinfandel duck with wild mushrooms, 140
FISH
    salmon
        chilled, with basil mayonnaise, 99
        Norwegian salmon, poached, 105
        supreme, Sausalito, 114

sea bass
    medallions with grape and saffron sauce, 138
    with salsa, Silverado grilled, 114
sole
    in red wine, 119
    Veronique, 92
    with capers, 114
steaks Sonoma-style, grilled, 113
swordfish with scallop sauce, grilled, 96

Gorgonzola Garlic Spread, 125

Italian Sausage
Catalina sausage isle, 112

LAMB
filet, Mandarine Napoleon, 87
leg of lamb
    in an almond sauce, 131
    with wine sauce, 140
rack of lamb, easy, 111

Mayonnaise, herbed, 101

PASTA
cappelleti, Rosa Mondavi's, 109
fettuccine
    a la Myra, 110
    Gorgonzola, 125
    pepperoni pasta, 122
    spinach pasta with shrimp, 89
    straw and hay, 122
    triple-cheese fettuccine, 135
lasagna, my favorite, 123
linguine
    with clam sauce, 136
    with porcine cream sauce, 122
primavera
    number one, 134
    number two, 135
tortellini Palermitana, 136
with mozzarella and cold tomato sauce, 135
with vodka, 122

Pesto see Sauces

Polenta
Maria, 126
with porcine wine sauce, Mario's, 126

PORK
en croute, 112
roast
    Castilian, 132
    Tuscany-style, 123
tenderloin, en croute with rosy sour cream sauce, 95

Quail
souffle with Madeira sauce, 87

Rice
alla Milanese, 126
Al Tartufo, 126

SALADS
fruit
    in apricot-honey sauce, 96
pasta
    summer salad, Margarit Biever's, 109
    tortellini, 139
seafood
    scallop, marinated, 101
vegetable
    artichokes and shrimp, 111
    Caesar salad, 92
    potato, German, 128
    watercress, 95
        and endive, 116

SAUCES
banana, 141
garlic, 94
green sauce, Frankfurt, 130
harlot's sauce, 137
marinara, 136
Neapolitan sauce, 137
pesto
    basic pesto, 137
    walnut, 137
porcine-tomato sauce, 122
teriyaki, Italian, 110
tomato, Mario's, 136

SHELLFISH
clams New York-New York, 105
lobster
    in pastry with saffron and Pernod, 87
    medallions with leeks and chanterelles, 97
    Pacific lobster with Champagne sauce, 140
scallops and shrimp coquilles, 94
seafood sausage, 112
shrimp
    crepes, Collavini, 125
    grilled, basil-prosciutto, 114
    scampi Trieste, 125
stew, Le Bernardin's, 113

Sorbet see Desserts

SOUPS
asparagus, creamed, 91
celery root, creamed, 138
garlic, 131
mushroom, Venetian, 121
potato, 121
pumpkin, 94
spinach
    cold, Corinne's, 102
    creamed, 96
tomato mousse soup, 138
zuppa alla Pauese, 121

VEAL
chops with Cognoc cream sauce, 118
cutlets Vienna-style, 129
osso bucco alla Milanese, 124
scallops
    Marseillaise, 118
    with prosciutto and peppers, 124
scalopine in Grappa sauce, 124

VEGETABLES
asparagus-leek quiche, 140
eggplant casserole, 141
escalibada, 132
garden symphony, 89
onions, stuffed, 106
potato pancakes with applesauce, 130
ratatouille, 120
red cabbage with apples, 129
stuffed vegetables provence-style, 119
tomatoes
    green tomato pie, 107
    with herbs, 108
with garlic sauce, 94
zucchini flowers, ricotta-stuffed, 107

Venison
medallions, with cranberries, 114
with juniper berry butter and pink peppercorns, 98

Vinegar
wine, homemade, 110

ACKNOWLEDGEMENTS

If I were going to credit everyone who helped me with this book I would have to go all the way back to my grandmother, Maria, who, along with my mother, Maria, showed me the wonders of what love and creativity can do in the kitchen. I suppose I could go back even further than that, to the ancestors of my ancestors, all of whom handed down information and attitudes about food and wine. I would also have to credit every friend who broke bread with me and shared a bottle of vino for I have learned from them all.

But I would like to give specific thanks to those who contributed time, suggestions, recipes, and information for the book. They include: Piero Antinori; Jobe Bernard; Margarit Biever; Jacopo Biondi-Santi; Carolyn Bloom; Mary Jane Blount; Jack Daniels; Judy Dew; Paul and Maureen Draper; Franco Dunn; Siegfried Eisenberger; Inez Ferrari; Kate and Brooks Firestone; Myra Hoefer; Jack Hooper; Sylvain Le Coguic; Robert Lipman; Wilma McIntosh; Tom and Carol Milam; Robert Mondavi; Marty Pogue; Don Reisen; Mary Robertson; Allen Russell; Sam and Vicki Sebastiani; Sylvia Sebastiani; Peggy Steine; Nikki Singer; Marimar Torres; Carolyn Van Dyke; Tom and Emily Wiseman; Frank Woods; Chateau Ste. Michelle; Fetzer Winery; St. Clement; Silverado; Sterling Vineyard; and the California Wine Institute.

Age appears to be best in four things, old wood — best to burn, old wine to drink, old friends to trust, old authors to read.

— Alonso of Aragorn